TO VIC,

BEST WISHES,

CUYLER "BUTCH"

BERWANGER

GO SOX!

M000274285

FIRST HEISMAN

The Life of Jay Berwanger

ALSO BY BRIAN E. COOPER

McCoy Group: A History of Commitment to the Customer
(McCoy Group, 2012)

Ray Schalk: A Baseball Biography
(McFarland & Company, 2009)

Red Faber: A Biography of the Hall of Fame Spitball Pitcher
(McFarland & Company, 2007)

FIRST HEISMAN
The Life of Jay Berwanger

December 10, 1935: The day Jay Berwanger's life changed forever.

Brian E. Cooper

CRESTWOOD PUBLISHING
Dubuque, Iowa

Copyright © 2014 by Brian E. Cooper
All rights reserved.
Published in the United States by Crestwood Publishing,
Dubuque, Iowa.
All rights reserved. No part of this book may be reproduced or
transmitted in any manner, electronic or mechanical, including
photocopying or recording, or by any information storage and
retrieval system, without written permission from the publisher.
Cooper, Brian E., 1954-

First Heisman: The Life of Jay Berwanger / Brian E. Cooper
Includes bibliographical references and index.
ISBN-13: 978-0-9885716-0-0

1. Berwanger, Jay, 1914-2002. 2. Football players – United States –
Biography. 3. University of Chicago.

Manufactured in the United States of America.

Crestwood Publishing
3462 Crestwood Drive
Dubuque, Iowa 52002-5117
www.crestwoodpublishing.com

Distributed by Cardinal Publishers Group

www.cardinalpub.com

First Edition

Front cover image: Special Collections Research Center,
University of Chicago Library.

Title page image: Corbis Images.
Cover and book design and layout: Carmen Goedken.

*To my wife, Ann, for her support and patience during this project –
especially since she doesn't even like football.*

ACKNOWLEDGMENTS

I am humbled by the generosity of the many people who assisted me, in ways large and small, in this endeavor. Some did so in their professional capacities. Others helped as a personal favor to me. However, time and again, folks went the extra yard out of respect for Jay Berwanger and his legacy. Whatever their motivation, I am most grateful.

This biography would be incomplete without the incredible cooperation and support of Jay's three children – John, Helen, and, especially, Cuyler ("Butch"). They gave their time (and patience). They shared personal stories. And they loaned photographs, memorabilia, and important documents to help me tell his story with accuracy and insight. In addition, John's wife, Pat, and Butch's wife, Jackie, also shared their observations and graciously opened their homes to this visitor from Jay's hometown.

Among other relatives who provided important assistance were Jay's stepdaughter Marianne Gerwig and his nephew Gary Lungwitz, who resides a short pass from Jay's boyhood home in Dubuque.

My research included a handful of trips to the Berwanger's alma mater, the University of Chicago. I spent dozens of hours in Joseph Regenstein Library – coincidentally, built on the site of the original Stagg Field – where Daniel Meyer's Special Collections Research Center staff and Ray Gadke, head of the microforms area, provided patient and professional assistance.

Additionally, I thank Will Hoyer for agreeing to proofread his father-in-law's manuscript, Tim Manning for proofing pages, and Carmen Goedken for designing the book from front cover to back.

With apologies for any inadvertent omissions, I sincerely thank these individuals and institutions for their help with this biography:

Individuals: Timothy Bachmann; Norma Banas; Ronald Beatty; Charles Benson; Cindy Bertaut; Cuyler "Butch" Berwanger; Jackie Berwanger; John Berwanger; Patricia Berwanger; Mirdza Berzins; Bradley T. Boyle; Brent Cook; John P. Davey; Elizabeth C. Deegan; Ernest Dix; Jack Dye; Raymond E. Gadke; Michael Gibson; Marianne Gerwig; Carmen Goedken; Archie Griffin; John Haarlow; Michelle Hellmer; Tim Henning; Dave Hilbert; Will Hoyer; Joel Katcoff; John Kuhl; Bud Legg; Gary Lungwitz; John McGlothlen; Tim Manning; Daniel Meyer; Dr. Bruce Montella; Martin Northway; Michelle Oberhoffer; Leonard Paul; Barby Pratt; Bob Quinn; Rudy Riska; Craig Schaefer; Jeff Sciortino; Eli Seamans; Mary Sharp; Robert A. Simpson; Bob Sokol; Kent Stephens; Kim Swift; Helen Berwanger Tierney; Tom Weingartner; Randall F. Weissman; Emory J. Westcott; Rob Whalen; Victor Winnek; Paula Wolfe; Rich Wolfe; Jim Wright; Kathy Young; and Frank Zarnowski.

Institutions and organizations: Camp Highland for Boys, Sayner, Wisconsin; Carnegie-Stout Public Library, Dubuque, Iowa; Center for Dubuque History; Chicago Public Library; Chicago Tribune; College Football Hall of Fame; Colorado State University Libraries; Cresco (Iowa) Public Library; Davenport (Iowa) Public Library; Dubuque Community School District; Dubuque (Iowa) Senior High School; Fort Dodge (Iowa) Public Library; Freeport (Illinois) Public Library; The Gazette, Cedar Rapids, Iowa; Glogau Photography (and Capitol and Glogau); Hinsdale (Illinois) Golf Club; The Heisman Trophy Trust; Iowa High School Athletic Association; Iowa Historical Society; Jay Berwanger, Incorporated; La Crosse (Wisconsin) Public Library; La Crosse (Wisconsin) Tribune; LaSalle (Illinois) Public Library; Loras College, Dubuque, Iowa; Loyola University, Chicago; Moline (Illinois) High School Booster Club; Oelwein (Iowa) Public Library; University of Chicago; and Washington High School, Cedar Rapids, Iowa.

When Jay Berwanger died in June 2002, obituaries from coast to coast featured the 88-year-old's status as recipient of college football's first Heisman Trophy. No one could have predicted that story angle in 1935, when Berwanger, more excited that the award came with his first airplane trip than the award itself, accepted a statue from the Downtown Athletic Club, an organization in New York City whose athletic director was former college coach John W. Heisman. After all, there were more prestigious awards at the time, including several All-America teams; the Douglas Fairbanks Award; *Liberty* Magazine's award; and the one Berwanger particularly coveted, the *Chicago Tribune's* Silver Football, awarded to the most valuable player in the Big Ten Conference. The University of Chicago star won all those awards – and more.

At first, I had trouble believing that no one had already written a biography of Jay Berwanger. No author from his native Dubuque, Iowa? Or from Chicago, where in 1930s he won acclaim as the best player in college football? I couldn't find a listing for any such book. When researchers at our local library had the same result, I committed to make Berwanger the subject of my third biography.

Born into a German-American family nearly a century ago, John Jacob Berwanger was the humble son of a Dubuque blacksmith. He lived and played in a different era. There were no youth tackle-football leagues. All high school fields were covered with natural grass, not artificial turf. And Heisman was the name of a coach, not a trophy. Players took the field with leather helmets and no face protection (more about that later). And once they were on the field, they stayed there. The game had no offensive specialists, no defensive specialists and certainly no "special teams." In light of the substitution rules of the day, athletes played both ways and thought nothing of it. Berwanger was in the center of that action, not only starring on offense, but also making jarring defensive stops as well as handling, punting, and place-kicking.

After winning honors as Iowa's best high school player of 1931, Berwanger accepted an honor scholarship from the University of Chicago, then a member of the Big Ten Conference, whose fading program was coached by the legendary Amos Alonzo Stagg. Berwanger's full-tuition scholarship (officially, for citizenship and academics as well as athletics) was worth a grand total of $300 a year. The best college player in the land still had to pay for his room and board.

Stagg was forced out before Berwanger joined the Chicago varsity, but the sophomore had the good fortune of playing under offensive genius Clark Shaughnessy, a future Hall of Fame coach. Though the Maroons were over-matched in the Big Ten, Shaughnessy and Berwanger managed to postpone the collapse of Chicago's football fortunes. His role as a "one-man team" brought Berwanger many national honors, including the first Downtown Athletic Club Trophy (its name for one year, before the club renamed it the Heisman Memorial Trophy).

This book focuses on Berwanger's life as a prep and collegiate player, of course. Readers wanting details of his high school and college games (as well as his exploits on the track) will find them here. But, just as there was more to Berwanger as a man, there is more to this book than game accounts. His campus celebrity. His role in a Hollywood movie. His Olympic aspirations. His foray into business ownership. His extra efforts to become a military pi-lot. His career as a football official, including a controversial call in the Rose Bowl. His decision, as the first pick in the first National Football League draft, to reject professional football. His donation of his name, time, and treasure toward his favorite causes. His heartache at losing two wives. His growing celebrity as the first Heisman winner.

I received several fortuitous bounces during this project. The first involved geography. I live in Berwanger's hometown, where I edit the local newspaper, allowing me convenient access to local archival material, from newspapers to yearbooks to public records. Further, aside from a few years during World War II, Berwanger always lived, studied, and worked in Dubuque or Chi-cago, separated by fewer than 200 miles, so research trips were manageable. Last but not least, Berwanger's three children supported my project, with younger son Cuyler "Butch" Berwanger taking the lead as my main con-tact. They not only shared their time in interviews, they let me borrow their father's papers, family scrapbooks and even the game films capturing him in action as Number 99.

My goal is that, as a reader, you will see Berwanger for who he was – a great football player for a few years who was a great man all his long life.

Brian Cooper
Dubuque, Iowa
June 2013

PROLOGUE

The score was only 6-0, but the way Washington High dominated Dubuque all afternoon, the margin might have seemed like 60-0. With only five minutes of the 1929 season opener remaining, Dubuque had not come close to scoring, while the hosts from Cedar Rapids seemed capable of advancing the ball at will. Yet, somehow, Dubuque managed to rebuff all but one of Washington's touchdown drives.

Watching nervously from the Dubuque sideline was John Berwanger. The sophomore had yet to play a down, and, the way this game was going, he doubted that he would. However, Dubuque blocked a Washington punt, recovered the ball on the hosts' 27, and started to drive. As the Red and Blue approached the Washington end zone, Coach Wilbur Dalzell suddenly called the 15-year-old's name. He ordered Berwanger to replace John Morris as running back.

The boy was so nervous that he could barely speak his name when, as required by the substitution rules of the day, he reported to the official. He looked toward his opponents. "From the bench the Cedar Rapids boys had been the size of houses," he recalled, "and I was afraid my heart could not stand a close-up view." He was so scared of the view, in fact, that he couldn't bear to watch the very game that he was about to change.

Berwanger had barely joined the Dubuque huddle when he heard his number called. He received the ball, cradled it in both arms, and headed toward the gap off right tackle. He didn't see what happened next, for one simple reason – he had his eyes closed. Nonetheless, he crashed through the line for a healthy gain. Dalzell's troops ran the play again, and again the eyes-closed Berwanger chewed up more yardage. The game clock continued to run. Dubuque ran the play a third straight time, and for the third straight play Berwanger took the ball, closed his eyes, and charged forward.

"I never once saw a chalk mark, or the hole I was supposed to hit, or a Cedar Rapids tackler," he said a few years later. "When my hands closed on the ball, my eyes would shut tightly and I would just run." He wound up on the ground, still clutching the ball and squeezing his eyes shut. The excited shouts of his teammates brought things into focus for him. "I opened my eyes then and, sure enough, there were the goal posts right ahead of me," Berwanger said. "That was my first touchdown. I'll never forget it."

That touchdown was the first of many by a player whose name will forever be associated with the most recognized award in American sports, the Heisman Trophy.

CHAPTER 1

More than a century before computer dating and their successor Internet matchmaker services, young people seeking dates and mates relied heavily on introductions through relatives and friends. Such was the case with Pauline Siems and John Berwanger, whose long-distance relationship started after they were introduced by a mutual acquaintance. Their parents were part of the 1880s wave of Germans immigrating to the United States.

Louis and Maide Siems, along with their infant daughter Pauline, sailed from Hamburg and settled in Chicago in 1882.[1] Over the next 11 years, four more children joined the family. Their father worked as a painting contractor and proprietor of a paint store at North Damen and West Roscoe, where the family occupied an apartment upstairs. Their residence was a half-mile east of German Sharpshooter Park, a shooting range and picnic grounds popular with German immigrants. In 1904, the site became home to Riverview Park, for decades one of the nation's leading amusement parks. A mile and a half to the east, a Federal League baseball team opened Weeghman Park in 1914; a couple of years later it was renamed Wrigley Field.

Pauline started working in her father's store as a girl, and she was still there, pushing 30 years old, when she met Berwanger, a blacksmith from Dubuque, Iowa, a thriving Mississippi River com-

Jay Berwanger, circa 1920, about the time he entered Marshall Elementary School in Dubuque. (Berwanger family collection)

munity 180 miles west of Chicago. Established by lead miners in 1833 at the intersection of Iowa, Illinois, and Wisconsin, his city was named for miner and fur trader Julien DuBuque (1762-1810), a Canadian of French descent. By 1890, when its population exceeded 30,000, Dubuque had become a leading city within the region bounded by Chicago, St. Louis, Des Moines, and Minneapolis. When immigration peaked, the miners had seen their operations fade; their children and grandchildren pursued other endeavors. The city was a hub for river commerce and the lumber industry. Dubuquers also built doors and windows for Farley & Loetscher Manufacturing as well as Carr, Ryder and Adams Co.; pumps and plumbing supplies for A.Y. McDonald and Morrison Manufacturing Co.; and wagons for A.A. Cooper.

Berwanger's parents arrived in Dubuque from Germany in early 1884, when his father (also named John) was 32 years old and his mother, the former Margarette Abresch, was 27 and late in a pregnancy. With them were two daughters – 7-year-old Augusta and 4-year-old Amelia. The Berwangers barely had time to unpack their trunks before John Berwanger Jr. entered the world (as a U.S. citizen) on February 24, 1884. Five more children followed – three boys and two girls – to make them a family of 10. The Berwangers resided on the west end of Fifth Avenue, on the northwest edge of Dubuque and near Eagle Point. They operated a small farm, and the head of the household also held various laborer jobs – at Roeber's Brickyard, at Linwood Cemetery, in a railroad shop, and, for the longest period, driving a horse-drawn wagon as an independent teamster. Margarette never learned English, but she was not alone, particularly in Dubuque. The great influx of Irish and German immigrants influenced life in Dubuque, where the Germans settled on the north side and the Irish on the south. Dubuque was home to a German-language newspaper, German Savings Bank,

Jay's mother, Pauline, as a 16-year-old. She was in her early 30s when she married John Berwanger and moved to his hometown, Dubuque, Iowa. (Berwanger family collection)

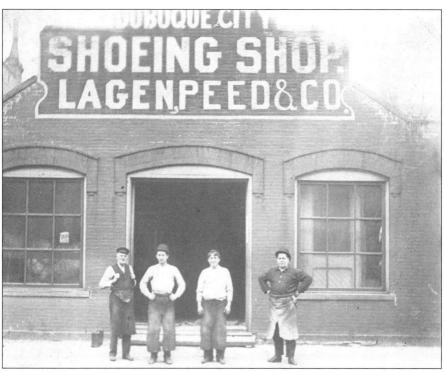

Jay's father John (third from left) was hired on at the Lagen, Peed blacksmith shop at 532 Locust Street in Dubuque and eventually became a partner. By the mid-1940s, he was the city's last blacksmith. (Berwanger family collection)

Jay's father, John Berwanger (1884-1966), was a farmer as well as a blacksmith. (Berwanger family collection)

Jay with his father, John, a blacksmith and farmer, circa 1920. (Berwanger family collection)

Germania Hall, German bands and choral groups, a German Presbyterian college and seminary, and several social and professional organizations for those of German heritage. The city's public schools had classrooms in which all subjects were taught in German. The Berwangers were Protestants in a city that remains predominantly Roman Catholic.

In 1900, the elder John Berwanger and his teenage namesake worked as laborers in railroad shops. Before long, they found other jobs. The father went to work for Myers Cox & Co., then a tobacco manufacturer. His 16-year-old son became an apprentice blacksmith, a four-year process during which he worked Monday through Saturday for a half-dollar a day. It was hot, heavy, and occasionally dangerous duty, yet the trade suited him. He made it his life's work. In his early years in the trade, John Berwanger Jr. worked at the Lagen & Sloan livery and boarding stable on the northeast corner of Fourth and Locust streets. By the end of the 20th century's first decade, about the time he met his future bride, he held an ownership position in Lagen, Peed & Berwanger, 532 Locust Street. (After a half-century in the business, he was Dubuque's last blacksmith, working at 2167 Central Avenue, adjacent to the Iowa Dairy Company, whose stable of more than 20 delivery horses received his exclusive attention.)

After a long-distance courtship, blacksmith John Berwanger married Pauline Siems, the paint store owner's daughter, and they set up housekeeping at 2327 Roosevelt Street, a few blocks east of his parents' farm. Their first son, Louis – named after his maternal grandfather – was born on the last day of April 1913. It was a difficult delivery, and any joy of parenthood was short-lived. Louis lived just 10 days. Eleven months after that, on March 19, 1914, John and Pauline Berwanger became parents again, and again the baby was a boy. They named him John, after his father and paternal grandfather, and gave him the middle name Jacob, honoring his father's brother.

With his father and grandfather also named John Berwanger, the boy was called "J.J." Over time, "J.J" became "Jay," and that was the name that would become familiar to generations of American sports fans.

Pauline Siems worked in her father's paint store, 2005 West Roscoe in Chicago, until about 1912, when she married John Berwanger of Dubuque, Iowa. Their son Jay was born in Dubuque in 1914. (Berwanger family collection)

CHAPTER 2

Jay Berwanger's early childhood coincided with World War I. It was not an easy time to be an American of German descent. Though the United States officially stayed out of The Great War for three years (1914-17), anti-German sentiment spread across the country. Encountering bias, suspicion, and outright hostility in their new country, many residents of German descent found it prudent to downplay their heritage. In the Berwanger family's home state, with anti-immigrant Governor William Harding stoking the flames of prejudice, Iowa made it illegal for German to be taught in the schools or even spoken in public. As the targets of abuse and vandalism – yellow paint was a popular weapon – individuals, institutions, and businesses changed their names to sound less German. Even Dubuque, home to a significant number of German immigrants, was not immune. Dubuquer Nicholas Gonner Jr., editor of the German-language Luxemburger Ga-

zette, was harassed so incessantly that he ceased publication in July 1918, sending his subscribers his other newspaper, the English-language *Catholic Tribune*. Yet, when the United States entered combat, the naturalized Americans served their new country faithfully. The first three Dubuque residents to die in World War I were German-

In his early years, while attending Marshall Elementary School in Dubuque, Jay was responsible for chores on the family farm. (Berwanger family collection)

Americans.[2]

During and after the war, Pauline and John Berwanger's family grew to include four more children – Dorothy (1916), Eleanor (1918), Elizabeth (1920), and Paul (1922). Jay enjoyed spending time outdoors, especially poking around his grandparents' farm up the road. In February 1919, three months after The Great War and a month shy of his fifth birthday, he started kindergarten at Marshall Elementary School. Over the next seven years, he managed to advance through the grades, impressing his teachers with neither his scholarship nor his conduct. However, when it came to performance on the playground, he was an honor student; his natural speed served him well in running races and sandlot football games.

After completing the sixth grade in the first month of 1926, he advanced to Jefferson Junior High, a hilltop school a half-mile south of his grade school. He went out for football as an eighth-grader and received what he described as "invaluable" instruction in the fundamentals from Jefferson coaches Julius Tickle and Wilfred Johannsen. When he was a 5-foot-1 end, Berwanger's eighth-grade squad won city bragging rights by defeating Dubuque's other public junior high, Washington.[3] In ninth grade, as he continued to grow, Berwanger shifted to halfback and took on additional duties at defensive end.

In January 1929, at semester break, Berwanger and dozens of classmates advanced from Jefferson Junior High to Dubuque High School, a castle-like

The longtime home of Jay's parents, John and Pauline Berwanger, when Roosevelt Street in Dubuque was barely a gravel path. (Berwanger family collection)

Berwanger credited his high school coach, Wilbur Dalzell, with emphasizing fundamentals and not creating "overnight heroes." (Dubuque High School yearbook)

structure of native limestone on the city's highest point, the western terminus of West Locust Street, at Clarke Drive. Opened in 1923, the school housed more than 700 students in Grades 10-12. A teacher and coach since 1922, before the high school moved to its current site, was Wilbur J. Dalzell. As a collegiate wrestler, Dalzell in 1918 became the first Indiana University student to win both its Big Ten Medal of Honor, for high achievement in academics and athletics, and the Jake Gimbel Prize as the Indiana upperclassman exhibiting the best mental attitude in athletic competition.[4]

Though he dabbled in college football a couple of seasons, when schools struggled to fill their rosters during the war years, the 145-pound Dalzell didn't display gridiron talent.[5] However, he learned enough about the game to coach it. His first job was at Harrisburg High School, in southern Illinois, where his teams went 17-6-1 over three seasons. He also coached basketball one season (4-9). He then moved to Dubuque, where he taught mathematics and physics and served as the assistant coach in football and track and head coach in wrestling. Eventually, Dalzell advanced to athletic director and head coach in all three sports; he remains the only coach in the Iowa halls of fame for each of those sports.

If Dalzell, who became head football coach in 1926, knew what he was getting in Jay Berwanger, he did not show any particular excitement. The young man did not command any headlines during the track season of 1929. In any case, the coach's approach was to bring along underclassmen slowly and deliberately, not only to give them more work on football fundamentals but also to shield them from some of the pressure of varsity competition. Years later, Berwanger observed, "I am grateful for the fact he did not allow any of his players to be overnight heroes. Rather, he confined himself to giving them a good groundwork in the apparent simpler stages of the game."

Fall practice for the 1929 football season opened with Dalzell and his three assistant coaches – James Nora, "Syl" McCauley, and Duane Wilson – assessing the talent. Berwanger reported in good shape, and the 150-pound sophomore's conditioning was attributed to a full summer of farm chores. "I worked with my dad on the farm all the spare time I had," he told an interviewer decades later. "In the summertime I worked in the harvest fields for friends, and that was the way we were able to make some extra money." (The interviewer also asked if his parents maintained discipline. "It was a German family," he replied with a smile. "I don't need to say more, do I?"[6])

Many of his teammates also held summer jobs offering plenty of conditioning. Several worked in the railroad shops or on rail crews. Howard Orvis, a tackle, worked in a freight warehouse. Lyal Holmberg moved barrels for Licorice Products Company. Allen Wallis was an attendant for show cattle taken to judging events around the Midwest. Even Dalzell – his players addressed him as "Coach" and, usually outside his presence, referred to him as "Dal" – stayed in shape over the summer, working for a landscape gardener; he also spent two weeks at a coaching school and one busy week on the golf course.

The Dubuque newspaper noted that in the first 10 days of preseason workouts – including a Friday the 13th scrimmage featuring 13 players on each side of the ball – the 15-year-old Berwanger was "coming along slowly. He, of course, has a lot to learn, but is trying hard." He needed to learn quickly; the season opener was less than a week away. And it would be a tough one.

Berwanger (middle of back row) had yet to fill out when he joined the Dubuque High wrestling team. In later years, he claimed that wrestling was his favorite sport. (Dubuque High School yearbook)

CHAPTER 3

Dubuque High's first opponent of the 1929 football season, Washington High School of Cedar Rapids, had an amazing record of athletic success. The foundation for its tradition was built during the tenure of Leo V. Novak, who coached football, basketball, track, wrestling, and swimming while also serving as athletic director.

In 1921, Novak's basketball Tigers went 20-1 and won the National Interscholastic Tournament hosted by the University of Chicago. He coached individual and team state champions in track, winning five consecutive team titles (1921-25) and a national meet (also at Chicago) in 1924. His football teams likewise earned state and national recognition. Novak received some undesired attention in December 1923 after his football team narrowly lost a national championship game to Scott High in Toledo, Ohio. Some 20,000 fans paid to see the battle. The post-game meeting to divide the gate receipts erupted into a fight. Novak knocked out a Scott teacher, but the altercation came to a swift conclusion when the Scott staffer holding the cash pointed his revolver at Novak.[7] By 1925, Novak, having worn out his welcome in Cedar Rapids, accepted a job with the high school in Parkersburg, West Virginia. However, his appointment was clouded by questions about his faculty status and whether local boosters were supplementing his income. Less than a year after that, Novak joined the staff at West Point, where for the next quarter-century he coached Army to success in track, cross country, and basketball.

In its post-Novak era, the Washington High football program lost some of its luster. Yet, coach Bill Kelly's inexperienced Tigers intended to continue their record of never losing to Dubuque. Berwanger was in uniform for his first varsity game, but not in the starting lineup. In the opening minutes on the Coe College field, Washington's Charles "Smitty" Smith intercepted

Karl Kenline's pass and raced 65 yards for a touchdown. Dubuque blocked the extra-point attempt, but, "The touchdown was so easily achieved that the Tigers assumed an easy, carefree attitude," a Cedar Rapids sportswriter noted. "During the first three quarters, the Tigers played a brand of football that might be classed as smooth, considering the greenness of the team and the fact that it was the first game of the season."

Though Washington dominated on both sides of the ball, Dubuque's defense somehow managed to keep the Tigers from returning to the end zone. The visitors made a stellar stand to open the second quarter, stopping Washington without a yard on four tries from the 4-yard line. Midway in the third quarter, Washington advanced to the Dubuque 8, where the defense held on three straight rushes before Toopey Redel's field-goal attempt fell short.

Only five minutes remained in the game, and Berwanger had yet to play a down, when Dubuque's Allen Wallis blocked Redel's punt to give the visitors possession on the Washington 27. Finally, Dalzell sent in his fully rested sophomore, who was so nervous that he had trouble speaking his own name when, adhering to the rules of the day, he reported to the official. Did Dalzell just want fresh legs on the field, or did he think he had a secret weapon? Either way, Berwanger changed the game.

Three straight plays, Berwanger got the call to carry the ball. Protecting the pigskin with both arms, he closed his eyes and charged straight ahead. He never opened his eyes until he was tackled. On the third run, he crossed the goal line. His eyes-shut approach caused him to not actually see his first varsity touchdown.

Washington's Verle "Bud" Schlack blocked Ray Airheart's dropkick attempt for the extra point, so the score remained 6-6. The hosts returned the ensuing kickoff to midfield and prepared to stage what they hoped would be the game-winning drive. However, Dubuque all-state guard Arnold Rieder intercepted a pass and ran it back to Washington's 40. With time running down, it was the Dubuque offense's last chance to win the game.

The Red and Blue again unleashed their sophomore. Berwanger repeatedly smashed through the Tigers' line. But he ran out of time. Dubuque had the ball on Washington's 12 when the game ended as a 6-6 tie. The Cedar Rapids sportswriter covering the game described the tie as a lost opportunity for the home team, saying the Tigers "lacked the punch for victory." He added, "Dubuque, however, supplied that necessary attribute in the person of John Berwanger, a rangy, hard-driving back, who personally conducted his team to the tying touchdown in the closing minutes of play after the cause of his team seemed hopeless." In his varsity debut, Berwanger covered 79 yards in just 10 carries.

Berwanger earned the starting assignment at fullback for the next game, a road contest against powerful Oelwein, which had won 14 straight, including a one-point win over Dubuque a year earlier. Though his battered team faced a squad with an impressive winning streak, Dalzell felt that his players were overconfident. The local newspaper noted, "They go about their work with a feeling that the Oelwein game is already in the bag, and unless Dalzell can get this idea out of their head, the boys are doomed for a let down, and a good licking along with it." On game day, neither team took a licking, but they got a soaking. Just a couple of plays into the contest, the skies over Oelwein opened up, and the rest of the game was played in a steady rain. Berwanger also returned kicks – and there were lots of them, as the teams traded punts while slogging about in the middle of the field. Dubuque's best scoring opportunity came late in the first half, when Louie Arthofer returned an interception to the 10. But Dubuque could not score. However, neither could Oelwein and its all-state running back, Everett Eischeid. Berwanger fumbled the wet football a time or two, but Oelwein couldn't take advantage. The game ended a 0-0 tie. Oelwein finished the 1929 season 6-0-3 to extend its unbeaten streak to 22 games.

Dubuque's offensive performance was less than satisfactory for Dalzell, who used an open weekend on the schedule to experiment with the lineup. "The backs seem to be improving," the local sports editor observed, "but the blocking in the line was not up to par." Berwanger was among those first-team backs practicing against the second-team defense. However, he suffered an injury during practice, and he did not see action on the rainy Saturday afternoon of October 12, when Dubuque hosted Freeport (Illinois) in the Dads Day contest. His absence did not hurt the team, which sloshed to a 21-7 victory. It was a miserable afternoon for the spectators, as was noted by workers at the concession stand. "Out of four cases of pop for sale at the football game last Saturday," the student newspaper reported, "only about four bottles were sold."

For the second straight weekend, Dubuque prepared to host another Illinois opponent, Waukegan, a Lake Michigan community north of Chicago. The Waukegan line averaged 173 pounds a man, compared to 157 for Dubuque. All during the week, Dalzell's practice sessions concentrated on the forward pass – how to execute it on offense and how to stop it on defense. However, when the teams squared off, it was raining so hard that the forward pass did not figure in the scoring. Dubuque struck quickly. In the first five minutes, John Morris sparked a drive by returning a Waukegan punt 43 yards, to the 22. Dubuque then ran on every down. On a second-and-goal from the 4, Karl Kenline crashed across the goal line. He tried to run on the extra-point attempt, but he fell down on the muddy field. The few spectators willing to put up with the dreadful conditions were treated to a thrilling game. "If it was not a sensational run it was a tackle, and so on they occurred throughout the game," the local sportswriter noted. Waukegan threatened all afternoon. The visitors attempted to trick the Dubuque defense with "spinner" plays. A Waukegan ballcarrier would twirl about in the backfield in hopes of deceiving the defense regarding where he would hit the line. On one drive, Waukegan used the spinner to reel off three straight first downs. But while the Dubuque defense bent – at one stage, it was backed up to its 11-yard line – it did not break, even in the closing minutes when Waukegan unleashed a series of passes. The hosts' early touchdown held up for a soggy Dubuque victory, 6-0. Berwanger, too injured to play the previous weekend, entered as a substitute but had little impact.

If conditions were poor for the Waukegan game, Dubuque might have anticipated even worse the next weekend at Clinton. After all, there was precedent. In their previous four meetings, the teams played in snow, mud, ice, and howling wind. In the days before the 1929 battle, though the weather outside was frightful – it included a chilling mix of snow and rain – Dalzell ran his troops through full practice sessions outdoors.

Meanwhile, on the national scene, bad news from Wall Street got worse. After a half-dozen years of extraordinary gains, fueled by lax credit policies for investors, stock prices peaked around Labor Day 1929 and then started to drop. But in this week, the New York Stock Exchange experienced particularly tumultu-

When Berwanger entered Dubuque High School in 1929, the castle-like structure was relatively new. It opened in 1923. (Author's photo)

ous trading sessions. On October 23 alone, stocks lost 6.3 percent of their value. The next day, prices took a lesser hit, but a record 12.9 million shares changed hands, earning the session the name "Black Thursday." The worst was yet to come.

With the markets closed for the weekend, Clinton hosted Dubuque in its sixth annual Homecoming game at Coan Field. For a change, the weather and field conditions were acceptable. The game was a contest of defenses and punters. Neither team could score. Berwanger again saw action as a substitute. Both teams mounted scoring threats in the fourth quarter, but their defenses were up to the challenge. The game ended 0-0. Dubuque's second scoreless tie of the season made its record 2-0-3.

Entering the final days of October and their week of practice for their own Homecoming game against Cedar Rapids Grant, the Dubuque players couldn't help but know about the dire news from Wall Street. Many of their fathers, grandfathers, and uncles – even those with modest incomes – had money in stocks. They had seen the market's incredible rise since the mid-1920s, and they bought shares on credit – with as little as 10 percent down. Of those who did not own shares, many worked for businessmen who did have money in the market. On the first day of trading of the week, Monday, October 28, prices plunged 13½ percent. The next day, October 29, 1929, investors tried desperately to cut their losses, trading 16.4 million shares while the market suffered another severe drop (11.7 percent). Bankers and government officials went to extraordinary lengths to shore up prices and public confidence, and the market staged a short-lived rally before dropping further. The catastrophic session, called "Black Tuesday," is forever associated with the start of the Great Depression. The Depression would serve as a backdrop of Berwanger's transition from teen to husband and serviceman.

Despite the numbing economic news of the previous week, some 3,000 fans converged on Dubuque Senior High to see the Red and Blue battle Grant. Berwanger ended up watching, too, due to an unspecified injury.[8] Nonetheless, Dubuque extended its victory streak in Homecoming games to eight with a 6-0 decision. The game's only points came on the first play of the second quarter, when Sheldon Allendorf capped a 60-yard drive with an 11-yard touchdown dash around end. The win took a physical toll on Dalzell's squad. The coach lightened the load in practice before their game at La Crosse (Wisconsin) Central High, but as their final tune-up, the preps scrimmaged against the University of Dubuque squad.

A Dubuque High traveling party of 20, including Berwanger and 17 other players, took the train to La Crosse. The visitors held a 22-0 lead in the fourth quarter when Ray Airheart aired a pass to Berwanger, who caught it on the La Crosse 26 and, displaying his raw ability, powered his way to a touchdown. Airheart's kick closed the scoring in the 29-0 shellacking.

The Red and Blue did not have much time to savor that easy win, knowing that their next game would be their toughest test of the season. The game pitted Dubuque and Davenport, two Mississippi River communities with undefeated football teams. Even with home-field advantage, Dubuque (4-0-3) was considered the underdog. Davenport, its sights set on the unofficial state title, was led by versatile junior Mike Layden. Another Davenport star was running back "Bus" Wellington. White-owned newspapers of the day routinely referred to the race of non-white athletes – African-Americans, especially. Thus, while a white player might have been described as a "powerful fullback," a talented player of color saw his race used as the adjective. Sportswriters occasionally expanded beyond the "colored" or "negro" tags used by their colleagues on the City Desk; one popular adjective was "dusky." The term shows up in many accounts of many games in which non-whites participated. The Dubuque paper referred to Wellington as a "negro flash." The same story appeared in the *Davenport Democrat*, but its editors removed the racial identification early in the article, and only in the final paragraphs referred to him as "the dusky flash."[9]

The game provided a black-and-white example of why Davenport was Iowa's top team. "The Davenport machine proved superior in almost every respect," a Dubuque sportswriter conceded. Trailing 6-0 for nearly half the game, Dubuque tied the contest early in the fourth quarter. However, Layden, who also made two interceptions, and Wellington broke it open with two offensive touchdowns to claim a 20-6 win. Berwanger saw no action in a battle that, according to the box score, featured but six substitutions all afternoon.

For the season finale, Dalzell and his team took the train to Fort Dodge, 190 miles due west. After going undefeated in its first seven games (4-0-3) before losing to Davenport, Dubuque struggled against 2-4 Fort Dodge. The Dodgers stifled Berwanger, who was a starter, and the hosts scored two touchdowns in the second quarter. The 13-0 decision closed Dubuque High's 1929 season at 4-2-3.

When Dalzell handed out postseason awards, he probably did so with his arm in a sling after breaking his shoulder while playing basketball. Berwanger, the only sophomore on the 1929 football squad, received his first varsity letter. Captain Arnold Rieder, a senior, earned *Des Moines Register and Tribune* second-team All-Iowa honors at right guard while left guard Erwin Wilke and running back Karl Kenline received honorable mention. However, no member of the Red and Blue squad earned accolades for his work in the classroom. The team carried a grade average of "C," with only Kenline making the Honor Roll. Berwanger's grade report showed a B in algebra, B-minus in Latin, C-plus in English and C-minus in history.[10]

Dalzell and Berwanger then turned their attention to wrestling. Though he received his greatest notoriety for his exploits on the football field, and was considered an Olympic track prospect, Berwanger's family said the sport he enjoyed most was wrestling. As a former collegiate wrestling star, Dalzell was a proponent of the sport. "Wrestling is the most beneficial of all sports for boys in general," he told an interviewer. "It develops muscles, muscles they did not know they have." The coach rated track and basketball as the most demanding activities, adding that football was the least strenuous. The athletic director scoffed at swimming, stating that it "softens the muscles."

The Dubuque High wrestling program was newly revived after a few seasons of dormancy. The yearbook photo of the 1929-30 wrestling squad shows 15 boys, all shirtless, posing with Dalzell. In the middle of the back row stands "John Berwanger" his ribs visible on his wiry frame. Dubuque had a three-meet wrestling season, and two of the contests were against Clinton. Berwanger won his three regular-season matches at 155 pounds, two of them by falls, and earned a varsity letter. Dalzell then entered Berwanger in a multi-state prep competition hosted by Northwestern University. In Evanston, Berwanger defeated a Chicago Lane Tech opponent but exited after losing to a Crane Tech grappler in the second round. (Dubuque's other entrant, 165-pounder Lyal Holmberg, lost his only match in overtime.)

Just one week after leaving the wrestling mat, Berwanger had a busy day at the inaugural Mississippi Valley Conference indoor track championships in the University of Iowa fieldhouse. Unlike most schools, Dubuque High did not display the school's name or insignia on its track jerseys. Instead, their tank tops displayed their city's nickname, THE KEY CITY. Despite the beneficial aspects of wrestling cited by Dalzell, Berwanger was not yet in track shape. His only points on that Saturday came in the pole vault, where he tied for third at 9-6. He was shut out in the mile medley relay, low hurdles, and long jump. During the season, Berwanger picked up points here and there in the field events and hurdles. In an outdoor dual meet against Clinton, he was part of an unusual seven-way tie for first in the pole vault at the modest height of 9-1. Berwanger qualified for the 1930 state meet after winning the long jump in the district qualifying meet. He also took fourth in the low hurdles and tied for third in the pole vault. At state, he leaped 18-8¾ in the long jump but failed to place.

The varsity letter Berwanger earned in track was his third of the school year, and it put the sophomore in elite company. Just four Dubuque High athletes won three letters during the school year; the other three were seniors. As soon as track ended, Berwanger participated in what remained of spring football drills.

Gargoyles guard the entrance of Dubuque High School. (Author's photo)

CHAPTER 4

The 1930 Dubuque High football team's season opener was also the school's first-ever night game. The venue was Municipal Athletic Field, near the city's riverfront at the foot of Fourth Street and the historic Shot Tower. The ballpark was home to minor league baseball's Dubuque Tigers, a Class D team that had just jumped on the bandwagon of hosting night games. Des Moines staged professional baseball's first night game under permanent lights on May 2, 1930, and by summer the home of the Dubuque Tigers had installed lights. The thought was that night games would shore up attendance, which was taking a beating during the Great Depression, because those who did have jobs would find it easier to attend. "Out here in Dubuque we have night baseball," writer John P. Mulgrew, using the pen name Jazbo of Old Dubuque, quipped in the *Chicago Tribune*. "The other evening we had a 13-inning game, which lasted so long there was talk of turning out the lights and calling it on account of darkness."

Dubuque High moved some of its football games from the school field on Saturdays – still a workday for many fans – to Municipal Field on Friday nights. The community responded positively. Nearly 2,000 fans turned out for the inaugural game under the lights, set for 8 p.m. Friday, September 26, 1930.

Dubuque faced a formidable opponent in Oelwein, which had not lost in 22 straight games. The visitors threatened early after recovering a Dubuque fumble in the first quarter. They advanced 54 yards, with backfield stars Burdell Eickenberry and Albert DeBow leading the charge, to reach the Dubuque 9-yard line. After the break between the first and second quarters, Oelwein pushed the ball another two yards. Then Dubuque's defense stiffened, throwing the Purple and Gold for a five-yard loss and, on the next play, recovering an Oelwein fumble. Dalzell's charges then mounted a drive of their own, started by Berwanger, gaining 15 yards on a dash around right end. Wearing Number 34 and playing halfback, which at the time required passing skills, Berwanger on the next snap lofted a 10-yard pass to Sheldon Allendorf, the team captain. After making the catch, the 135-pound Allendorf ran another 30 yards, deep into Oelwein territory. Dubuque stuck with its passing attack. Berwanger connected with Jack Nelson near the end zone. When Nelson was tackled, he landed with the ball resting on the goal line. Touchdown. After missing the placekick for the extra point, Dubuque buckled down and took its 6-0 advantage into halftime.

After intermission, an inspired Oelwein offense threatened. "It looked very much during the second half that Oelwein was out for blood," the *Telegraph-Herald* reporter observed. On the visitors' first play from scrimmage, from their own 23, DeBow burst through the entire Dubuque defense. He covered 72 yards before he was caught five yards from the end zone. But again, the Dubuque defense held, stopping Oelwein on four straight running plays. Though the visitors possessed the ball most of the second half, they came no closer to scoring, and Dubuque's first-half touchdown was the game's only score.

"Although the entire squad gave a good account of itself, the outstanding players for the senior high were Berwanger, who outpassed and outpunted his opponent; Nelson; Allendorf; and Holmberg, the latter being an important factor in the line," the Dubuque sportswriter noted. "Eickenberry and DeBow clearly were the shining lights of Oelwein," whose undefeated streak ended.

What optimism Dalzell and his squad felt after their opener was crushed the next week in the first of three road games, all three in Illinois. The first was in Moline, where Coach George Sennett's school the previous week hosted its inaugural night game. The Dubuque contest, staged on a beautiful Friday evening, brought some 3,500 fans to Browning Field. Moline dominated Dubuque, 39-6. The star of the game was Kenneth Esterdahl, whose two touchdowns included a 55-yard return of a booming Berwanger punt in the first quarter. Dubuque scored its only touchdown in the fourth quarter, when the game was out of reach, by blocking a punt deep in Moline territory and executing a nine-yard drive. Berwanger attempted to kick the extra point, but the play went awry. A Rock Island sportswriter said of the proceedings, "It must have been discouraging for Coach Dalzell." Indeed.

Dubuque suffered further discouragement and embarrassment the next two weekends. In a night game at Freeport, where the Pretzels had not won since 1928, Dalzell's crew lost again 13-7. Freeport jumped to a 7-0 lead. Dubuque responded with an apparent score of its own on Berwanger's 36-yard run, but the touchdown was called back on an offside penalty. The drive resumed when Berwanger passed to Allendorf for nearly 40 yards and then took the ball across the goal line from two yards out. Berwanger also kicked the extra point to deadlock the game. However, Freeport star Swede Schmelzle closed out the scoring with a five-yard touchdown, his second of the evening, to open the fourth quarter. The final score was 13-7.

Dubuque's 19-0 loss at Waukegan the following Saturday afternoon was never close. In their Homecoming game, the hosts avenged the previous year's loss in Dubuque. They scored all three of their touchdowns in the first quarter, with fullback Don Merriman doing the honors. Dubuque could muster only four first downs all day.

After going 0-for-Illinois, Dubuque prepared to host an Iowa school, Clinton, which was 5-0 and had state-title aspirations. Despite losing three straight, the Dubuque newspaper reported, "the boys feel that they should start winning soon and regard this game as a good chance to hang up a victory." During the week of practices, Dalzell focused on offense. The game was scheduled as the fifth annual Dads Night, where the fathers of Dubuque players were invited to walk the sidelines while their sons did battle. "The Clintonians are primed for a hard battle tonight," the Clinton paper noted, "and while confident of notching their sixth successive victory, are not confident to the point of overconfidence." In front of about 2,000 fans, including about 500 who traveled 60 miles from Clinton, the teams waged what the local sports editor described as "one of the bitterest struggles registered on the local lot in moons." Dubuque surprised Clinton with its aggressive play.

The star of the game was Allendorf, who twice snapped off 30-yard runs and then scored a first-quarter touchdown on a one-yard plunge, and Lyal Holmberg, whose work at center – on offense and defense – opened holes for the Dubuque running backs and wreaked havoc for the Clinton offense. Holmberg blocked at least two punts. Dubuque had the ball on the visitors' 4 when a Clinton substitute drew a flag for violating the rule that, upon entering the game, a substitute could not speak to his teammates for one play. (The intent of the rule was to prevent coaches from using substitutes to relay messages.) The officials moved the ball from the 4 to the 1, and Allendorf took it in from there for a touchdown. On the extra-point try – whether scored by run, pass, or kick, it was worth one point – Berwanger rushed off-tackle and reached the end zone. The score was still 7-0 at intermission when members of the Clinton pep club gave an impressive demonstration on the Dubuque field. Dressed in white uniforms with red trim and carrying red flares, they waited for the ballpark lights to be turned off and then assembled in various formations before concluding with a snake dance.

When play resumed, Dubuque nearly scored an insurance touchdown. Fred Holtz blocked a Clinton punt, picked up the ball and was running unmolested toward the goal line. However, the referee blew his whistle and brought the ball back to where Holtz contacted the punt. "It was a free ball and Holtz had the right of way to advance it," the Dubuque writer complained. "He would have scored a touchdown had not the referee stopped the play." Clinton took advantage of the decision and kept the Red and Blue out of the end zone. The teams traded punts most of the second

As a 15-year-old sophomore at Dubuque High, Berwanger rushed for his first touchdown while holding his eyes closed. (Dubuque High School yearbook)

half, with Berwanger kicking for Dubuque. The hosts had another scoring opportunity late in the game, when senior defender John Ludescher rushed across the line, blocked a Clinton pass, caught the ball in the air and dashed for the goal line. He was dragged down at the 6-yard line. After Dubuque executed a couple of running plays and advanced the ball to the 4, time expired. Dubuque had its upset victory, 7-0. In their excitement, local students and fans moved their celebration from the ballpark to downtown, where their shouts and car horns could be heard for more than an hour after the final gun.

Despite the tough and close battle, sportsmanship was not a casualty. Noted the Dubuque sportswriter, "Defeated as they were – and unexpectedly on their part – the Clintonians took their medicine as only real sports will." His Clinton counterpart, noting that the game was more one-sided than the score indicated, suggested that the ineffectiveness of Coach William Livermore's squad was due to overconfidence after all. He wrote that the victory was "well-earned by a Dubuque team that was unquestionably superior to the Clintonians for the night at least," and listed Allendorf and Berwanger as the stars. The setback in Dubuque turned out to be Clinton's only loss of 1930 (7-1).

Next up for Dubuque (2-3) was a trip to Davenport. The previous season, Dubuque hung close most of the game before Davenport, led by Mike Layden, pulled away for a 20-6 win. With the return of Layden, a senior and future prep All-America back, Davenport was expected to be as tough as ever. Some 2,500 to 3,500 fans converged on the Davenport field on Saturday afternoon, November 1. Dubuque's Red and Blue knew they could not afford any mistakes, but they made one early – and it was by one of Dalzell's steadiest performers. In the second quarter, with the wind at his back, Davenport's "Bus" Wellington uncorked a long punt. Allendorf backpedaled to attempt the catch at his own 10-yard line, but the ball hit off the captain's hands and bounded into the end zone. Davenport's Gerald Preston outraced Allendorf, fell on the ball, and claimed an easy touchdown. Layden kicked the point to make it 7-0. After intermission, Wellington lofted a pass to Layden at the goal line. That toss slipped through Layden's grasp but continued on into the arms of Preston, who recorded his second touchdown of the afternoon. The pass for the extra point failed, but it didn't matter. Dubuque didn't score, and Davenport owned a 13-0 victory. Though it was in a losing effort, Berwanger was credited with "a sparkling game" after making many long gains.

Layden, who with Preston earned star recognition in the game, was also a standout in basketball and track at Davenport High. He went to prep school for one year and then enrolled at Notre Dame, where he closed his collegiate football career playing for his brother Elmer, one of the Notre Dame "Four Horsemen" of the 1920s. "There wasn't any pressure on me," Mike later said of the sibling connection, "But there was pressure on Elmer because my father told Elmer to play his best 10 men and his brother."[11] Elmer Layden, whose coaching resume included a stint at Loras College in Dubuque, later became commissioner of the National Football League.

After the tough Davenport game, Dalzell gave his starters two days off in addition to their regular Sunday, figuring the rest would be more beneficial than drills. When the full team returned on Wednesday afternoon, however, he worked them hard. Another out-of-state team was on the schedule: Central High of La Crosse. The visitors from Wisconsin were not up to the task, however, falling 40-0 and looking bad doing it. La Crosse's prospects suffered a blow when its captain, Frank "Pebbles" Stone, suffered a first-quarter injury and never returned. La Crosse got no closer to Dubuque's goal line than the 12, and that was in the third quarter, when the matter was all but decided. Allendorf made up for his fumble against Davenport with several outstanding runs, including a 52-yarder and a meandering 80-yard interception return for a touchdown.

About the only surprise of the evening was that, amid all the scoring, Berwanger had but one point – a run following a touchdown. Then again, Berwanger, whose longest runs were of 21, 25, and 10 yards, was not on the field at the finish. With the game out of reach, Dalzell and La Crosse coach Mark Sutton substituted extensively. They "were sending them in as fast that they could think up names," the Dubuque newspaper noted, which added that Berwanger nonetheless had a "brilliant" game. Dubuque High improved its record to 3-4 with two games to play, keeping hopes of a winning season alive.

As he prepared his team for a Friday afternoon game against Grant High in Cedar Rapids, Dalzell adjusted his starting lineup, inserting Carl Badger at fullback in place of Wayne Anthony. It was an opportune move. In the opening minutes on the Coe College gridiron, Grant lost a fumble on its 41-yard line. After Berwanger rushed for eight and 15 yards, the Grant defense stiffened. On fourth-and-eight from the 16, Berwanger passed to Badger, who shed a would-be tackler and rumbled into the end zone. The visitors converted the extra-point kick. After Grant tied the game, 7-7, Berwanger resumed his show. He raced 40 yards on one play and chewed up 16 yards on the next. He passed for three yards, ran for three more, blocked as Anthony gained two, and finally smashed through the Grant line for a seven-yard touchdown. For good measure, Berwanger ran the ball across for the extra point, making it a 14-7 contest.

Dubuque extended its lead to two touchdowns early in the fourth quarter. Berwanger's pass to Allendorf gained 35 yards before Grant stopped him inches from paydirt. On second-and-goal, Allendorf crashed across. His point-after kick missed, but the officials granted Dubuque the point anyway due to an offside penalty.

Down 21-7, Grant kept battling, and it received some help from Berwanger, whose punt from his end zone careened out of bounds at the Dubuque 20. The defense was then about to sack Grant passer Alvin Hurst, who wildly flung the ball to the end zone and Chris Schamberger, his left end. Schamberger did not hold onto the ball for long, but long enough to give Grant a touchdown. Grant's run for the extra point failed, and the home team short-circuited its next drive with a fumble on the Dubuque 20. Dalzell's Red and Blue returned home with a 21-13 victory.

With a 4-4 mark and the opportunity to close the season with a winning record, Dubuque prepared to host Fort Dodge. Played the Saturday afternoon before Thanksgiving, the game was the centerpiece of Dubuque High's 10th annual Homecoming weekend. Activities included a parade through the business district, a play ("A Typical Homecoming") and a snake dance. The school's classrooms and hallways were filled with red and blue balloons, streamers, and pompons. Though their football team had as many wins as losses and was facing an undefeated opponent, Dubuque's enthusiasm was high. After all, Senior High was 8-1 in Homecoming games, including eight straight wins.

Coach Fred Cooper's Fort Dodge squad came to town with a 5-0-1 record, intent on finishing the campaign undefeated and claiming a share of the mythical state title. Cooper knew how to coach winners: His wrestling squads had claimed three state titles the previous four seasons (and in a few months would tie for another championship). The visitors touted four future all-state football selections, including first-teamer Harry Largent, an end. Cooper's team also planned to retain a special trophy – a football painted in each school's colors.

After forcing Fort Dodge to punt in its first possession of the game, Dubuque started on its own 20 after a touchback. The offense went nowhere, so it became Berwanger's turn to punt. He shanked his kick out of bounds just nine yards past the line of scrimmage. It was a costly mistake. Fort Dodge made quick work of the 29 yards, scoring on two rushes by Don Geyer. The attempt for the extra point failed. The prospective state champions had another drive under way late in the first quarter when Allendorf intercepted a pass and returned it five yards to midfield. Berwanger, no doubt hoping to make amends for his awful punt, played a key role in the ensuing drive. On the first play of the second quarter, he rushed for six yards, to the 30. Next, he connected with Allendorf on an 11-yard pass play. A couple of plays later, with the ball on the 15, Berwanger rushed off-tackle for a first down. He then completed a short pass to Fred Holtz at the 3. From there, Berwanger carried the ball across for the tying touchdown. Like Fort Dodge, Dubuque also failed on its extra-point try.

Dubuque stopped the Fort Dodge offense again and then mounted a 50-yard scoring drive. On its first play, Berwanger passed to Robert Knapp, who had just entered the game at end, for 20 yards. The Red and Blue gained nine yards on the ground before Berwanger tossed to Allendorf, who caught the ball and outran the defense. Berwanger plunged across the goal to notch the extra point. Dubuque 13, Fort Dodge 6.

The visitors tried a passing attack to open their first drive of the second half, but their strategy backfired early. Allendorf grabbed his second interception of the afternoon, giving his team the ball on Fort Dodge's 22. Berwanger burst through for 11 yards, and gained another yard on a plunge. Dubuque then scored an insurance touchdown when John Ludescher ran around right end for the final 10 yards. The extra-point attempt failed, but Dubuque held a 19-6 lead.

Fort Dodge had not gone through the season undefeated by giving up in tough spots. Berwanger provided an opportunity when he fumbled away the ball on an outside run. The visitors drove to the Dubuque 11, but could get no closer, thanks to a couple of tackles for loss by Holtz. The teams held each other scoreless in the fourth quarter. The 19-6 decision spoiled the visitors' bid for an undefeated season and a claim on the mythical state championship; their victory over Mason City on Thanksgiving Day could not ease their disappointment.

For Dalzell and his Dubuque squad, the win over Fort Dodge meant four victories in their final five games and a winning season (5-4). The football lettermen soon afterward elected their captain for 1931: Jay Berwanger. The vote was unanimous.

In December, when *The Des Moines Register* and its sister paper, the *Tribune,* announced their all-state teams – a tradition the newspapers started in 1914 – only one Dubuque player received a spot among the first five teams. It was not Berwanger or even the captain, Allendorf, whose work on both sides of the ball drew rave reviews all season. Instead, the honor went to senior guard Lyal Holmberg, who made the Second Team. Berwanger had a solid season, but not outstanding enough to place him among the best 10 halfbacks. Instead, he was lumped in with the 45 halfbacks making Honorable Mention. Though buried in the fine print as a junior, Berwanger would make the headlines his senior season.

CHAPTER 5

The Berwangers were not wealthy, but they were the first on their stretch of Roosevelt Street in Dubuque to have electricity and indoor plumbing. "Electricity meant that Mom could hear the soap operas on the radio," Jay's sister Eleanor recalled. "Sometimes other ladies in the neighborhood would join her."

Eleanor had pleasant memories of the Christmas season. "Jay would take the horses and wagon, cross the Wisconsin bridge (spanning the Mississippi River) to get us a beautiful big tree in the Wisconsin," she wrote decades later. "Mom and we three girls would string popcorn to hang on the tree. We had beautiful ornaments, and before electricity was available we had candles on the tree." It was holiday tradition that Grandpa Siems and his brother, Uncle Louie, would visit from Chicago. When the children left the house to visit their Berwanger grandparents a short distance up Roosevelt Street, Eleanor said, the Siems brothers trimmed the tree, all the while "fighting over how it should be done." She recalled, "They always gave each of us $5. One year, my $5 was lost among the wrapping paper – a big tragedy."[12]

A couple of weeks after Christmas 1930, Jay lost his paternal grandfather and namesake. John Berwanger Sr. died in his home at age 78. The patriarch, who had come to the United States from Germany 47 years earlier, had been ill several months. Fellow members of the Harmony Lodge of Odd Fellows served as pallbearers, with burial in Dubuque's Linwood Cemetery, where the deceased was once employed as a laborer. The funeral took place on his son John's 47th birthday.

That winter, Jay was again a dedicated member of the wrestling squad. He was the first to show up for afternoon practice and among those (along with Harold Zimmer and Russell Rafoth) who wouldn't go home until so ordered by coaches Dalzell and Jim Nora. Due to when he started high school and eligibility rules in place at the time, these would be his last full seasons of wrestling and track.

The Dubuque High wrestling program, revived the previous season after several years of inactivity, achieved only modest success. Dubuque's bid for a .500 season ended in the final match of the final dual meet, a 20-19 loss to New Hampton.[13] Berwanger wrestled at 165 pounds, one class below heavyweight. He was undefeated in seven bouts entering the championship match in the district tournament, which determined qualifiers for the 1931 state tournament. Already assured a state berth as a district finalist, Berwanger lost the district championship to Earl Turnure, representing Eldora State Training School, an institution for young incorrigibles. Prospects of a Berwanger-Turnure rematch at the state tournament in Ames evaporated when Berwanger lost a tough first-round match. Berwanger's season closed at 7-2, while Turnure became one of three individual titlists from the training school, which tied Fort Dodge for the team championship.

Berwanger then returned to the track, where his strength, speed, and versatility were in full display. Over the course of the 1931 season, he competed in the 100-yard dash, low hurdles, high hurdles, shot put, discus, pole vault, long jump, triple jump, javelin, and sprint – and led the team in scoring. Though the Dubuque High team was young – Berwanger was one of only three returning letterwinners – by season's end it won the district championship. At districts, Berwanger qualified for the state meet in four events. He won the 120-yard high hurdles and also qualified in two events

Jay's grandfather, John Berwanger Sr., came to Dubuque from Germany in the 1880s. He operated a small farm, worked in a railroad shop and a cemetery, and made deliveries with his horse-drawn wagon. (Berwanger family collection)

in which he set school records, the low hurdles (25.8 seconds) and long jump (21-3½), as well as the shot put.[14] He did not earn a medal at state – and it is not recorded whether Berwanger or his fellow qualifiers actually competed. If they did, the city and school newspapers failed to report on their performances. During the Great Depression, Dubuque and other schools occasionally passed up competitions because they lacked the money for travel. Dubuque's daily newspaper regularly reported prep track results, but it carried no account of the state meet in Ames, where Davenport claimed another team title. The weekend after state, in the Mississippi Valley Conference meet at Davenport, Berwanger finished second to the host school's Mike Layden, in the high and low hurdles, who had just won state titles in those events. Berwanger also placed fourth in the discus.

Berwanger entered a postseason event, the inaugural Tri-State Relays, sponsored by the *Dubuque Telegraph-Herald*. The meet at Columbia (now Loras) College featured prep and collegiate athletes from Iowa, Illinois, and Wisconsin. Berwanger won an event rarely contested at the high school level, the triple jump, won the 220-yard low hurdles, and finished second in the 120-yard high hurdles. For all that, he received the trophy for the meet's outstanding junior athlete. He qualified for the Midwest States Track and Field Meet, sponsored by the *Chicago Herald-Examiner*, the following Saturday at Chicago's Soldier Field, where he advanced to the low-hurdle finals but finished last. By now, Berwanger's potential as a decathlete was coming into focus. One man who recognized those possibilities was the starter and referee at many of his meets: Ira Davenport, local civic leader and former Olympic medalist.

After his regular high school track season in 1931, Berwanger won the triple jump and low hurdles in a regional meet sponsored by the Dubuque Telegraph Herald, qualifying for a Midwest meet in Chicago's Soldier Field. (Author's photo)

CHAPTER 6

In August 1931, Wilbur Dalzell, just back after taking a coaching course at the University of Michigan, mailed letters to his 50 Dubuque High football prospects, encouraging them to get into shape and reminding them that practice sessions would start in just 10 days (on September 1). His captain needed no reminder. He was ready to go, thanks in part to a conditioning drill he created for himself. Working the horse-drawn plow on the family farm, he challenged the animals, holding the plow handles and tugging against their natural horsepower. Both sides put up a good fight.

The 1931 season would be the first of football competition for the recently formed Mississippi Valley Conference, which previously had crowned champions in only basketball and track. Conference members were Clinton, Davenport, Dubuque, Iowa City, and the two Cedar Rapids schools, Grant and Washington. When Dubuque High opened practice, it still did not have an opponent scheduled for its season opener, less than three weeks away, though Dalzell had a prospect in LaSalle-Peru High School of Illinois.

The afternoon before the opening day of classes and the first sanctioned football practice, players received their gear and went through a coach-less workout under the direction of their captain. The next afternoon, Dalzell took the helm. With 11 lettermen returning, he knew his team could improve on last year's 5-4 record. But how much better could they be?

In addition to football, Berwanger had classroom responsibilities. He took four courses during the semester, receiving C-pluses in typing and English, a B-plus in economics and a B in algebra. In the Fall 1931 semester, he also received Physical Training credit through his participation in athletics. Somehow, he mustered only a C in Home Room.

Though he had played well as a junior, Berwanger's football performance was not particularly noteworthy. He was talented and versatile – a presence on offense, defense and in kicking – but he had not stood out as even the top player at his school. But over the subsequent year, he grew, he matured, and he gained confidence without losing his modest and unassuming manner. Bigger, stronger, and faster than ever, Jay Berwanger was about to surprise fans, opponents, and pundits alike. He was poised for greatness.

For the season opener, Berwanger, 22 teammates, Dalzell, and team manager Russell Rafoth piled into a bus early the morning of Saturday, September 19, for the 150-mile trip to LaSalle, Illinois. Though the game at Social Center Field lacked the buildup and hype a 21st century fan might expect, it matched teams that would vie for state-champion status in their respective states. That season, LaSalle-Peru would go on to place four players on the All-Illinois Eleven.

In consideration of the unseasonably hot afternoon – it was at least 90 degrees – teams received four rest periods per half.[15] The substitution rule was relaxed, so that players removed for substitutes could re-enter during the same half. LaSalle dominated the game in virtually every statistical category

The Berwanger siblings, circa 1934, from left: Elizabeth, Paul, Dorothy, Eleanor, and Jay. (Berwanger family collection)

– except in points scored. The host Red and Green amassed 17 first downs to one for Dubuque. That the visitors managed to stay close was due to their defense, a bit of luck, and Berwanger. The Dubuque captain rushed for 124 of his team's 136 yards. Eighty of those yards came on one run. On a second-down play in the second quarter, Berwanger crashed through the right tackle hole, shook off several LaSalle-Peru tacklers, and raced across the goal line. Four years later, Berwanger described that run as his most exhausting experience in football until a long dash in the penultimate game of his collegiate career: "I thought the last 10 yards were four city blocks." Carl Badger's kick for the extra point hit an upright and bounced back onto the field. Though outplayed throughout the first half, Dubuque managed to take its 6-0 lead into intermission.

Early in the third quarter, with LaSalle advancing the ball to the Dubuque 8, Dalzell made wholesale substitutions. However, Berwanger was not going anywhere. Number 42 stayed on the field. The insertion of fresh Dubuque players made no difference on the sweltering afternoon, as the Red and Green moved to the 1-yard line before Leonard "Sheik" Kaszynski plunged off tackle for the tying touchdown. The extra-point effort failed, keeping the battle tied at 6.

By all rights, the game should not have been this close. LaSalle-Peru mounted several offensive drives, but three of them ended at the Dubuque 17, 5, and 20. A fourth LaSalle-Peru bid for a go-ahead touchdown ended late in the game when Berwanger intercepted a pass at his goal line and returned it to the 26. Had Dubuque been able to notch a first down or two, it could have run out the clock and escaped with no worse than a 6-6 tie. But the visitors struggled to gain any yardage. On third down, Kaszynski intercepted a Berwanger pass at the Dubuque 30. LaSalle-Peru had barely enough time for a final drive. With the clock winding down and their energy sapped, the Dubuque boys battled the LaSalle-Peru offense, fatigue, and the summer-like heat. They halted a LaSalle-Peru rush just 18 inches from the goal line with five seconds to play; the hosts called a timeout. Coach Dean Johnson set the play that would decide the game. With some 700 spectators cheering LaSalle-Peru on, all-state quarterback Willard "Benny" Benson crashed through the middle for the winning touchdown. The affair was decided, and the ensuing extra-point kick was a mere formality, but Dubuque jumped offside on two consecutive tries. After the second offense, officials credited LaSalle-Peru with the point. Final score: LaSalle-Peru 13, Dubuque 6.

Though it was a game Dubuque deserved to lose, subsequent events would show that Dalzell's squad came within five seconds of an undefeated season. LaSalle-Peru nearly made it through the season undefeated and with a mythical state title. Those hopes died in the second-to-last game, when Hall won by a touchdown. LaSalle-Peru, which outscored its opponents 287-31 in 1931, finished 7-1-1.

Dubuque faced another tough opponent on the road for its second game, Oelwein. When the teams met the previous year in Dubuque, Dalzell's charges broke Oelwein's three-season undefeated streak, 6-0. Oelwein sought revenge. Excitement in anticipation of the Dubuque-Oelwein game of 1931 might have provided fans some respite from their worries about the economic malaise enveloping the country. The Great Depression was worsening. On September 24, 1931, the Dow Jones Industrial Average suffered one of its worst single-day drops ever, losing more than 7 percent. While unemployment in the Dubuque community and the country surged, teachers faced the prospects of pay cuts. High school students couldn't help but notice the impact of the Depression. In a telling statement that nonetheless had a lighter element, someone overheard the future Class of 1932 valedictorian, Alma Bardill, in exasperation exclaimed, "Oh, WHY did the Depression have to come right now when we're having hard times?!"[16]

Though Berwanger was by now a confident presence on the gridiron, the same could not be said of all his teammates. One running back got so nervous that in games he would forget his right side from his left. "We put black tape on his right wrist and white tape on his left and called plays going to the right side 'black' and those going to the left 'white,'" Berwanger wrote a few years later. "By this method he kept track of which way the plays were going."

On the afternoon of September 26 at Oelwein's municipal ballfield, Dubuque repeated its 1930 conquest by another 6-0 score. As he did the previous year, Berwanger beat the Purple and Gold, this time with a 20-yard run in the first quarter. He also contributed on defense. In the third quarter, Dalzell played his entire second string. In the fourth quarter, Oelwein mounted a threat, advancing to the visitors' 11 before being set back by a penalty and a stiffening Dubuque defense. "The outstanding star of the game was Berwanger, Dubuque's left halfback. He was the main ground gainer for Dubuque and he was a ... tower of strength on defense," his hometown paper reported. "Numerous threats by Oelwein were broken up by stellar work of this Dubuque performer."

For its home opener against Moline, Dubuque High oozed school spirit. The morning of the Friday night game, students filled the auditorium for a pep rally. On the agenda were cheer sessions, comments from players and even a performance by junior Grant Lawrence, who did a tap dance "appropriate for the football season." That evening, 90 minutes before kickoff, students staged a parade from the school to the municipal ballpark about 2½ miles away.

In their 1930 meeting, Moline had thrashed Dalzell's squad, 39-6. Dubuque turned the tables in 1931, shutting out the Illinoisans, 13-0. Berwanger contributed to Dubuque's first touchdown in a couple of ways. On the final play of the first quarter, he boomed a punt that the Moline returner couldn't handle, and Dubuque's Irvie Prior recovered the fumble on the 5. "Captain Berwanger made two drives himself and in his last charge took out the entire middle of the line," the Dubuque newspaper said. Berwanger crashed through again on the extra-point try to make the score 7-0. If his running, passing, and defense were not enough, Berwanger's punts gave Dubuque an advantage in the field-position game. However, the affair did not always go Dubuque's way. At one point, the student newspaper noted, "Dalzell gave (tackle Paul) Sheffield such a cold look that he melted like an ice cream cone." After a scoreless third period, during which Dubuque stopped a Moline drive on the 10, the hosts added an insurance score with five seconds to play. Berwanger highlighted the 55-yard drive with a 30-yard run and then a pass to Wayne Anthony for a five-yard touchdown.

Having settled the score with Moline, Dubuque High prepared to visit Iowa City. For many years, the teams always played each other on Thanksgiving and always in Iowa City. And Iowa City always won. However, the teams had not met since 1923, when Iowa City won 7-0 during a blinding snowstorm. In its preview article, the *Telegraph-Herald* reported that it could cite no occasion when Dubuque beat Iowa City on the gridiron. That streak came to a speedy and decisive end on a rainy Saturday afternoon at Shrader Field. The game was only 10 seconds old when Berwanger connected on a pass to Melvin Vonah, who raced 50 yards for a touchdown. Berwanger booted the extra point. Vonah and Berwanger chewed up yardage the remainder of the first quarter. Early in the second quarter, Prior fell on a loose ball near the Iowa City goal line. Harold Zimmer then rushed for the touchdown. In what turned out to be easy for such a historic win – Dubuque's first in conference competition and first ever over Iowa City – Dalzell played his second team for three-quarters of the contest. Even Berwanger, the game's offensive star, spent some time on the bench. The contest also marked the emergence of sophomore running back Theatrice Gibbs, the team's only African-American player, who in two years would be the team captain. He was believed to be the first of his race to captain an American high school football team.[17]

The following Friday, designated Dads Night, Dubuque High knew it had its hands full with the visitors from Cedar Rapids Washington, the one-time state and national power. On the opening kickoff, Washington star Joseph Schneider nearly went the distance, covering 85 yards before being tripped down by a diving Harold Glab at the 5. Dubuque rebuffed four straight rushing attempts and took over on its own 1. However, after the home team's drive stalled, Berwanger was tackled in his own end zone before he could snag the errant center snap and punt the ball. The safety gave the visitors a 2-0 lead.

On the first play of the second quarter, Berwanger broke through on an off-tackle play and romped on a 40-yard touchdown sprint. Though the point-after kick failed, Dubuque held a 6-2 lead and momentum. The Red and Blue offense began to pound the left side of the Washington defensive line, with guard Melvin Paul leading the blocking assault. The visitors tried substitute linemen, but they too couldn't stop Berwanger, Gibbs, John Ludescher, and Wayne Anthony. Berwanger scored again to put Dubuque ahead, 12-2. However, the Cedar Rapids crew battled back, sparked by Toopey Redel's wild 55-yard touchdown run. He reversed direction, swirled, swiveled, and escaped each Dubuque player at least once. "It was the cleverest piece of footwork ever seen on the field," Dubuque sportswriter C.A. "Scoop"

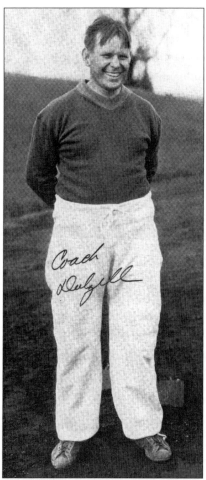

Wilbur Dalzell coached Berwanger in football, wrestling and track at Dubuque (Iowa) High School. Dubuque school officials, honoring his four decades of directing young athletes, renamed the local stadium Dalzell Field. (Dubuque High School yearbook)

Wilhelm noted. Though trailing 12-8, Washington reclaimed control and threatened to take charge in the second half. However, on three separate drives deep into Dubuque territory, Redel fumbled away the ball. After one of those turnovers, Dubuque faced a fourth-and-two. Berwanger got the call, rammed through the line for the first down, and kept going until he reached the end zone. Paul's extra-point kick made it 19-8. Dalzell then directed his charges to play it safe and protect their lead against Washington's increasingly desperate comeback attempts. After breaking up a series of long passes, a scoreless final period ended and Dubuque High collected one of its biggest victories ever. "It was truly a great game," Wilhelm concluded. "The Senior high never played better." After this game, the Dubuque sports editor for the first time touted Berwanger for higher recognition, referring to him as "a player of all-state caliber." However, the senior's best was yet to come.

The next afternoon, Berwanger and teammates Paul, Sheffield, and Robert Schwind traveled to Iowa City to watch the University of Iowa and Indiana battle to a scoreless tie. It was hardly a marquee match-up: Iowa finished the season 1-6-1 while Indiana was 4-5-1, with half of its victories coming at the expense of the University of Chicago. Whether the trip afforded Hawkeye coach Bert Ingwersen an opportunity to woo the Dubuque visitors, especially future all-staters Berwanger and Paul, was not reported. In any case, Ingwersen was out of the job after the season anyway.

Even the Dubuque junior varsity enjoyed success in 1931. After a particularly exciting victory – a 6-0 win at DeWitt featuring a 90-yard kickoff return to open the second half – the boys whooped it up on the ride home. As the bus rolled through town, the driver noticed that the din was diminishing, little by little. Eventually, he turned around and found himself alone inside the bus. "A pair of legs disappearing upward into the air outside of one window was the explanation of this," the student newspaper reported. "The entire squad was riding triumphantly down the avenue on the top of the bus."

Dalzell had scouted Dubuque's next opponent, and he warned his players that they would have their work cut out for them against Clinton, a veteran squad featuring several lineman who were also outstanding wrestlers. In their meeting the previous season, Dubuque's 7-0 victory turned out to be Clinton's only loss. Dubuque entered the 1931 game at Clinton short-handed due to injury and civil unrest. Paul, the outstanding guard, was unavailable due to a sprained ankle. Two reserves who were members of the Iowa National Guard, William O'Brien and Marwin Brown, missed the game when they were called to active duty. The governor summoned the National Guard to deal with Southeast Iowa farmers who were blocking veterinarians from mandatory testing and inoculating of cattle against tuberculosis. Incidents included a mob of 500 farmers breaking into a jail to free a compatriot, angry farmers blocking roads and hurling clods at veterinarians and their escorts, and bayonet-brandishing Guardsmen confronting mobs. The revolt lasted months.

When Dalzell and 22 players arrived for Clinton's Homecoming night battle, they found Coan Field saturated by 18 straight hours of rain. The precipitation ended by kickoff, and the soggy conditions seemed to have no adverse effect on Berwanger. He rushed for four touchdowns and reeled off several long runs. His 34-yard touchdown run, followed by Badger's extra-point kick, allowed Dubuque to take a 7-6 lead into halftime. Clinton would get no closer. "The third period opened calmly enough and there was no warning of what was to follow," the *Clinton Herald* reported. What followed was Berwanger's burst for another long touchdown. "Breaking loose through tackle, he threaded his way through outstretched arms and when he got into the open, he was off like a mustang, covering the 67 yards to the goal line in non-stop flight. That was the beginning of the end." After Berwanger scored two more touchdowns – from 12 and 24 yards out – and ran for an extra point, Dalzell took pity on his vanquished hosts and rested his captain the rest of the evening. Dubuque's final touchdown in the 33-6 rout came on Gibbs' 59-yard interception return in the fourth quarter. The Clinton newspaper described Berwanger's 25-point night as "the best individual performance seen here in years," and said Dubuque High (5-1) "probably will rank at the season's close as the best in the state." Among the spectators in Clinton was Jesse Day, coach of conference rival Davenport, who, the Dubuque student newspaper quipped, "got a few more gray hairs added to his crop when he saw Berwanger running wild against the Clinton aggregation." The next afternoon, Dalzell and assistant coach Duane Wilson scouted Dubuque's final two opponents as Davenport whipped Grant, 32-6.

Berwanger followed his four-touchdown effort in Clinton with a two-touchdown night in Dubuque. The 20-6 victim was Freeport (Illinois). Berwanger's sparkling play was a 75-yard touchdown run in the third quarter. The captain picked up about 20 yards along the sideline and then cut back toward the center of the field, where he eluded the Freeport safety, Joseph Abate, and continued across the goal line unmolested. With a three-yard plunge in the final seconds of the first half and extra-point runs after each of his touchdowns, Berwanger logged a 14-point night. The Pretzels' chances suffered a blow in the second quarter when their quarterback, Howard Leamy, was knocked unconscious while attempting to tackle John Ludescher. The Freeport sportswriter was effusive about Berwanger. "What was scheduled to be a football game between 22 players was turned into an exhibition of individual brilliance of one player while 21 others set the stage for each performance for this big, 6-foot-2, 178-pound giant with the shoulders of a bull and the muscles of an elephant, which molded together with marvelous suppleness and continued with a natural penchant for football, made him the perfect football player last night."

The Freeport writer described Berwanger's punishing style: "He ran with his knees pumping high and his body weaving about. Once past the line of scrimmage he was a demon to stop and ordinary methods were of no avail. One man was either pushed into the earth with his stiff arm, shook off by his weaving motion, or dragged a few yards, and after two or three black-jerseyed gridders swarmed on him, he could be finally brought to a stop. He had plenty of speed to go with his other assets, too." Freeport's lone touchdown, on a 54-yard run by halfback Harold Reizer, represented the last points Dubuque allowed in 1931. With an open weekend on the schedule before the final two games, Dalzell gave his players a few days off. Berwanger and teammate Paul Sheffield took advantage of the break by going hunting, a pastime Berwanger enjoyed most of his life.

In seven games, Berwanger had logged 10 rushing touchdowns and passed for two additional scores. The Dubuque star had emerged as a man among boys. Opponents' strategy focused on one thing: "Stop Berwanger." As the season moved toward its climax, a student sportswriter ventured out in search of a feature story. He endeavored to ask the football players whether they had any superstitions or "mascots" (good-luck charms). The reporter apparently lacked his own mascot, because he had little luck in securing interesting replies. Berwanger was not much help. The reporter said that when asked the question, the football star "pushed some of the blond hair out of his eyes and looked uneasy." He replied: "I don't know if you'd call it a mascot, but it generally works. If I find money on the field, it'll bring good luck," he said. "At least it has in the conference games."

Before the next conference game, at winless Grant High of Cedar Rapids, the Dubuque High student body gathered around the team bus for a send-off. Standing atop the bus, cheerleader Harold Roddy led the assemblage in several yells. A 14-member band provided musical support as the students serenaded the team with "Alma Mater" and "The Victory March." In Cedar Rapids that night, the slippery condition of the Coe College field might have limited Berwanger somewhat – his longest run was only 15 yards – but he passed effectively and collected two touchdowns, both on one-yard dives. Dubuque claimed an 18-0 victory. "The way Jay Berwanger mowed down the Grant players with his high knee action reminded us of a machine gun in action," a writer for the student newspaper remarked. *Cedar Rapids Gazette* sportswriter Earl Coughlin became a qualified believer: "Dubuque high school may not have the strongest prep team in the state, and its captain, John Berwanger, may not be the best of Iowa's scholastic halfbacks, but … the river city machine and its main cog displayed enough speed and power to warrant the belief that it will require an extra fancy outfit to take their number."

If such a fancy outfit existed, it was Davenport. Though it had graduated several standouts, from last year's state championship team, the Quad City contingent was again undefeated entering the contest. The game was Dubuque High's Homecoming contest, which the home team had won nine straight times. This Homecoming game had more at stake than a winning streak or even the first football championship awarded by the conference. The winner was virtually assured of being declared a state champion.

Homecoming activities began with a rally in the auditorium during the school day Friday. The football squad marched in, accompanied by the band, and took seats in the center section. The program included a singing quartet, a skit, a dance performance, and remarks by a couple of alumni and Dalzell. A cheerleader introduced each player and recited his accomplishments. That evening, some 700 Senior students staged a snake dance through the streets of Dubuque. The string of revelers, with the prior permission of management and without strong objection from patrons, weaved through three movie theaters – the Avon, Grand, and Spensely – during screenings. Afterward, hungry students might have stopped by George's diner, nicknamed "The High School Store," where a pint of milk, potatoes, vegetable, slice of pie and Jello sold for a nickel each and two hamburgers went for 15 cents.

The afternoon of the big game, some 3,500 fans – perhaps the most ever for any prep or collegiate contest in the city – jammed the stands and pressed up to the edge of the field. Members of the reserve football team and two basketball teams assisted with crowd control, working hard to keep spectators away from the south sideline. The stands included about 300 boosters from Davenport. Those who didn't make the trip could receive updates from a radio reporter using a field telephone. Also present was Jack North, sports editor of the *Des Moines Tribune,* whose job included picking the All-Iowa teams for the *Tribune* and its sister *Des Moines Register.* However, North witnessed the game not from the press box or even the sidelines; he served as the field judge. For years, North (born Jacob Norenbersky) moonlighted as a football and basketball official. As *Register* columnist Maury White noted years later, "Because of being the famed picker of all-state teams, his services (as a sports official) were eagerly sought by high school teams with strong candidates." Thus, Dubuque officials contracted North to make the 400-mile round trip to work the Saturday afternoon game. It would be the biggest game of 1931 and the final contest of Berwanger's prep career.

Starting with the opening kickoff at 2:30, North worked a rough game. Berwanger suffered a broken nose in the first quarter, when he signaled for a fair catch on a short punt but was creamed by Elmer Soeder of Davenport. (None of the players had a face guard on his helmet.) The resultant major penalty advanced the ball to Davenport's 14. If Berwanger was feeling the effects of the hit – on the next play, he lost eight yards trying to get around end – he shook them off and stayed in the game. He connected on a pass to Vonah for seven yards to conclude a scoreless first quarter. As the second

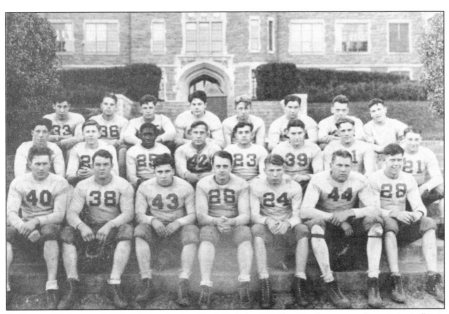

Dubuque High went 8-1 in 1931, winning the Mississippi Valley Conference and receiving a "state champion" designation from The Des Moines Register and Tribune, whose sports editor served as field judge for Berwanger's his final prep game. He made Berwanger (Number 42, middle row) honorary captain of the papers' all-state team. (Dubuque High yearbook)

period opened, Berwanger gained 10 yards, to the 5-yard line, and then crashed through for a touchdown. Badger's kick for the extra point fell short. Dubuque 6, Davenport 0.

At another point in the contest, a Davenport lineman made a strategic mistake. He tried trash-talking the Dubuque star. "Hey, Berwanger! You look great when (Mel) Paul opens your holes for you!" Berwanger decided he had something to prove. From then on, Berwanger mostly ran to the left – opposite Paul's side and directly into the strength of Davenport's line. The lineman must have regretted the taunt: Berwanger continue to chew up yardage, and the Davenport stalwarts took such a beating that, as one sportswriter described it, they "split out into a sieve in the waning moments of the game, permitting even Senior's subs to gain yardage."

Nonetheless, though it could not mount an offensive attack all afternoon, Davenport hung close, thanks to its defense and a bit of luck. When they weren't struggling to wrestle Berwanger to the soggy turf, Davenport players were starting their offensive drives deep in their own territory – courtesy of some of the most accurate punts of Berwanger's career. After starting a drive at its own 9 and making only one first down, Davenport punted to Berwanger, who unleashed a 42-yard return to the 15. On the next play Berwanger advanced the ball to the 8, but then Anthony lost a fumble on the 2. The next Dubuque drive, which spanned the third and fourth quarters, stalled on the Davenport 9. The score remained 6-0.

With each exchange of punts, Dubuque gained field position. The home team's second touchdown capped a six-play, 35-yard drive, with Berwanger rushing four times and Theatrice Gibbs twice. Berwanger scored a touchdown from the 2, rushing to the left – again challenging the stronger side of Davenport's line. The pass for the extra point failed, leaving Dubuque's lead 12-0. After Davenport's offense failed again – the visitors never crossed the Dubuque 35-yard line – conference and state honors were within Dubuque's grasp. In the final minutes of the championship game, Berwanger and Gibbs again alternated hitting the tired and demoralized Davenport line. They pounded it 11 times. On the 12th play, with time nearly expired, Berwanger crossed the goal line for his final high-school touchdown. Gibbs' rush for the extra point failed, but it didn't matter. Coach Dalzell sent in a substitute and summoned Berwanger to the sidelines, no doubt to the applause and cheers of the thousands assembled. Jay Berwanger's prep football career ended. As soon as the post-touchdown kickoff was blown dead at the Davenport 30 and Dubuque began celebrating the 18-0 victory.

"Davenport need offer no alibi for defeat," Quad Cities sportswriter Bob Feeney told his readers. They "went down before a stronger, heavier team that boasts a halfback of far more than ordinary ability. Berwanger weighs 175 pounds, and while he isn't exceptionally fast he runs with tremendous force. He swings his knees high and has a long stride." Prophetically, Feeney added, "He'll be heard from as a university star in a few years."

As Dubuquers reveled in their team's biggest victory ever, the players celebrated in their locker room. According to the student newspaper, activities included giving Berwanger "a much-needed shave." Their captain, who rushed for 17 touchdowns and passed for two others during the 8-1 campaign, outdistanced the rest of the Mississippi Valley Conference in scoring. To no one's surprise, he was named first-team all-conference. Later, the player who managed only honorable mention standing a year earlier joined The *Des Moines Register* and *Tribune's* first-team all-state roster. On top of that, the papers made him the honorary captain of the squad, effectively the state's player of the year. Guard Melvin Paul joined him on the first team, while tackle John Welbes made the second team. Quarterback John Ludescher joined the fifth team while Irvie Prior, Billy Thill and Glenn Paisley received honorable mention. Meanwhile, The *Register* and *Tribune* listed Dubuque High as one of its state co-champions despite its season-opening loss; the other champs were undefeated. That Dubuque's loss occurred out of state – in the final seconds at LaSalle, Illinois - helped Jack North justify Dubuque's designation as state champion.

By the time those honors hit the papers in December, Berwanger was practicing with the wrestling team, preparing for his final few weeks of high school competition. With athletics, schoolwork, and chores on the farm, Berwanger had no time for other extracurriculars. Outside of the sports page, his name rarely appeared in the student newspaper. One exception occurred late in his senior year, in the "Patches" gossip column. "A mysterious yellow paper appeared in the Patches box. On it were words to this effect: Who would think that Jay Berwanger would correspond with strange women? By unrevealed means we have learned that he has been writing to a girl in Oelwein, Iowa, whom he knows only through seeing her picture in a current newspaper." Another report placed the young lady in a different Northeast Iowa community, Guttenberg. In any case, Berwanger denied the accounts. Meanwhile, with the football season over, speculation grew over which college the school's top athlete would choose.

CHAPTER 7

As 1932 opened, the end of Jay Berwanger's high school athletic career was days away. Dubuque High School was a three-year institution, educating sophomores through seniors, and like dozens of his classmates, Berwanger started high school in January 1929, at the beginning of the spring semester. His six semesters of athletic eligibility would expire at the end of the fall semester of 1931-32. His track eligibility ran out in 1931, and his opportunity to wrestle would end before the district or state wrestling tournaments. Nonetheless, Berwanger would help the wrestling team as long as possible, competing until he was no longer eligible.

On January 27, 1932, in his final athletic appearance representing Dubuque High, Berwanger wrestled as a heavyweight and pinned his Cresco High opponent, junior Clarence Tass, in 6:05. Berwanger was one of only three Dubuque victors in the team loss to Cresco, a state powerhouse. Can anyone cite any other athletic competition in which the lineup included future winners of the Nobel Prize and a Heisman Trophy? Among Cresco's winners the night of Berwanger's final meet was 145-pounder Norman Borlaug, who later in life saved millions of lives through his Nobel Peace Prize-winning research that developed high-yield wheat to feed impoverished countries.

Though he had already accumulated enough credits to earn his diploma, Berwanger stuck around for the spring 1932 semester. He was advised to take more challenging courses in preparation for the rigors of college academics. He enrolled in geometry and two physics classes. It is likely that Dalzell was his teacher for physics and perhaps geometry, too. Berwanger posted his highest set of grades ever – a B-minus, B and B-plus. He also weighed his college options.

Meanwhile, the Depression's grip on his hometown tightened.

Depositors staged a crippling run on Federal Bank and Trust and, days later, Union Trust and Savings Bank closed. The bank failures wiped out $3,376 in Dubuque High School activities funds. School officials assessed the losses and calculated that they could sustain most events and programs, including publication of the school yearbook. However, they cancelled the basketball game against La Crosse and disbanded the golf team. The Depression effectively ended countless high-schoolers' dreams of a college education. Yet those dreams remained alive for Iowa's best football player.

John Berwanger at one point questioned whether his older son needed a college education. After all, it didn't take a college degree to be a blacksmith or farmer. Besides, the Berwangers were people of modest means; how would they pay for college? Eventually, perhaps after being assured

that Jay's athletic skills would greatly ease any financial burden, John Berwanger acceded. Jay would pursue college – and colleges would pursue him.

Throughout the existence of intercollegiate football, player recruitment and eligibility have been sources of controversy, intrigue, and corruption. In the late 19th and early 20th centuries, most institutions and conferences had rules against granting athletic scholarships, using players who were not students, and engaging in other unethical tactics to gain the upper hand. The regulations were difficult to enforce and frequently

Walter Eckersall was a three-time All-America for the University of Chicago (1904-06). (Special Collections Research Center, University of Chicago Library)

ignored. With or without rules, alumni and coaches went to extraordinary lengths to secure the services of their prized prospects. Just after the turn of the 20th century, Chicago prep star Walter Eckersall committed early to the University of Chicago Maroons. That decision did not deter the University of Wisconsin and University of Michigan from trying to persuade Eckersall to change his mind. Chicago officials accused Michigan of breaches of "every ethic of intercollegiate sport" in the effort to make Eckersall a Wolverine. As the start of the 1903-04 academic year approached, Eckersall still had not enrolled anywhere. Acting on a tip, legendary Maroons coach Amos Alonzo Stagg personally rushed to a Chicago railroad depot and removed Eckersall from the station platform before the young man could board a train for Ann Arbor. Eckersall enrolled at Chicago and stayed put. He was worth Stagg's effort. The plucky back became a three-time All-America. Soon after Eckersall's eligibility expired, however, Chicago expelled him, reportedly for bad debts, loose morals and other indiscretions.[18]

Major colleges engaged in some level of recruiting, but coaching staffs were small and thus unable to do much scouting at prep games. Colleges often relied on reports from alumni and boosters, high school coaches and newspaper clippings. Loyal and zealous alumni were more than willing to contact prospects on the behalf of their alma maters. The Eckersall recruiting episode notwithstanding, Stagg tried to portray his university as being above all that. In 1927, Chicago's Stagg described alumni of U.S. universities as "the most active agents in developing athletic immorality." However, he added that college authorities often go along with it. "In their anxiety to boom their institutions," he said, the colleges "lend themselves to questionable cooperation," including seeking out athletes and coming up with money to help athletes receive tuition remission or scholarship aid.[19]

After Berwanger was named Iowa's top prep football player of 1931, officials and boosters of several major colleges tried to steer him their way. Chicago won out. (Berwanger family collection)

In the first three decades of the 20th century, most colleges instituted programs to "subsidize" top athletes through tuition remission, room-and-board allowances, campus jobs, and training tables. In 1922, the Big Ten Conference, wracked with allegations and confirmed cases of violations, hired its first commissioner, John L. Griffith. His first assignment was to provide leadership in the enforcement and interpretation of amateur rules. At the outset, Griffith noted that conference rules effectively endorsed the involvement of alumni in recruiting prep athletes. The commissioner encouraged university athletic directors to shut down the slush funds that many alumni organizations operated to recruit and subsidize athletes – funds that the universities either specifically knew about or assumed were in place. By the late 1920s, only a handful of institutions did not give subsidies; among members of the Big Ten Conference, only Illinois and Chicago were on the list.[20]

Through official or unofficial channels, most of the Big Ten members made their interest in Berwanger known. They included 1931 co-champions Michigan, Purdue, and Northwestern. Also pursuing him were Minnesota and two schools that in 1931 had just one conference win between them, Chicago and Iowa.[21] In addition, it is likely that Dalzell put in a good word for his alma mater, Indiana University. Northwestern demonstrated its interest by having future College Football Hall of Fame inductee Ernest "Pug" Rentner, an All-America halfback, visit Berwanger in Dubuque.[22] Michigan benefited by having a loyal alumnus in Dubuque, retailer Carl Mehlhop, talking up the Wolverines, who went 8-1-1 overall in 1931 and were about to earn designation as a national champion in back-to-back seasons.

The Big Ten program in Berwanger's home state remained in disarray. The University of Iowa was trying to recover from sanctions, including suspension from the conference, in the wake of recruiting and eligibility scandals. The offenses included payments to athletes from an alumni-fueled slush fund operated with the knowledge of key university administrators. In the winter of 1931-32, Iowa hired Ossie Solem away from home-state Drake University, which had just finished its fourth straight 5-0 season in the Missouri Valley Conference. In Solem's 11 seasons in Des Moines, his Drake teams were 54-32-5. It became Solem's job to rebuild the Iowa program. One of his first orders of business was to convince quality players to join him in Iowa City. Dick Crayne, an all-state running back and track champion from Fairfield, Iowa, committed to the Hawkeyes. Now, could Solem land another prize in the big kid from Dubuque? One who hoped so was local dentist Max Kadesky, an Iowa booster from Dubuque. The Dubuque High School alumnus starred on the University of Iowa's first two unbeaten teams (1921 and 1922) and earned second-team All-America recognition.

A few weeks after taking over the Iowa program, Solem visited Dubuque to address the banquet honoring Dubuque High's graduating lettermen. They had plenty to celebrate. In addition to its football championship, Dubuque won the conference basketball title with a 10-0 record. During his speech in the Hotel Julien banquet hall, Solem intended to inspire Berwanger and other Dubuque boys to become Hawkeyes. The effort fell flat. "He didn't do a good job," Berwanger said more than 60 years later. "During the course of his speech, he said he had heard rumors that some of the players were thinking of leaving the state. He said if any of the boys crossed the Mississippi River, they should be considered traitors to the state of Iowa. That didn't go over well with us, and none of us went to Iowa."[23] Though Solem might have talked himself out of Berwanger's services, and the other universities had solid and successful programs, there was one thing they lacked. They didn't have Ira Davenport.

CHAPTER 8

Before, during, and after the Jay Berwanger era at Dubuque High, a familiar figure in the city's athletic and civic life was Ira Davenport, owner and manager of Dubuque Boat and Boiler Works, a shipbuilding concern. He was a former chair of the Republican Party in Democrat-laden Dubuque County; nonetheless, the community elected him to the local school board, a non-partisan position, in the early 1920s. Davenport occasionally coached football. He directed military veterans representing the local American Legion post and coached two seasons at Loras College, going 0-5-2 in 1920 and then 7-1 in 1921. He received local notoriety for all this, but it was as an athlete two decades earlier that Davenport earned international acclaim.

As a high-schooler from Pond Creek, Oklahoma, Davenport attracted national attention for his achievements in the sprints and quarter-mile. Representing University Preparatory School in Tonkawa (Oklahoma), he recorded the prep nation's fastest 100 yards of 1908 when he blazed the century in 9.8 seconds.[24] He earned an invitation to a national interscholastic meet sponsored by the University of Chicago. The university's athletic director and coach of football and track was Amos Alonzo Stagg, who recognized that hosting prep competitions in various sports was an excellent recruiting tool. Davenport hit the trifecta in Stagg's invitational on a rainy June day, winning the 100-, 220- and 440-yard dashes, the latter in a meet-record 51.2 seconds. The *Chicago Tribune* observed that his victories "seemed as easy for him as falling off a log. He simply ran the legs off the competition." With Davenport its lone representative, his school finished second in the team standings. University Preparatory School was at the time considered a "feeder" school for the University of Oklahoma, but Davenport did not follow that course. Within three months, he was back in the Windy City, enrolled in Stagg's University of Chicago.

Ira Davenport was a business owner in Dubuque, where he became young Jay Berwanger's mentor. Davenport was key to Berwanger's decision to enroll at Chicago.

Stagg switched Davenport to the quarter-mile and half-mile. As the 20th century's first decade closed, Davenport a national leader. The freshman gained notice in Eastern track circles with his performance in the 1909 Penn Relays, when he turned a blazing lap to anchor his team to a come-from-behind victory in the one-mile relay. Appearing hopelessly out of contention, some 15 yards behind Michigan and Harvard when he took the baton, Davenport caught the leaders entering the final straightaway and broke the tape two yards ahead of the closest anchorman. When Stagg and his relay team returned from Philadelphia, Chicago students staged a celebratory rally, at which Davenport was asked to describe his heroic run. Over the next couple of years, Davenport rose from national to world prominence, and he became a leading prospect for the U.S. Olympic team in 1912.

Though Davenport's name showed up on Stagg's football roster, he was first and foremost a track man. In the fall of 1911, when Davenport was a senior, he planned to skip the football season to concentrate on his bid for the Olympics. However, when the team suddenly found itself without a quarterback, Davenport reported for football practice. It was a controversial move; critics warned that a football injury could ruin Davenport's opportunity to represent his country the following summer in Stockholm. Those worries nearly became reality. In Chicago's first scrimmage of 1911, "Davy" suffered a sprained shoulder. That was that. Stagg removed him from the football team, and Davenport focused only on track.

Davenport made the U.S. Olympic team in the 400 and 800 meters. In Stockholm, American Jim Thorpe grabbed the headlines with his victories in the pentathlon and decathlon. However, Americans were responsible for other exciting achievements, including a record-smashing race involving Davenport. He found himself in the thick of the fastest 800 final ever, with four runners in gold-medal contention just 25 meters from the finish. Davenport beat the previous world record but finished just a step short of gold. He wound up third in 1:52.0, behind fellow Americans Ted Meredith (1:51.9) and Mel Sheppard (also 1:52.0). In the 400, he narrowly missed advancing to the finals.

After the Olympics, Davenport worked a half-year at an automobile dealership in Racine, Wisconsin, and then spent one year as purchasing agent for Woods Electric Automobile Company in Chicago. In January 1914, after an engagement of a year and a half, he married Dubuque native and former University of Chicago student Phyllis Schreiner. On the first day of 1915, Davenport started a job in his wife's hometown – construction superintendent of Dubuque Boat and Boiler Works, the nation's second-oldest boatbuilding enterprise.[25] A half-dozen years later, he owned the company.

The businessman had an eye for track talent, and he had his eye on Berwanger. As early as Berwanger's sophomore year at Dubuque High, Daven-

A 1912 Olympic medalist, Ira Davenport starred at the University of Chicago. (Special Collections Research Center, University of Chicago Library)

port chatted with the versatile young athlete at meets. In the spring of 1931, Berwanger's final season of track, Davenport suggested that Berwanger apply his speed, agility and coordination to the decathlon. He suggested that Berwanger, like Davenport, could become an Olympian.[26]

Davenport stayed in touch with his alma mater, and he also assisted at University of Chicago track meets. When Berwanger was a senior, in the spring of 1932, Davenport took him to visit the university. Though the young man had often visited the Windy City – his maternal grandparents and other relatives lived there – it was his first time on the Midway campus.[27] Decades later, in an article for the *Chicago Tribune*, Berwanger modestly recalled his campus visit. "Knowing that I was an athlete of sorts, he (Davenport) brought me into Chicago and introduced me to the boys at the Psi Upsilon fraternity house, who were very cordial to me." Davenport also made sure that Iowa's best prep football player met Stagg. It was not noted, but it might have been on this visit when he also met Davenport's Chicago teammate Austin Menaul, a 1912 Olympian in the decathlon and pentathlon, who served as a volunteer coach. As soon as Berwanger returned to Dubuque, he mailed his application for admission to the University of Chicago.

With that level of attention from Davenport, it's impossible to know for certain whether other colleges even had a chance to win Berwanger's services. According to notes on Berwanger's official high school record, the University of Chicago was the only school to receive his transcript, suggesting that Berwanger applied to only one school. However, his decision was not based on athletics alone. Location and career opportunities were other considerations. "I figured if I did something (in sports) – got some recognition and so forth – it would do me more good in Chicago than, say, Iowa City or up at Ann Arbor," he explained decades later. "And I liked the new (academic) program that (President Robert) Hutchins had up at the university, so when I got accepted and got an honor scholarship, I went there."[28]

When it came to promoting and recruiting for the University of Chicago, Davenport had several things going for him. He had the athletic credentials. As a leading Dubuque citizen, he had credibility. And, even during the Great Depression, he had jobs. Soon after choosing Chicago, Berwanger started a summer job at Davenport's business. The physical labor in the hot and dirty Dubuque Boat and Boiler Works facility enhanced Berwanger's conditioning, but it was not enough for him. After work, he often ran the four miles home, where farm chores awaited.[29]

The University of Chicago's official policy, like that of the Big Ten Conference, prohibited athletic scholarships. However, the university found a place for Berwanger on its list of 16 incoming freshmen receiving honor scholarships covering tuition for two years. (The scholarships could be renewed for his junior and senior years.) According to the Dubuque High newspaper, Berwanger's scholarship was due to his "athletic ability and high scholastic standing." In reality, he was an adequate student but no superstar. He ranked 77th out of 238 seniors, barely placing him among the top one-third of his graduating class.[30] A news article based on a University of Chicago press release stated that the honor scholarships were awarded on the basis of "scholarship, character, leadership and service." Also on the recipient list were basketball star Bill Haarlow and football prospects Tom Flinn and Steve Remias. Haarlow and Remias had top academic credentials, and each was his class president. (Chicago's scholarship offer failed to seal the deal with Remias, who wound up attending the University of Michigan.)

The scholarship system – at Chicago and elsewhere – was the topic of a "Talking it Over" column by the *Chicago Tribune* sports editor, Arch Ward. After receiving a couple of complaints about athletes receiving scholarships from Chicago and the University of Washington, Ward stated that, even if the undocumented reports were true, he had trouble mustering any outrage. "There undoubtedly are some schools which condone proselytizing and recruiting, but the fact that an athlete is obtaining an education on a free scholarship doesn't necessarily reduce the institution concerned to the ranks of the semipros," Ward wrote. "What I am trying to say is that I see no crime in trying to help a boy through college. That even goes for an athlete."

That defense was insufficient to please the University of Chicago, whose publicity director filed a lengthy response and noted, among other things, that nearly one in five incoming freshmen had received a scholarship of some sort and that all decisions are made independently by faculty members outside the athletic department. "For a good many years the university has suffered athletically because it has held to the theory that a good athlete must also be a good student," Bill Morgenstern wrote. "There are indications, however, that the next year will see the truth of that theory demonstrated, so far as Chicago is concerned. There were a good many athletes who were able to measure up to the faculty's standards."

Berwanger's full-tuition scholarship was worth $300 an academic year. He received no financial assistance for books or room and board. After working the summer in Davenport's factory and on the farm, Berwanger in mid-September packed up and headed for Chicago and the next chapter in life.

CHAPTER 9

That the University of Chicago coat of arms depicts a phoenix is appropriate. In mythology, the phoenix rose from the ashes. The university was phoenix-like in that, virtually overnight, it rose from marshland to a great institution of higher education. Few universities, if any, can claim such a rapid transformation from non-existence to national prominence.

The University of Chicago was founded in 1890 by the American Baptist Education Society. It appropriated the name of a three-decade-old Baptist institution that had gone belly-up a few years earlier. Oil tycoon John D. Rockefeller pledged $600,000 – worth roughly $15 million today – to operate the university. Rockefeller, who at the time had never even visited Chicago, made his gift contingent on others coming up with $400,000 for land acquisition and construction.[31] The Baptists failed to come up with the match themselves, so they turned to Chicago business leaders. It was not easy: Chicago had won the bid to host the Columbian Exposition in 1892, marking the 400th anniversary of Christopher Columbus' arrival on the continent. Fundraising for the exposition diverted many donors' discretionary dollars from other initiatives. However, university proponents succeeded in raising the $400,000. The campus site was donated by Chicago department store mogul Marshall Field, who gave 10 acres, then worth an estimated $100,000, in the newly annexed Hyde Park area, south of downtown. The ambitious project was on.

John D. Rockefeller Sr. (left) provided the seed money to create the University of Chicago, and he selected William Rainey Harper (right) as its first president. (Special Collections Research Center, University of Chicago Library)

Rockefeller's choice as the charter president

was, to no one's surprise, his close friend William Rainey Harper, a brilliant 35-year-old professor at Yale University. Harper envisioned a start-up university that would be world-class from the start. It would emphasize graduate-level research and training but would also offer undergraduate education, a divinity school, a university press and even community outreach education. Unlike many other institutions, it would educate year-round with an ambitious summer program.

With the funding and his appointment in hand, one of Harper's first official acts was to recruit a football coach. Harper saw football – winning football – as an essential publicity- and morale-builder for his yet-unbuilt university. He had someone in mind from the start: Amos Alonzo Stagg, the former All-America with whom he was acquainted through their time at Yale. Harper wrote to Stagg, asking for a meeting. "I have a very important matter about which I wish to talk to you. I am very anxious to see you at an early moment." The early moment came at an early hour – a breakfast meeting at the Murray Hill Hotel in New York. Stagg recalled the conversation:

"Dr. Harper then unfolded his plans for the University and broached the subject of my heading up the athletic department, first offering me a salary of $1,500.00. The whole idea was new to me and I kept still and just thought. Dr. Harper did not wait long but said, I'll offer you $2,000 and an assistant professorship. Still I kept silent and thought. Decision and action were dominant characteristics in Dr. Harper's make-up and probably thinking that the question of salary, which was furthest from my mind, was causing my hesitation, he enthusiastically burst in with "I'll give you $2,500 and an associate professorship, which means an appointment for life."

Stagg mailed his answer to Harper in late November 1890: "After much thought and prayer I feel decided that my life can best be used for my Master's service in the position which you have offered."[32] The interval between Stagg's acceptance and the opening of the university two years later gave ample opportunity for Stagg to get cold feet about Chicago and consider other offers. Ultimately, Harper persuaded Stagg to honor his commitment. That Stagg secured a tenured associate professorship and headed the nation's first physical education department, one treated on a par with academic departments, was unprecedented. As Stagg biographer Robin Lester noted, the action "began the professionalization of college coaching in America."[33]

Designing and constructing the university buildings occurred at a frenetic pace. Meanwhile, just a dozen blocks to the east, laborers in Jackson Park worked feverishly to build Daniel Burnham's Great White City, site of the

Columbian Exposition world's fair. The site spilled over into Midway Plaisance, a linear park that stretched from Jackson Park to Washington Park at the west edge of the university campus, which came to be called the Gray City. A prospective professor visited the university construction site and was not impressed. He reported seeing "unfinished gray stone buildings scattered loosely over the immense campus which was nothing more than a quagmire with a frog pond at the south end."[34]

Soon enough, the campus, with buildings constructed on cloistered quadrangles, came into focus. The first structures copied the English Gothic style of architecture, including towers, spires, cloisters, and gargoyles. While some critics complained that their design dripped with pretentiousness – Rockefeller himself questioned the need for a Gothic façade on the gymnasium – trustees stuck to the plan, arguing that the building design would create and convey (to undergraduates especially) an atmosphere of academic seriousness and tradition.

The concurrent construction projects at the University of Chicago and the Columbian Exposition marked a pivotal moment in the city's history. "With their unified designs, both the Gray City and the White City symbolized the civic cooperation Burnham and (university trustee and civic benefactor Charles L.) Hutchinson believed was as responsible for Chicago's growth as its unsheathed competitiveness," historian Donald L. Miller wrote. "These paired 'cities' were built at the same time to inspire a new Chicago, not to mirror what the present city was, as the skyscrapers in the Loop did. Condemned by modernist critics at the turn of the century and today, the quadrangles of the University of Chicago, historian Neil Harris wrote, 'survive as one of the country's most remarkable expressions of commitment to a scholarly or priestly dream.'"[35]

Burnham's Great White City was not finished on time, so the Columbian Exposition opened 401 years after Columbus' arrival, in 1893. Meanwhile the University of Chicago opened on schedule in the fall of 1892. However, construction of the campus still had a long way to go. Stagg, chair of the Department of Physical Culture and Athletics, described the situation:

"When I reported for duty in September 1892, no buildings had been completed and the carpenters still were at work in Cobb Hall, the one structure nearing completion. We entered the building over bare planks, and in lieu of knobs on the doors, the teachers carried square pieces of wood to insert in the doors to turn the latches."

His football program was similarly unprepared.

CHAPTER 10

The inaugural day of classes at University of Chicago classes, October 1, 1892, also marked the first day of football practice. Thirteen boys and young men reported. "Some never had played, most of them very little; three were graduate and three divinity students well up in years," Stagg recalled, "and all the other colleges in the Chicago territory had been practicing for nearly a month." Noting that the new university had many "eager students" without time to spare for football, Stagg reduced the time and intensity of practice sessions in hopes of attracting more players.[36] After just one week of practice, with the 30-year-old Stagg taking part, the university squad posted a 12-0 win over nearby Hyde Park High, a school that over the years would supply the University of Chicago with a wealth of athletic talent. "There was no secrecy about my presence in the line-up, and no objections by our opponents," Stagg said years later. "The game was too young and weak for such a situation to be thought particularly unusual."[37]

Football in 1892 more closely resembled soccer and rugby than 21st-century football. The game was played with an egg-shaped rugby ball. A football of prolate dimension – technically, where the polar axis is larger than the equatorial diameter – did not arrive until 1896, and even then the ball was rounder than the one used today. The field was 110 yards long, and games lasted 90 minutes. A touchdown was worth four points, and a point-after-touchdown kick was worth two points; the kick had to be attempted from five yards outside the point on the goal line where the touchdown was scored. Reflecting the rules' emphasis on kicking, a field goal (five points) was more valuable than a touchdown (four). Safeties then, as now, were worth two points. Substitutes were allowed only for seriously injured players or those kicked out of the game by the referee. The offense had three chances to advance the ball five yards to gain a first down, and the forward pass was

not part of the game. Many of the tactics in those games are illegal today –
including mass play, pushing, flying wedges, and even heaving one's own ball
carrier over opposing players.

Three weeks after the first practice, the University of Chicago hosted
its first collegiate game. The opponent was Northwestern University, from
north suburban Evanston, which started its football program 10 years earlier.
About 300 students, "many of them young women," gathered in South Side
Park, an off-campus site rented for the occasion, to root on their respective sides in a game that was unfamiliar to many Americans. "Both factions
went there to carry away scalps and both made a deal of noise," the *Chicago Tribune* reported. Northwestern had an apparent first-half touchdown
disallowed on a fumble. In the second half, Chicago rooters "went wild"
when Stagg, playing halfback, appeared to score a touchdown on a long run.
"But their ardor was dampened when the referee declared the ball had not
touched the third man, and the run was of no service." The fumble-filled
contest finally came to an end as a scoreless tie. (In a rematch in Evanston 11
days later – a drizzly Wednesday afternoon – Northwestern posted a hard-
fought 6-4 victory.)

When Lehigh at the last minute backed out of its game against the
University of Michigan, scheduled for November 12 in Toledo, Michigan
wired a last-minute invitation to Chicago. Stagg and his players scrambled
and caught the last train that would get them to Ohio in time. "Michigan
had not bothered to change the advertising and the crowd did not realize
that Lehigh was being represented by eleven impostors from Chicago until
the second half," Stagg recalled. Still, Chicago made it "interesting" for their
hosts, losing by only an 18-12 margin. The visitors racked up $217 in travel
expenses, but they came home with $264 as their share of ticket proceeds.[38]

The first victory in University of Chicago football history came in the next
game, at the expense of the visitors from the University of Illinois, 10-4. The
former All-America Stagg himself scored the winning touchdown. Illinois
later exacted revenge on its home field in the season finale, 28-12. Chicago
closed its first season 1-4-2, but the Maroons would not experience another
losing season for nearly two decades (1910). In the interim, Stagg built a
football powerhouse.

In only the second season of Stagg's reign, the University of Chicago and
University of Michigan agreed to play on Thanksgiving Day 1893 in the
Windy City. The schools envisioned a Big Game event like those staged in
the East by Harvard, Yale and Princeton. Michigan fans filled special trains

from Ann Arbor to see the holiday spectacle on the hosts' new on-campus field, at 57th and Ellis. They went home satisfied but chilled when Michigan prevailed easily in the snow, 28-10. Chicago's season record dropped to 4-4-2, but in December 1893 and January 1894, it won indoor games against Northwestern and previously unbeaten Notre Dame to finish 6-4-2. The indoor contests were staged at Tattersall's, an exhibition hall often used as a horse market, at West 16th and South Dearborn streets.

After the traditional close of the 1894 campaign, the first in which the university's teams went by the nickname "Maroons," Stagg took his squad on a publicity- and cash-generating barnstorming tour of the western United States. In December 1894 and January 1895, the Maroons covered an exhausting 6,200 miles and played four games, including two against Stanford, to finally end their season with a record of 11-7-1.

Situated in the preeminent city of the Midwest, with the nation's most railroad connections, and supported by a strong base of ticket-buying fans, Stagg could offer visiting teams more revenue by playing in Chicago than they usually realized in their home stadiums. As a result, the University of Chicago rarely played road games. Between 1896 and 1905, nearly 90 percent of the Maroons' games were on their home gridiron. An extreme example was 1894, when, excepting their barnstorming tour of the West, the Maroons played at home for 14 of their 15 games. At that, their lone "road" game was at Northwestern, a mere 20 miles away. Chicago's approach was to schedule weaker visitors early in the season, not only to give Maroon players a tune-up but to chalk up victories that could spark fan enthusiasm (and ticket sales) for the rest of the season.[39] Over the 10-year period from 1896 through 1905, after which the Chicago schedule was cut in half for several seasons, Chicago dominated 42 early-season guests by a combined score of 1,232-37. One frequent victim was Monmouth, a small college from western Illinois, which from 1896 through 1903 lost seven games to Chicago by a combined score of 292-4. The final game in that series was a 108-0 drubbing. (Monmouth came back one more time, in 1932, and lost 41-0.) To be fair to Monmouth and other small-school victims, larger universities also found themselves losing to Chicago. In 1904, the University of Texas traveled to Chicago and experienced a 68-0 whipping for their trouble. The University of Chicago yielded only 28 points in 14 contests in 1899, just 27 points in 1902 (21 of them coming in a loss to Michigan) and five points (all to Indiana) in their 10-0 season of 1905.[40]

Stagg parlayed his coaching skills, a sophisticated recruiting system (under the auspices of the Chicago Alumni Club), worshipful publicity emanating from a newspaper-rich city, and support from a community and alumni caught up with football fever to make the Maroons one of the best-known programs in the "West." Their first championship in the Western Conference, (until 1987, it was officially the Intercollegiate Conference of Faculty Representatives) came in 1899 when they won four conference games, beating their opponents by a combined 166-0. In non-conference action, Chicago and Iowa spoiled each other's bids for unblemished records by trading field goals in a 5-5 tie. Iowa, which would join the conference the next season, finished 8-0-1. Chicago, which later had another 5-5 tie (against Pennsylvania), wound up 12-0-2. In addition to their 1899 title, the Maroons also claimed

the championship of the conference (subsequently known as the Big Ten) in 1905, 1907, 1908, 1913, and 1924.

The university's football fortunes were viewed as critical to the university's fortunes overall. Stagg biographer Robin Lester recounted President Harper taking the unusual step of addressing the football team at halftime of an 1895 game in which the Maroons trailed Wisconsin, 12-0.[41] "Boys, Mr. (John D.) Rockefeller has just announced a gift of $3 million to the University," Harper said. "He believes the University is to be great. The way you played in the first half

Amos Alonzo Stagg, shown in 1906, was the first and only head football coach at the University of Chicago (1892-1932). The university forced Stagg to retire after Berwanger's freshman season, before he became eligible for varsity competition.

leads me to wonder whether we really have the spirit of greatness and ambition. I wish you would make up your minds to win the game and show that we do have it." Final score: Chicago 22, Wisconsin 12. High expectations and regard for the football program only served to increase the authority and influence of Stagg, who also served as athletic director and coached track and, briefly, baseball. Football paid the bills and helped build the university's visibility and reputation. The coach wielded great power on campus, and he used it, year after year. In 1901, Stagg decided to install electric lights at the practice field. "In the latitude of Chicago, in the autumn months, practice by artificial light is imperative if the class work of the players is not to be interfered with," he explained.[42]

In 1905, as President Harper lay dying of cancer, Chicago achieved its greatest gridiron success. The Maroons capped their first perfect season with a dramatic 2-0 victory over previously unbeaten Michigan on Thanksgiving Day. (The Michigan punt returner whose mistake resulted in the game-winning safety, William Dennison Clark, carried his shame for that play for the next 27 years. He killed himself in 1932.[43]) American society and its institutions of higher education in 1905 turned up the heat and looked critically at football's influence, impact, and injuries, which included 18 fatalities (three in college games). The ways and means of recruiting and enticing prep players, devolving into open bidding involving dubious college aid programs and generous alumni, was building cynicism and outrage among faculty and fair-minded fans. The University of Chicago was a prime target. Edward S. Jordan, writing in *Collier's* magazine in November 1905, classified Chicago as the leader in corrupt programs. "Western educators who have helplessly watched this campaign place the University of Chicago first among the violators of the trust which rests upon all universities for the conservation of academic ideals," he wrote. After noting the denials of university officials, including President Harper, Jordan continued, "Nevertheless, the University of Chicago possesses and makes use of larger official resources for the maintenance of athletes than any other university in the West. To athletes sought after in the annual bidding contest between friends of the rival colleges the resources of Chicago appear most seductive." The *Collier's* article alleged that more than 100 students were receiving partial or full tuition remission under a "student service" program for campus work (some of which required little work by the athletes.) "In the information office of the university alone thirty-nine men do service on the relay plan." Jordan revealed that football star Walter Eckersall was "simply an 'athletic ward' of the University of Chicago, retained under her system of official 'maintenance' as a factor in building her athletic prestige." (During this period, amid allegations and damning evidence that Hugo Bedzek had boxed professionally, an offense that should have cost him his college eligibility, Stagg looked the other way and continued to play the All-America in 1905.[44])

Stagg was given an opportunity to preview the *Collier's* article and have his response published in the same issue. The coach cast himself as an unwilling victim – a victim of the very system he helped create: "I believe that the growing tendency among college students to demand athletic directors and coaches to openly solicit the attendance of football experts, has in line a dangerous tendency, which, if allowed to run, can not but in time undermine the highest integrities and fundamental purpose of a true American university."[45] Soon after the death of Stagg's ally Harper in January 1906, as the reform movement was gaining steam, an internal investigation revealed that no fewer than 25 Chicago athletes received scholarships for work they never performed.[46]

Worse than the abuse of scholarships were the debilitating injuries and deaths on the football field as well as unsporting and violent conduct. People from professors to presidents sounded the alarm. The 1905 season was barely under way when President Theodore Roosevelt convened a White House meeting with representatives from the collegiate football powers in the East – Harvard, Yale, and Princeton – to discuss the problem. Many accounts suggest that Roosevelt threatened to ban football; that was not the case. However, the president gave his guests the assignment of immediately drafting an agreement promoting reform. Their result was a statement that they would follow "in letter and spirit the rules of play." Their non-binding pledge was soon forgotten.

The Harvard-Yale game, a bloody affair marred by inattentive officiating and marked by Harvard administration's unsuccessful attempt to remove its team from the field, signaled the failure of Roosevelt's intervention. Chancellor Henry McCracken of New York University, whose institution was the opponent when Union College's Harold Moore suffered a fatal football injury on November 25, convened two conferences to discuss the reform or abolition of the game. Columbia University already had its answer: The nation's largest institution abolished football, which its president, Nicholas Murray Butler, called "an academic nuisance." Union College, which had experienced tragedy on the gridiron, also dropped the sport.[47]

At the first McCracken conference, in early December 1905 in New York, a majority of the 12 colleges and universities represented rejected a proposal to abolish football; instead, they resolved to reform it. Further, the group sought to expand its influence – and counter that enjoyed by Eastern powers Harvard, Yale, Princeton and Pennsylvania – by inviting all football-playing colleges to a subsequent conference. Organizers hoped to exclude from the meeting those who were profiting from the game, including coaches, alumni, and hangers-on. A few days later, the official Intercollegiate Football Rules Committee, made up of Eastern officials and Stagg, held its regularly scheduled meeting. They discussed and debated several proposals, including the forward pass and the requirement to make 10 yards in three tries for a first down. When they failed to reach consensus, their influence waned.

Meanwhile, the second McCracken meeting resulted in the creation of the InterCollegiate Athletic Association (ICAA), forerunner of the National Collegiate Athletic Association (NCAA). Its charter president, Major Palmer E. Pierce of the U.S. Military Academy, recalled the atmosphere that brought about the association: "The rules of play were severely handled by the public press. The Football Rules Committee was charged with being a self-constituted, self-perpetuating and irresponsible body, which had degraded a once noble sport to the plane of a gladiatorial contest." Pierce and Walter Camp, head of the Intercollegiate Football Association, hammered out some rule changes intended to open up the game and make it safer. The amendments included legalization of the forward pass (with restrictions), a neutral zone at the line of scrimmage, offensive gain of 10 yards (instead of five) required for a first down, 60-minute games (instead of 70) and the ejection of players guilty of "fighting or kneeing" an opponent.[48] Pierce, whose Army career took him to the rank of brigadier general and assistant chief of staff of the American Expeditionary Forces in France during World War I, served as NCAA president for 21 years (1906-13 and 1917-29).

The rules changes that Pierce helped formulate allowed a forward pass only if it originated behind the line of scrimmage and five yards to the right or left of center. There were risks associated with the rewards of attempting a forward pass. If a team's passed ball failed to touch a player before hitting the ground, it turned over possession to the defense. Only one forward pass could occur on each set of downs.[49] There were no limitations on who was eligible to receive a forward pass.

On the University of Chicago campus, outraged alumni and students protested the proposed reforms, including those to eliminate the athletic training table (such as that provided at Hitchcock Hall, the nicest dormitory on campus, where the top athletes lived); ban preseason training; slash the schedule to five games; and bar graduate students as players. However, the bigger threat was abolition of football altogether. On the first day of February 1906, University of Chicago faculty, considering football beyond reform, unanimously voted to suspend the sport for two years if other members of the conference concurred. However, cooler heads prevailed, and Chicago and other schools in the Big Nine Conference retained football – but with some restrictions. The changes included the abbreviated schedule, no longer playing on Thanksgiving, banning practices before the regular opening of the school year; and varsity eligibility for just three seasons only.

"Where properly managed, there can be no objection to a training table, but it is too easy of prostitution into free board and room for athletes," Stagg stated years later. "I confess that I was opposed to doing away with the training table, fearing for the physical conditioning of the athletes, but I have changed my mind. Looking back, I cannot see that its abolition has had the least effect on the conditioning of the men." At one stage, faculty considered a recommendation to ban so-called professional coaches, such as the University of Michigan's Fielding Yost, and others who were not faculty members. All this was too much for Michigan, which after two unhappy years seceded from the Big Nine; the Wolverines did not return until 1917.[50]

On September 24, 1906, Stagg returned from a three-week trip to Chautauqua, New York, and discovered several of his players, including returning All-America Walter Eckersall, practicing at Marshall Field. He evicted them, ordered the stadium locked tight, and reminded them that under conference rules, the first football practice cannot begin until the start of classes – which at Chicago was October 1. On that date, Stagg had the gates unlocked and went about teaching his team about the forward pass. (Eventually, the starting date for practices was moved up to mid-September.)

The dramatic changes in the rules left a great many questions in the minds of players, coaches and officials. Legendary Yale coach Walter Camp traveled to Chicago to explain the revisions to Stagg and dozens of other Western coaches in early October. The seminar at the Edgewater Beach Hotel made it clear that the rules were not necessarily clear. Even Camp confessed to being perplexed about some elements of the 26 rule changes, conceding it probably would come down to the interpretation of game officials each Saturday afternoon.[51] Whatever Stagg's opinion of the forward pass, onside kick, and other changes in the rules, he resolved to learn and implement them. He soon became regarded a leader in pursuing the more open style of play allowed under the rules.[52] After his team went 4-1 in the first season under the new rules – the loss was a 4-2 decision to Minnesota – Stagg supported the changes. "There are great possibilities in the new rules and with another season I look for a far better game of football," he said. "The forward pass and the on-side kick have been used only in a plain, elementary way. Given more time I believe the coaches will perfect these two possibilities to an amazing value." The rules committee relaxed the penalty for an unsuccessful forward pass, but it was still tough: Instead of losing possession of the ball, the offense would be assessed a 15-yard penalty. After another 4-1 campaign in 1907, Stagg told delegates at the annual rules meeting, "I object to the too great element of chance which has resulted from the present rules surrounding the forward pass. The best feature of football has always been that the best team can win on its merits, and I dislike to see this condition upset. I believe in chance, but not in so much of it as is now possible. In many cases this year the forward pass allowed teams to get down the field by sheer chance." He called for a way to ensure that only players eligible to receive a forward pass – ends and backs – are touching the ball. "I am just as enthusiastic over the forward pass as I ever was," he said, "and would not think of cutting it out and reverting to the old style of game."

The forward pass was far from the only challenge facing Stagg. After President Harper's death in early 1906, a faculty council investigated the questionable practice of awarding of "student service" scholarships to athletes who performed little or no service. However, little or nothing was done with the final report, and the faculty, perhaps resigning itself to the abuse or turning its attention to other issues, did not press the matter. [53]

One of William Rainey Harper's first initiatives upon becoming charter president of the University of Chicago was to recruit a top football coach. He hired Amos Alonzo Stagg. (Special Collections Research Center, University of Chicago Library)

After the rules changes and reforms, which soon allowed one more game to be put back on the schedule, Stagg's Maroons remained a force. They won the conference in 1907 and 1908 (5-0-1) and came close in 1909, when they were 4-1-1 in the conference and tied Cornell (New York) in a non-conference matchup. However, the tide was shifting. Chicago's conference rivals, mostly public universities whose admissions standards were considered less stringent, experienced growth in undergraduate enrollment that made Chicago one of the smallest schools in the league. Even with Stagg's intervention with professors to keep players eligible and with administrators to secure admission for prized recruits, it was harder to field championship teams. The Maroons won their only conference championship of the 1910s in 1913, when they went 7-0 (with no non-conference contests).

Meanwhile, Western teams came into their own, reversing the dominance of the Eastern elite schools, and football was transforming from a game for the upper crust to one marketed for the masses, Stagg biographer Lester observed. "The scale of the football enterprise on the Midway remained more like that of the elite eastern schools; Chicago and those eastern teams found themselves far behind after the nationalization and democraticization of football in American had its effect by the late 1920s."[54]

Still, in the early 1920s, Stagg's teams hung in there. They went a collective 13-2-1 over three seasons (1921-23). Chicago then won the Big Ten championship in 1924 with the unusual record of 3-0-3, edging out Illinois and Iowa (both 3-1-1). It would be Chicago's final conference title and the final time the Maroons would record more Big Ten wins than losses.

As Chicago's football fortunes faded in the second half of the 1920s, university administration was experiencing its own transition. In selecting their fourth president to serve in the decade, trustees opted for youth and innovative thinking over experience. They hired 30-year-old Robert Maynard Hutchins, dean of the Yale Law School. During Hutchins' presidency (1929-51), he established many of the undergraduate curricular innovations that the University is known for today. These included a curriculum dedicated specifically to interdisciplinary education, comprehensive examinations instead of course grades, courses focused on the study of original documents and classic works, and an emphasis on discussion, rather than lectures. While the core curriculum has changed substantially since Hutchins' time, original texts and small discussion sections remain a hallmark of a Chicago education.

However, unlike his predecessors, Hutchins didn't like football – especially its influence on campus life and academic priorities. He considered college football a corrupted distraction to higher education's primarily purpose. That did not bode well for Amos Alonzo Stagg and the university's athletic boosters.

CHAPTER 11

In mid-September 1932, Berwanger left Dubuque and moved into an off-campus apartment at 1219 East 53rd Street, four blocks north of Stagg Field, and reported to the University of Chicago football team. He was among 11 freshmen Stagg invited to report early and practice with the varsity for two weeks. Under Big Ten Conference rules, freshmen were not eligible for intercollegiate athletics; they could not even compete against freshmen from other schools. Thus, freshmen spent all season standing in as the upcoming opponent during varsity practices or engaging in intra-squad scrimmages. Berwanger most likely was in attendance when his new teammates walked all over their guests from Monmouth (Illinois) College in their season opener, 41-0.

The final Monday morning of September, Berwanger and more than 700 other freshmen gathered in Leon Mandel Assembly Hall, where President Robert M. Hutchins delivered the opening address of freshman orientation week. In addition to listening to speeches, the freshmen took placement examinations, went on tours, enjoyed social activities, and registered for classes. Berwanger signed up for a math-intensive schedule. Over the three quarters comprising his first academic year, he took physical science, social science, plane trigonometry, algebra, plane geometry, and gym (officially "physical culture"). He received 16 units of credit from

Jay's father, John, was a blacksmith and farmer, and his mother, Pauline, maintained the seven-member household. They named their oldest surviving son John, after his father and grandfather, but nearly from the start the boy was called Jay. (Berwanger family collection)

his entrance exams.[55]

Berwanger had plenty of adjustments to make – to university life, to university academics, and to life in what he called a "larger environment."[56] Under the Hutchins' "New Plan," Chicago students were not required to attend their classes or take tests during the school year. Students received marks of "S" or "U," indicating satisfactory or unsatisfactory progress in each course, but those ratings had no bearing on whether they received credit. Everything was based on their performance on comprehensive examinations administered at the end of the term. It was a pass-or-fail proposition. Hutchins once described letter grades as "useless," but the university later resumed issuing them. "The only utility for grades at the University of Chicago is for transfer purposes, as an accommodation to other institutions who are not as enlightened as we are," Hutchins once told an audience of registrars visiting Chicago. He went on to tell the visitors that most of their offices were overstaffed. The campus paper noted that convention organizers had invited Hutchins to give the "welcoming" speech.

After the first day of orientation, all the freshmen football players reported for their initial practice. Among them were Berwanger, the other freshmen who had been working out with the varsity, and Mel Paul, Berwanger's Dubuque High teammate. A total of 40 players were on hand, roughly half the total of previous seasons. The coach of the freshmen, Amos Alonzo Stagg Junior, the 31-year-old son and namesake of the Grand Old Man, attributed the drop-off to a change in university policy. No longer was credit in "physical culture," which could be satisfied by participation on an athletic team, a graduation requirement. The younger Stagg publicly expressed little concern about the shorter roster, noting that the absentees probably were not varsity material anyway.

Many of those who *did* report for freshman football were not varsity material, either. Ernie Dix had not played one down of football at Calumet High School, on Chicago's South Side. However, Dix, who had worked in his father's hardware store instead of going out for sports, decided to try Big Ten football. In the locker room before his first practice, Dix tried to put on his equipment. He was baffled. A fellow freshman helped him figure out the shoulder pads. The teammate was Berwanger. "I found out later that he was a great football player (in high school)," Dix recalled.[57] Thus began a friendship and business relationship that would last the next 70 years.

That a star like Berwanger would help an inexperienced teammate instead of deriding or teasing him was indicative of the Iowan's character and personality. However, the equipment episode reflected the direction of University of Chicago football – a spiral that one of the greatest college players ever could only slow temporarily. The Maroons had not posted a winning season in Big Ten play since 1924 (3-0-3). In the subsequent eight seasons, they went just 8-30-1 in conference games.

Glories of decades past were not enough to satisfy current students. During the 1931 season, when the team was mired in a 2-6-1 campaign, the *Daily Maroon* sparked controversy by publishing an anonymous student's letter calling on Stagg to retire, and another student publication, the alternative *Phoenix*, satirically expressed its view that Stagg was responsible for the drop in Chicago's football fortunes.[58] Nonetheless, Stagg expressed optimism. "I look forward to the impending football season – my forty-first at the University of Chicago – with more anticipation and confidence than I have had reason to feel for many seasons. I expect it be to be very satisfactory," he wrote. With a nod to the effects of the Great Depression, Stagg also noted that ticket prices had been reduced, allowing Chicago students to purchase a "C" Book, containing tickets to all university athletic events, for $5.

In the run-up to the Yale game at New Haven, Stagg staged a two-hour scrimmage between his varsity and the freshmen, with the underclassmen simulating the Yale offense. The varsity had all it could handle. The *Daily Maroon* noted, "Jay Berwanger, all-state halfback from Dubuque, Iowa, was the most consistent ground-gainer, and in addition, showed unusual passing ability." Added a city newspaper, "Part of the gains registered by the freshmen yesterday, however, were due less to the Yale plays than to the eye-opening running of Jay Berwanger, freshman halfback from Dubuque, who picked holes with a sure instinct and ran through them. Berwanger's relentless driving and a few long passes captured by (Ralph) Balfanz and (Rainwater) Wells, freshman ends, would have been good for several Yale touchdowns had the scrimmage been a regulation game."

After the varsity netted a 7-7 tie at Yale, Stagg's alma mater, the Chicago campus was anticipating an easy home victory over Knox College. Suddenly, the game against the visitors from Galesburg, Illinois, became back-page news. The top story: Stagg would leave his post as athletic director by July 1, 1933. For the time being, he was still the football coach, but Stagg was on borrowed time. University policy stated that trustees had to issue an invitation each year for anyone they wished to keep beyond age 65, and Stagg received those extensions. Through most of that period, Stagg quietly lobbied to stay beyond age 70. However, President Hutchins opposed further extensions. He thought it would be easier to make changes if he had a new athletic director, someone to oversee the football coach.

Simultaneous with disclosure of Stagg's forced retirement as athletic director, trustees announced the hiring of his successor, T. Nelson Metcalf, athletic director at Iowa State College in Ames. One of Metcalf's first tasks would be to decide who would coach the football team in 1933. Would Stagg receive another extension? Meanwhile, the Grand Old Man made it known that he had no intention to retire from coaching. "I expect to be good for 15 to 20 years of active service," the 70-year-old icon said in an official statement. "I went into athletic work because it offered the largest opportunity for service through contact with young men. No scheme of life which removes that contact would meet with my ambitions." Stagg said he had "no protest" about the retirement policy, but added, "I feel too young and aggressive to step altogether out of my particular work, and, frankly, I am not content to do it. Whether I remain at Chicago or go elsewhere, I wish to be active in the field of coaching." He held out hope that he could continue at the Midway.

The next afternoon, on the field named after him, Stagg's Maroons struggled against Knox. Were they distracted by the retirement announcement or overconfident against a weak opponent? Whatever the reason, the game was

The abandoned west stands of Stagg Field, under which scientists secretly developed the first atomic bomb. This photo was taken in 1947, two years after the bomb ended World War II and a dozen years after Berwanger's last football game there. (Seymour Katcoff photo, courtesy of Joel Katcoff)

scoreless at halftime. As the varsity combatants headed to the locker rooms for intermission, the Chicago freshmen took the field for a brief scrimmage. The 25,000 spectators – half of them were Boy Scouts and "schoolboy patrolmen" who were guests of the university – received a glimpse of the Maroons' future. They couldn't help but notice Number 21 on the freshman Blue squad, Jay Berwanger. According to one newspaper account, he "took the ball for every offensive play, and was in on almost every tackle on defense." Back home, the Dubuque paper said coaches tried to keep a lid on Berwanger's outstanding work in hopes he would not become a "marked man" by opposing teams when he joined the varsity. "Berwanger has a lot of ability and a very likeable disposition. Whether or not he lives up to the high expectations they seem to have for him in Chicago, we in Dubuque are still back of him!"

After the freshmen exhibition, the Chicago varsity wore down the Knox defense and scored three fourth-quarter touchdowns to post a 20-0 victory. Discussion and debate about Stagg resumed. Some people, aware of Stagg's age and the football team's recent struggles, believed it was time for a change. Others remained loyal to the Grand Old Man. A *Daily Maroon* editorial took a shot at Stagg's critics, who "are the kind that are with you when you win and against you when you lose. The wolves – that's what they are called. And now, it can be easily imagined, that some of the wolves are crowing. But, for every one of them there is a group of twenty to overshadow any debasement of that which really is." Among those surprised and angered by the move to oust Stagg were members of three fraternities and the freshman football team, who circulated petitions calling for his retention as football coach. The *Daily Maroon* reported that every member of the freshman football team – many of whom said they came to the university because of Stagg – signed the petition "with enthusiasm." In the 1980s, Berwanger recalled being upset with Stagg's ouster. Memories have a way of fading, especially after 75 years, but one member of that team, Dix, did not remember signing a petition. However, he did recall a particular encounter with the Grand Old Man during practice. "I remember going out for a pass one time and knocking him on his ass," the former benchwarmer chuckled. "My only claim to fame."

The petition drive probably was still a topic of conversation a week after the announcements, when the varsity football team hosted a banquet for the freshmen. There might also have been talk about how some freshmen had breached the campus tradition that only "C men" (varsity letterwinners), seniors, and their girlfriends may use the "C" Bench, a concrete amenity installed in 1903 outside Cobb Hall. A poster ominously warned uncooperative freshmen, "Beware of the Botany Pond."

After the Thursday dinner, the university band headed a torchlight procession to a bonfire and pep rally for the varsity's home game against Indiana. Two days later, the Maroons prevailed over the Hoosiers, 13-7, to claim their only Big Ten victory of the season. The win turned out to be Stagg's last for Chicago (but not his last *in* Chicago).

Petition drives to retain the coach gained momentum, and Stagg, sensing that a lifetime appointment was not in the cards, campaigned to coach Chicago football for at least one more year. He stated that he had already turned down offers from three universities because he hoped to stay on the Midway. Meanwhile, the rumor mill immediately speculated on Stagg's successor, starting with three of his former players: Walter Steffen, a Chicago judge; H.O. "Fritz" Crisler, who was in his first season at Princeton, between stints at Minnesota and Michigan; and multi-sport coach Pat Page, who was head coach at Indiana for five seasons before joining Stagg's staff. Theirs were only the first of roughly a dozen names mentioned in connection with the job.

Months before all this became public, Hutchins offered Stagg two opportunities to stay at Chicago, though neither involved coaching or athletics administration, at no loss of compensation (when his retirement allowance was figured in). One job involved working with alumni and high schools, and the other was chairmanship of the Committee on Intercollegiate Relations. The first opportunity went by the boards somewhere along the way, and Stagg curtly rejected the other eight months after it was offered – only after it became official that he would be neither athletic director nor football coach.[59] His pension was $3,000 a year for life – which the University of Chicago paid for many, many years.[60]

Not long after the announcement of Stagg's forced retirement, Berwanger's freshman football season ended prematurely, cut short by a broken nose during a scrimmage. All concerned decided to not risk further injury to Chicago's leading prospect for next season's varsity. His second broken nose in less than a year would lead to an innovation in football equipment that would one day become common.

CHAPTER 12

As his broken nose healed, Berwanger prepared for his freshman track season and paid greater attention to his classroom work. He needed to pass his all-or-nothing comprehensive examinations in the spring to be eligible for varsity sports during the 1933-34 academic year. The comprehensive exams, administered *en masse* in large halls, were graded blindly. Students' names did not appear on test materials, only assigned numbers – so even a sympathetic professor had little or no opportunity to give an athlete the benefit of the doubt. Each comprehensive exam was usually worth nine hours of credit, and most students sat for four of them a year.

Athletic eligibility at an academically challenging institution such as the University of Chicago was an ongoing concern, especially under Hutchins' New Plan. Having just seen the varsity football team struggle through the 1932 season after losing three top sophomores after comprehensives, followers of the Maroons showed particular interest in Berwanger's academic progress. In a letter to his successor reviewing the prospects for the 1933 football program, Stagg wrote, "If Berwanger is eligible, you will inherit the fastest and the best set of backs that have ever represented the University of Chicago."[61] To hear Berwanger tell it decades later, they had no reason to worry. He viewed academics as just another challenge he could meet. However, his transcript suggests that he had it easier on the gridiron than the classroom. His first-quarter progress mark in physical science was "unsatisfactory." Yet, he improved his physical science mark to "satisfactory" in the winter and spring quarters, while replacing trigonometry with college algebra and then plane analytic geometry in subsequent quarters.

In addition to athletics and academics, Berwanger also had to make time for a job. His $300 scholarship covered his tuition for the year, but, star athlete or not, he had to pay for all other expenses, including room and board.

Perhaps to save money, he changed residences during his freshman year, joining two roommates in an apartment at 57th and Dorchester, a quarter-mile
east of the university fieldhouse. No-work jobs for star athletes were believed
to be a thing of the past, but nonetheless Berwanger's assignments were
not terribly grueling. He performed odd jobs around Bartlett Gymnasium,
including handing out shower towels when Chicago hosted prep tournaments, and dispatched maintenance workers in the university hospital. Later,
as a resident of the Psi Upsilon house, he helped serve meals to his fraternity
brothers.

Berwanger's first appearance on the track for Chicago was a December
intrasquad meet pitting the freshmen against the varsity. He entered four
field events and recorded three second-place finishes and one third, single-
handedly accounting for 10 of the freshman squad's 17 points. A few weeks
later, the campus newspaper revealed that Berwanger aspired to make the
U.S. Olympic decathlon team in 1936. "He is still pretty green," head coach
Ned Merriam said of the 18-year-old, "but he has a great deal of natural
ability, and should improve enormously." In late January, at a triangular exhibition involving the Chicago freshmen, varsity, and alumni, Berwanger won
the long jump (21-6), placed second in both the high and low hurdles, and

Though freshmen were ineligible for varsity competition, the Chicago track program issued awards
for intrasquad competitions. Berwanger won plenty of ribbons in 1933. (Author's photo)

placed among the top four in three other field events.

For some or all of Berwanger's collegiate track career, he received help from volunteer coach J. Austin Menaul. A former teammate of Berwanger's Dubuque mentor, Ira Davenport, Menaul knew a thing or ten about the decathlon. In fact, he is credited with winning the first decathlon ever, in 1912 at Northwestern University. Later that year, on the cruise to compete in the Stockholm Olympics, Menaul suffered an injury that forced him to scratch from the decathlon, but he finished fifth in the pentathlon (both won by Jim Thorpe). Menaul became a livestock buyer at the Chicago Stockyards and, after work, he helped coach Maroons track. It is not known whether access to Menaul as a coach was part of Davenport's pitch to convince Berwanger to attend Chicago.[62] In any case, Menaul had a willing and talented student.

Though freshmen could not compete against athletes from other colleges, the rule did not preclude coaches conducting "telegraphic meets." Also called "postal meets," in these novelty competitions each team conducted each of the events on the program in its respective facility. Teams then exchanged, via wire or letter, their athletes' times and distances, from which placing and team scores were determined. These meets provided more incentive for athletes than an intrasquad meet. The University of Iowa and University of Chicago scheduled such an affair for their freshmen for Thursday afternoon, February 9, 1933, when bone-chilling cold gripped the Midwest. In Chicago, the temperature outside plunged to minus-19. However, inside the fieldhouse Berwanger was hot, leading the Chicago contingent in four events and placing in two others.

Jay poses after the Purdue game of 1934, his junior year. Playing his first college game attended by his father, he passed for two touchdowns and rushed for another. However, despite his heroics, Purdue prevailed, 26-20. Jay also suffered a knee injury in this game, which might explain his stance in this photo. (Berwanger family collection)

The day the Maroons and

Hawkeyes staged their telegraphic meet, Windy City newspapers reported that the University of Chicago had hired its next football coach. Throughout four months of speculation and rumor, incoming athletic director Nelson Metcalf kept a tight lid on his selection process. His secrecy was helped by geography: Metcalf conducted his search while fulfilling his contract at Iowa State, nearly 400 miles from Chicago and its pesky sportswriters. However, in late January, a reporter did get Metcalf to confirm that one of the "three or four" candidates still under consideration was Clark D. Shaughnessy, head coach at Loyola University of New Orleans. Meanwhile, an informal group of former Chicago lettermen called the Order of the C, scheduled a meeting to decide its recommendation. Even before convening in a Loop hotel, these alumni made it clear that they wanted Metcalf to pick a Chicago alumnus. The "C" men invited Metcalf to their meeting. He replied by telegram that he could not attend, and he urged the group to postpone its session pending "outcome of negotiations." That night, a group of former lettermen placed a long-distance call from the Atlantic Hotel to Metcalf and asked the status of his selection process. Metcalf surprised them by revealing that he had already submitted his recommendation to university officials. Contacted by a reporter at 11 p.m., one or more administrators disclosed Metcalf's choice: Clark Shaughnessy.

CHAPTER 13

Metcalf's selection of 40-year-old Clark Shaughnessy to be the second football coach in University of Chicago history was welcomed and praised, not only on the Midway but across the country. Shaughnessy, a former backfield star at the University of Minnesota (1911-13), was regarded as a gridiron genius, an offensive innovator whose teams at Tulane and Loyola of New Orleans played a thrilling style of football. He was experienced and successful, having won two-thirds of the games in his two previous jobs. His 11 seasons as head coach at Tulane (1915-20 and 1922-26) included a 9-0-1 campaign in 1925 and an invitation to the Rose Bowl. University administrators nixed the trip to Pasadena, and Shaughnessy took his talents to Loyola (1927-32). Any reservations that the new coach was not a Chicago alumnus were short-lived. Shaughnessy's selection, along with the anticipated elevation of Jay Berwanger to the varsity, pumped new optimism into Maroons supporters.

Meanwhile, Amos Alonzo Stagg prepared to open the next chapter of his famed coaching career. Four days before Shaughnessy's name hit the headlines, the Grand Old Man agreed to coach the College of the Pacific. He took the job without ever visiting the campus in California. Its president, Tully C. Knoles, traveled to Chicago and finalized the contract during a meeting in Stagg's home. Knoles, a letterman in football, baseball, and track at the University of Southern California, had been president of Pacific, the state's oldest college, since 1919, when the institution was located in San Jose. In 1924, the college relocated to Stockton, about 60 miles east of San Francisco. In 1894, when he was 18 years old, Knoles rode his bicycle 38 miles to see Stagg's Maroons defeat Stanford 24-6 in one of the nation's first intersectional games. (Stanford's team manager that afternoon was a future U.S. president, Herbert Hoover.) Now, Knoles and other College of the

Pacific officials aspired to move their football program to the highest level, creating greater visibility and prestige for the Methodist school of about 750 students. They believed Stagg was just the man to make that happen. They were right.

Though Stagg welcomed his new opportunity, he still regretted leaving Chicago, partly because it wasn't his choice and partly because of his four-decades-long connection to the university. "Every time I think of it," he said, "I get a lump in my throat." Another reason was he knew that the Maroons would be a better team in 1933. He told Shaughnessy, "I confess I quite envy you for Zimmer, Berwanger, and Cullen, all weighing over 180 lbs., are exceptionally fast, and Zimmer and Berwanger exceptionally clever." After

Considered a genius at offense, Clark Shaughnessy became University of Chicago's coach in 1933, Berwanger's first varsity season. (Special Collections Research Center, University of Chicago Library)

mentioning a few other backs, including Tommy Flinn ("a sterling little 150 pounder") and Vinson Sahlin ("fast but not a sprinter"), Stagg summarized, "We have never had anything like such a group of backs even in the golden period of John Thomas and '5 Yards' McCarthy." His comments to Shaughnessy came in a letter that was cordial, gracious and instructive. "I want to offer you my hearty congratulations and best wishes on your appointment as my successor as football coach," Stagg wrote. "It is my hope that you will equal my forty-one year record, and that you will also have the satisfaction of a reasonable amount of success throughout your career." Stagg summarized which current assistant coaches were and were not available to help Shaughnessy during his transition and spring drills, named former players who might assist during the spring, and detailed what each coach should be paid.

Before he left the Midway, the Grand Old Man donated to the nearby Rosenwald Industrial Museum (later the Museum of Science and Industry) his Milburn electric automobile. The Maroon-colored vehicle had been a gift from some former players in 1919, when Stagg was hobbled with back problems. During his rehabilitation, Stagg supervised workouts from the vehicle, chugging about the practice field in his "private grandstand."

The paths of Stagg and Shaughnessy did not cross immediately. By the time Chicago's new football coach arrived for spring drills, the former coach was using vacation time to do the same in California. Stagg received a hero's welcome in Stockton, where he was greeted by four bands, an American Legion contingent, College of the Pacific students, and local business leaders. Welcoming activities during those five weeks included a parade, a banquet in Sacramento, a Shrine luncheon in San Francisco, an American Legion event, the Stanford-California dual track meet (where Stagg served as referee), a Yale dinner in San Francisco, and a joint luncheon of the Big Ten and Chicago alumni clubs of San Francisco. He returned to the Windy City to fulfill the final two months of his contract as Chicago athletic director and to deliver his goodbyes. When a *Hyde Park Herald* reporter asked his prediction for the 1933 Maroons, Stagg said, "I regard the prospects as the best ever. They can't fail to have a good team, if the players are eligible. There's promise of the fastest backfield ever at Chicago for I've never seen such fast backs as Captain Zimmer, Berwanger, Cullen, and Flinn." Stagg also issued a friendly challenge to Shaughnessy for a game between the College of the Pacific and University of Chicago. (The game finally took place in 1938, when the Maroons were in their death spiral, Stagg made the most of his homecoming with a 32-0 victory.)

Though he was the track team's best freshman in no fewer than seven events, Berwanger did not complete the season. He set aside his spikes to focus on football. Berwanger wanted to be part of spring workouts under the new coach. He was not alone. Zimmer, Cullen, Flinn, and Bart Smith left the track team for football practice. The custom was that Stagg would neither pressure nor demand that his players abandon their spring-sports teams in favor of spring football drills. Shaughnessy told track coach Ned Merriam that he intended to respect that tradition. However, knowing how their presence would help Shaughnessy and the football team, Merriam gave the football players on the track team his blessing to leave the squad for spring football. The track squad was not the only spring sport to cede players. Junior-to-be Ellmore Patterson set aside his tennis racket and headed for the gridiron.

The cooperation of Shaughnessy's new colleagues and the players' desire to work with their new coach from Day 1 resulted in 56 players, reportedly a record and twice the average during Stagg's final years, checking out football equipment. More than 40 reported for the first meeting and practice. Writers from the Chicago papers were on hand to document the proceedings.

There was no question that a new man was in charge. "Shaughnessy proceeded with startling rapidity to lay out the lines along which future teams will be developed," the *Chicago Tribune* reported. "The first thing I want to tell all of you is that I'm your friend. I've picked up quite a few things during 23 years of football. One of them is that football teams are made off the field as much as they are on it. I'm no person to be afraid of. Anything in the world I can do for any of you I'll do it gladly. Come to me first with your problems. My address is Room 404, Windemere Hotel. I mean it."

Turning to matters on the gridiron, Shaughnessy said, "We're out here to win. I want you to get that in your heads and get it in to stay. We're going to take our lickings, but we won't admit them till after they're over. We're going to pick out a style of play that's flexible, that has variety, speed, and deception, and we're going to depend on it against superior bulk." He put the squad on notice: Attendance would be taken every day. Tardiness meant running six or eight laps, and missing practice entirely earned an offender 15 to 20 laps.

The new coach said that a player who can do one thing better than anyone else on the team will stay on the team. "If every one does his specialty in the right way at the right time we won't need a brilliant all-around team. We can always win. We're going to put great emphasis on kicking, for one thing, both offensively and defensively. It's 25 percent of the game."

An offensive genius who would be hailed for bringing back the T-formation, where the halfback lined up directly behind the quarterback and was flanked by both halbacks, Shaughnessy said the traditional names for certain positions would be put aside in favor of more descriptive terms. The key lineman, "a heavy fellow who knows how to drive," commonly called a "tackle," would be known as the "pivot man." Next to him would be a "heavy guard." Instead of calling him the "center," Shaughnessy introduced "ball snapper," pointing out that he would not necessarily play in the center of the line. One end would take a position as a fifth member of the backfield. Though Shaughnessy was credited with changing the course of football's offense, his ideas on names for the positions never caught on.

In his first meeting, Shaughnessy gave fair warning to those playing a particular backfield position. "The poor devils who are quarterbacks on my teams are in for a hard time," he said. "We're going to spend a lot of time on field generalship. I won't have a mechanical quarterback. I want a man who knows what to do at every time and every place. And he must be liked and respected by the whole team." The whole team voted to have spring workouts from 3:45 to 5:45 p.m. weekdays for the next six weeks. "A high wave of optimism pervaded the Maroon camp," an Associated Press article observed. Nelson Metcalf, the new athletic director, was on hand and "also beamed confidence." Their work was not confined to the practice field. Sessions with Shaughnessy included nearly as much mental work as physical rigor. His detailed and lengthy "chalk talk" sessions were standard procedure. Though most of Stagg's former assistants scattered, one who stuck around was the Grand Old Man's son, Lonnie.

During spring drills, Shaughnessy worked on building his own staff. He hired Julian Lopez, one of his former players and assistant coaches at Loyola. Familiar with Shaughnessy's complicated offensive schemes, Lopez mostly worked with the Maroon backfield. Lopez, a lawyer, had turned to coaching when the New Orleans bank where he worked failed. (After four seasons as Shaughnessy's assistant coach, Lopez joined the Federal Bureau of Investigation and moved up its ranks, becoming the first Hispanic to attain the grade of special agent in charge. He retired from the FBI in 1960.[63])

In the varsity's intrasquad scrimmage culminating spring drills, Berwanger ran for three of the White squad's four touchdowns. His first score in the 24-0 exhibition came on a spinner play – he twirled to confuse defenders at to where he intended to hit the line – and dashed around left end for a

50-yard touchdown. At the conclusion of spring workouts, the university officially welcomed Shaughnessy and Metcalf to their new positions with a reception that included a dinner and a vaudeville show put on by students.

In addition to preparing his new team for the fall campaign, Shaughnessy worked to ensure that he would have the services of the player some experts had tagged as the Big Ten's best prospect since Illinois' Red Grange (1923-25). Jay Berwanger's availability was dependent upon his performance on his comprehensive exams, and published comments referring to the question – from Stagg down to a student trainer – indicated the level of concern. "Rumor has it that Coach Shaughnessy is determined that Jay Berwanger will be able to play this fall … has him studying about 14 hours a day, we hear," wrote the *Chicago Americans* Leo Fischer. Berwanger finished his spring quarter, took the comprehensives, and returned to Dubuque, where he worked, worked out, and awaited his test results. Berwanger admitted that he was worried about one particular exam. "If I'm not eligible, it's because I took too darn much math during my freshman year," he told an interviewer, adding that, if necessary, he would quit the boatyard and enroll in summer school to regain his eligibility. "I'm going to play football next fall, he said, "or know the reason why."

Berwanger (second from right) worked at Dubuque Boat and Boiler Works the summers before and after his freshman year at the University of Chicago. (Berwanger family collection)

For the second straight year, Berwanger's summer job was at Ira Davenport's Dubuque Boat and Boiler Works. He was not the only football star on Davenport's payroll that summer. Another was Dubuque native Oran "Nanny" Pape, seven years Berwanger's senior, who the previous fall played his third and final season in the National Football League. One newspaper feature article reported that Berwanger's job was riveter, while another stated he was a reamer, drilling the holes through which the rivets were secured. Either way, Berwanger's assignment required and built strength. A photo accompanying a *Chicago Daily News* feature in August 1933 shows him posing with a rivet gun, his biceps bulging. "Berwanger is in almost perfect shape," reporter James S. Kearns wrote. "Besides his work in the boat yards, he has been swimming, golfing and canoeing as often as he could manage during the first two months of the summer." He also got together a couple of evenings a week with some of his former Dubuque High teammates to toss and kick the football. "Berwanger has outgrown many of these companions in the last two years," Kearns observed, pegging the 19-year-old at 200 pounds, some 25 pounds heavier than his weight during high school. As if that were not enough conditioning, Berwanger resumed his practice of running the four miles between the boatyard and his home.[64] "There is one thing about Berwanger that makes him a standout in athletics," a writer revealed. "He has never smoked and nor has he ever drank any alcoholic beverage stronger than 3.2 beer. 'I don't like cigarettes or booze,' Berwanger says. 'I'm going to wait until I'm through competition before I'll start in celebrating whatever is to be celebrated.'"[65] (That statement to the contrary, there is evidence that Berwanger drank – even relaxing over drink with Shaughnessy before games – and smoked during his playing days and beyond.)

Cause for a celebration arrived July 12, 1933, when the University of Chicago issued results of the comprehensive examinations. Berwanger passed. Varsity football and national glory awaited.

CHAPTER 14

Berwanger wrapped up his summertime responsibilities in Dubuque and returned to Chicago around Labor Day 1933. Classes and official football practices did not begin for another 10 days, in accordance with the Big Ten rule prohibiting issuance of equipment or any supervised football activity until September 15, but he was working hard at Stagg Field nonetheless. He was among several athletes who accepted jobs to reassemble the steel stands at the football stadium. The others included football players Ewald Nyquist, Robert Perretz, Walter Maneikis, and Ray Pokela; and basketball players Bill Lang and Bill Haarlow. They were paid for their labors. "Did someone say something about subsidizing football players?" said Leo Fischer of the *Chicago American*. "Just try lugging heavy steel stands around for six hours a day and you'll soon realize whether 35 cents an hour is a 'subsidy' or not. Anyhow, none of them is going to get rich playing football at that rate – but they do have a lot of fun." A photo accompanying the feature story showed Berwanger and five crew mates, shirtless and holding yard tools as props, mugging for the camera. "Some of these names may not be familiar just yet to Maroon football followers," the caption stated, "but they'll be well enough known before the season ends, from all indications."

However, Berwanger was already well-known, though he had yet to play a down of varsity football. His name, as well as that of new coach Clark Shaughnessy, appeared in virtually every preseason article mentioning the University of Chicago. Writing the Big Ten preview for the North American Newspaper Alliance, Wisconsin coach Clarence Spears described the specimen from Dubuque as "the most talked-of freshman back in this section of the country" and "a triple-threat back of great speed and size, of whom much is expected."

As the student workers assembled the stadium grandstand, they no doubt discussed news that trustees of their school and Northwestern University were discussing collaboration and cooperation – up to and including merger. They cautioned that their talks were informal and preliminary, the outcome might be limited to sharing facilities and reducing duplicated programs, and the like. However, before the end of the football season, the possibility of a full merger – with more details and suggestion of certainty – returned to the headlines.

Expectations were high as Chicago started fall practice. Yet, experts tempered fans' optimism with a dose of realism. The Maroons appeared respectable through the first string, they acknowledged, but overall the team lacked size, experience, and bench strength. Sportswriter Fischer said that Chicago would be improved but not of championship caliber – despite having Berwanger, who "has speed and power, is a tremendous punter, and from his preliminary work is being touted as a combination of all it takes to make an All-American." The *Daily News'* Ralph Cannon described Berwanger as "tall and lithe – of the George Gipp type. A lot of responsibility will rest in him. If he is another Grange there will be plenty of excitement on the Midway …" Of the top prospects on last fall's strong freshman team, all but end Ralph Balfanz, a speedster from Abilene, Texas, passed his comprehensive exams and began practice.

When it came time to assign players their jersey numbers, Shaughnessy made an unusual choice for Berwanger: Number 99. Decades later, Berwanger, with a modest smile, recalled Shaughnessy's explanation. "He said something like this. He said I was as near to perfect (100) as he could figure it, and he couldn't use 100, so he used 99."[66]

Shaughnessy's offensive system was more complicated than most, and players had lots to learn and remember. In 1933, the team's calls in the huddle started with a number corresponding to a particular formation. Numbers in the 70s and 80s were reserved for pass plays. For runs, the next number would be two digits, the first associated with a specific backfield position. The quarterback was 3, the right halfback 4, the fullback 5, and the left halfback 6. The second digit of the number specified what hole the runner should hit. The odd digits were to the right and even digits to the left. The left guard hole was 2, left tackle was 4, and around left end was 8. Over center was zero. Finally, another two-digit number was given, the second digit giving the count upon which the ball was to be snapped. Thus, "23" meant the snap was the third count but "32" meant the second. Berwanger offered an example of "28, 30, 23." That meant Formation 28, player 3 (quarterback) going through the 0 hole (over center), with the snap coming on the third count. "At Chicago we came out of the huddle and the quarterback would say: 'All right?' Then if no one answered he would start calling off a string of numbers in rhythm. These numbers meant nothing except to establish the rhythm. If the last number of the huddle signal had been 2, we knew we were to start on the second number. If it had been 3 we knew we were to start on the third number, and so on." A call of "46, 75, 52" translated into formation 46, pass play 75, and the snap on the second count. That was a lot to remember, especially in game situations. He said, "Calling these signals, however, is a little more difficult than learning them."

The players learned their signals and plays in secret. Shaughnessy closed the workouts to all outsiders. He later relaxed the restriction, allowing the public to observe practice once a week. The team practiced twice a day until classes began the first Monday in October. Shaughnessy's morning session was held in the fieldhouse, where he conducted chalk talk and walked his charges through new plays. "He is very exacting as to detail, yet is not the punishing type," observed Cannon. "He never uses stronger cuss words than "damn" or "hell" and his one fault, perhaps, in handling the boys is expecting them to grasp his intricate formations as readily as he dishes 'em out. When they don't, he drives 'em." Indicating his intention to focus on fundamentals, and reflecting a concern that injuries would expose his team's lack of depth, Shaughnessy rarely conducted full-contact scrimmages. He knew the stakes. So did the *Chicago Tribune's* Wilfrid Smith. "It's one thing to step into the Western conference as coach of a university which has never won a football title or seldom placed in the first division," he wrote. "It's quite another proposition to take charge at Chicago, which ranks second in all-time standings of games won and lost, and which has a host of old grads and former players forming a critical advisory board. Then, too, only a most courageous coach would accept a position from which A.A. Stagg, Chicago's Grand Old Man, was practically forced to resign after 41 years of service. Lack of material, lack of interest by the faculty in varsity sports, and other complications are familiar charges on the Midway." Smith expanded on the dichotomy between athletics and academics at Chicago. "Athletes generally matriculate at universities having winning teams. Chicago and her alumni must overcome this. The men now on the squad should not be bothered with eligibility, long a bugaboo at Chicago. Chicago wants athletes, but it wants only intelligent athletes." And Chicago needed more athletes. After 2½ weeks of twice-a-day practices, and with the season opener just days away, Shaughnessy put out the call for more bodies. "New men do not need any previous experience," the student newspaper announced, "and will be given personal attention in order that they will be on a par with the entire squad by the week of the Purdue game" (in two weeks). Simultaneously, the new athletic director, Nelson Metcalf, announced a 12-point plan for change in the university's athletic and intramural programs. Point 2 stipulated that no student would be cut from an athletic team.

As Shaughnessy prepared his team and waited for walk-ons, university officials promoted ticket sales by pointing out that their 1933 season ticket package was the least expensive in the conference. A fan could purchase tickets to all six of the Maroons' home games for a total of $6.60.

The first of those half-dozen games was against Cornell College, a small school from Mount Vernon, Iowa. Chicago regarded it as little more than a practice game, another one of the mismatches put at the start of the schedule to tune up the team for the tougher conference battles to follow. However, two years earlier, when Cornell was the guest for the opener, the Maroons' margin of victory was only 12-0. To temper public expectations, and perhaps with an eye of boosting ticket sales, Maroons' coaches warned that in 1933 Cornell would be no pushover. They cited Cornell's 12-7 victory over Iowa State Teachers College (now the University of Northern Iowa) the previous weekend. However, in recognition of the potential mismatch and the fact that Chicago assistant Kyle Anderson scouted Cornell's season opener, Metcalf honored Cornell coach Richard Barker's request and spelled out the formations Chicago planned to use: variations from single-wing and punt (shotgun) formations.

The Chicago sideline had a new coach and a new look. Shaughnessy got rid of the uniforms from the Stagg era and outfitted his team in white jerseys, pants of light yellow "airplane cloth," and maroon headgear. For their occasional road games, the team switched to maroon jerseys, white headgear, and the same light yellow pants. Fans noticed one other difference involving equipment: Berwanger's helmet sported a facemask. The mask consisted of two bars of spring steel covered by sponge and leather – one horizontal across his jaw and one vertical from the middle of the other bar to the top of the helmet. Its purpose was to protect Berwanger's nose, which had been broken each of the previous two seasons. Doctors had warned that a third break could end his playing career. The mask was created by athletic trainer Wally Bock, who later worked 21 seasons for major league baseball's Cleveland Indians.[67] In an era when most players wore no face protection – a few still played without helmets – the device added to the Berwanger mystique. Sportswriters often referred to him as "The Man in the Iron Mask." In any case, it did its job: Berwanger suffered no more facial injuries. Some of his teammates started sporting less elaborate single-bar faceguards.

Another change in the post-Stagg era ended the quarter-century-old tradition of singing "Wave the Flag," which contained a reference to Stagg, after football games, faculty banquets, and interfraternity performances. The Maroon faithful were informed that "Wave the Flag" had been retired in favor of "Chicago Loyalty:"

Chicago we're true to you
Our Alma Mater ever dear
Chicago we're true to you
That we are loyal never fear,
(Rah, Rah, Rah)
Chicago we're true to you,
We greet you now with cheer and song,
With deeds of worth and tested courage strong,
Chicago we're true to you.

However, vocalists were informed that should anyone be inspired to still sing, "Wave the Flag," the line referring to Stagg – "With the Grand Old Man to lead them" – was to be replaced with "With Coach Shaughnessy to lead them."

Stagg was gone but hardly forgotten. Shortly before the season opener, Captain Pete Zimmer received a telegram addressed to the Delta Kappa Epsilon fraternity house. It was from the Grand Old Man himself. "Best wishes to you and team for the season," Stagg told the captain. "Get hot for every game." Stagg also sent a telegram to Shaughnessy. "Best wishes for the season. Hope you win all your games. Give my love to my old colleagues in the department." As the team gathered in the locker room before running onto Stagg Field, Shaughnessy read Stagg's message and posted it on the bulletin board.

Jay Berwanger's varsity football career and the Clark Shaughnessy era at Chicago began together at 2:30 the afternoon of Saturday, October 7, 1933. The city's official temperature was a football-friendly 55. The game attracted 20,000 to 25,000 fans, most of them Boy Scouts and other youngsters enjoying free or discounted admission. Another sporting event expected to draw a crowd on Chicago's South Side that afternoon, Game 4 of baseball's City Series between the Cubs and White Sox, had been postponed out of respect for

Cubs owner William Veeck Senior, whose funeral was that morning. A mile east of the ballpark and four miles north of Stagg Field, the pleasant weather and Chicago Week designation attracted nearly a quarter-million patrons to the Century of Progress Exposition. Visitors streamed through the world's fair gates at the rate of 12,000 per hour while Berwanger and the Maroons played Cornell, and the pace picked up during the evening. By the end of the night, 242,184 guests had attended the fair, making it the second-busiest Saturday since the exposition opened more than five months earlier.

The Chicago-Cornell game was the mismatch that many anticipated – a 32-0 romp – but it was exciting nonetheless for fans hoping that a new coach and new personnel would restore winning football to the Midway. "There was unmistakable evidence of a new spirit on the gridiron and in the stands," wrote *Chicago Tribune* sports editor Arch Ward. "Chicago had poise, strength, and a certain obvious assurance. Its work was striking even when the caliber of opposition is taken into consideration." Added the *Chicago Herald-Examiner's* George Morgenstern, "So, after eight bad years, the Midway is looking up sky-high." One of a half-dozen sophomores making his varsity debut, Berwanger lived up to his advance notices. On Chicago's first offensive drive of the season, the Maroons faced fourth-and-five on the Cornell 20-yard line. They gave the ball to Berwanger, who churned through for the first down. A few plays later, on fourth-and-goal from the 3, Berwanger crossed the goal line standing up and then kicked the extra point. It was the first touchdown of his collegiate career.

On Chicago's next possession, Berwanger capped a 62-yard touchdown drive with a one-yard plunge. He then missed the point-after kick. Immediately after Zimmer had his apparent 52-yard punt return for a touchdown negated by a penalty, he passed 15 yards to sophomore end Rainwater Wells, who ran 30 yards more for a touchdown. Berwanger's kick for the extra point missed wide, leaving Chicago with a 19-0 lead at halftime. The Maroons struck quickly in the third quarter after returning a punt to the Cornell 37. Ewald Nyquist rushed 17 yards up the middle. On the next play, Berwanger rushed through the center of the line, cut to his left and outran the defensive backfield for his third touchdown. He converted the point-after kick to make it 26-0. Berwanger's fourth touchdown run of the afternoon was a 36-yarder in which he ran up the middle and began "mowing down tacklers like a scythe." After seeing Berwanger miss half his extra-point kicks, Shaughnessy gave the opportunity to quarterback Vin Sahlin. His drop-kick missed.

On defense, the Maroons stymied Cornell at every turn. Late in the game, with the score 32-0, Cornell's Fred Shadle engineered a pass-filled drive against the Chicago reserves, who gave up at least four of Cornell's five first downs. When the visitors reached the 6-yard line, Shaughnessy sent in his starters, who promptly recovered a fumbled lateral and preserved the shutout.

Despite scoring 26 points and unleashing punts one sportswriter described as "a joy to behold," Berwanger expressed dissatisfaction and bewilderment with his performance. "I couldn't get started Saturday against Cornell," he said. "I don't know what was the matter." Two of Berwanger's touchdowns came on essentially the same play, described by an analyst as a "rejuvenation of the old-time split buck." The Maroons went into an unbalanced line formation, with both guards to the right of the center. Sahlin took the snap, faked a handoff to Zimmer as he headed left and handed the ball to Berwanger, who ran between the guards on the right side of the line and found paydirt.

The weak opponent notwithstanding, Shaughnessy's Maroons drew rave reviews. "For those who have been skeptical about whether this boy Berwanger is redder than Red Grange, as his advance agents claim, it might as well be announced right here that he made four of the five Chicago touchdowns and kicked both points after touchdown," Morgenstern wrote. Said Leo Fischer of the *American*, "Berwanger's debut which might be called the debut of the new athletic regime on the Midway as well as the initial appearance of the handiwork of Clark Shaughnessy, new gridiron mentor at Chicago, was the outstanding event of the game."

The day after his first victory as University of Chicago coach, Shaughnessy sat down and penned a letter to his predecessor, opening with the salutation, "Dear Mr. Stagg." Shaughnessy

Decades before it became required equipment, a faceguard was installed on Berwanger's helmet to protect a twice-broken nose. Trainer Wally Bock designed the device, which was made of spring steel covered by sponge and leather. Berwanger was often called, "the man in the iron mask." (Courtesy of the College Football Hall of Fame)

first thanked him for the pre-game telegram. He told the Grand Old Man that his son and namesake "is a big help," that they "spend many hours together, and that Lonnie has already scouted Michigan and Illinois." Summarizing the previous afternoon's game, Shaughnessy said, "We apparently had no opposition to speak of. The Cornell team was light and we ran rough shod over them by just being bigger and stronger rather than by skill." Looking ahead, the new Chicago coach confided, "Am afraid we won't arrive in time for Purdue or Michigan but will have a dandy team before the season ends unless injuries ruin us. Am not scrimmaging at all to speak of – but we need it badly. Sort of a 'devil and the deep sea' situation – trying to avoid injuries." He concluded the full-page letter, "Thanks again for your message. Excuse the informality and handwriting – am just up against it for time and know you will understand."[68] Shaughnessy had to turn his attention to getting his team past Washington University without injury and preparing for Purdue and the rest of Chicago's Big Ten schedule.

CHAPTER 15

Their team's dominance in the 1933 season opener pleased Chicago fans, but no one was confusing little Cornell College with Michigan or Purdue. The Maroons had such an easy time of it against Cornell that they did not need to use more than eight or nine of the 80-plus plays in their playbook. Shaughnessy observed that his new team had left plenty of room for improvement – and he had a way to help the players see it, too. He had arranged for a camera operator to take motion pictures of the Cornell game from the Stagg Field grandstand. He showed the film at team meetings. The most glaring shortcoming was that the weakside linemen did not hold their blocks long enough before engaging the defensive secondary. As a result, Cornell defensive tackles and ends caught many ballcarriers from behind. The team's lack of depth, evident even against the Purple, was a widely publicized liability. The squad got a small boost when Jim Gold, a sophomore lineman, earned his eligibility by retaking and passing a comprehensive exam in September. Ed Cullen, the track captain, returned to the football team and worked out at quarterback as well as center, the position he played in high school. Shaughnessy devoted practice time to teaching players additional positions, in case they had to substitute for injured teammates. The squad, which at one point had 43 players, would be down to 37 after the third game.[69]

While Shaughnessy worked his players hard, practicing plays until they were run to perfection, he also injected a bit of fun into the proceedings. He presented Bob Perretz, a husky sophomore guard, with a two-pound box of candy – the bounty he promised to the player making the first tackle of each game. The coach offered the prize with the stipulation that the recipient pass along "most of the contents to some pleasant nonathlete." The newspapers did not identify the young lady who received Perretz's gift.

Members of the LaSalle Street Coaches, some 125 Chicago alumni and supporters who enjoyed getting together at the LaSalle Hotel and second-guessing the Maroon coaching staff, invited Shaughnessy, elected him into membership and then tweaked him about his candy prizes. The new coach replied that many boxes of candy awaited alumni who could tell him how to score from midfield.

Shaughnessy preferred to run an offense in which the quarterback called the play from formation rather than in a huddle. However, anticipating that in a no-huddle offense his players might struggle to hear the signals over the crowds in Big Ten stadiums, the coach experimented with a "huddle-shift." This huddle was a 1-4-4-2 diamond, with the two lines of four players each standing at right angles to the line of scrimmage. Once the play was called, the players shifted positions within the huddle, standing closest to the position they would take when getting into formation for the play.

The University of Chicago's 1933 football schedule was, again, laden with home games. From the previous eight seasons (1925-32) through Berwanger's career (1933-35), Chicago traveled for exactly two games each season. Even with its home-field "advantage" and its practice of scheduling weak non-conference opponents the first game or two of each season, Chicago had enjoyed just one winning season since 1924 (7-3 in 1929, despite a 1-3 mark in the Big Ten).

The travel roster for the Washington University game listed 33 players, and Shaughnessy's fervent hope was to return from St. Louis with all 33 men still available to play the following Saturday. He did not have the team scrimmage during the week. "The Maroon phobia about injuries is not due to

In addition to being a force on offense and defense, Berwanger also handled punts and place-kicks for the University of Chicago. (Chicago Tribune photo. Reprinted with permission)

any special dread of Washington," the *Chicago Tribune* explained the morning before the contest. "It is due to their intense desire to be at the very peak of physical condition for their game against Purdue a week from tomorrow, the real test of their new found prowess. Coach Shaughnessy is frank to say that he has no relish for tomorrow's encounter, particularly since it is away from the home lot." The coach also expressed concern about the St. Louis weather, which even in mid-October could feel like that of summer.

At 11:30 a.m. the day before the Washington University game, the Maroons boarded a train at Chicago's Dearborn Station for the six-hour trip to St. Louis. The Wabash Railway Co. advertised that it planned to add cars to accommodate Maroons boosters. The round-trip coach fare was $6 and $10.70 for first class. The team arrived at Wabash's Delmar Station in St. Louis, which was closer than Union Station to the Washington University campus, on the west edge of the city's massive Forest Park, site of the 1904 world's fair. The team checked into the Forest Park Hotel.

Jimmy Conzelman, a former halfback at Washington, was in his second season coaching his alma mater. The 35-year-old had plenty of experience. After college, he was a member of the Great Lakes Navy team that won the 1919 Rose Bowl. A teammate, George Halas, recruited Conzelman for his Decatur Staleys (later the Chicago Bears) in the fledgling American Professional Football Association (forerunner of the National Football League). Before returning to Washington University, where he was to stay eight sea-

The Maroons expected good things from sophomore Jay Berwanger (second from right) in 1933, his first varsity season. From left are Vinson Sahlin, Pete Zimmer, Berwanger, and Ewald Nyquist. (Special Collections Research Center, University of Chicago Library)

sons, Conzelman had been a professional player, owner, and championship coach. (The multi-talented Conzelman – his resume included newspaper publisher, playwright, author, orator, actor and advertising executive – returned to professional coaching in 1940 and entered the Pro Football Hall of Fame in 1964.) In their 1933 season opener, Washington, a member of the Missouri Valley Conference, posted a 22-7 win over McKendree College, from Lebanon, Illinois, a Little Nineteen Conference school that went undefeated in 1932. The next week, Conzelman's squad battled Illinois but withered, gave up two fourth-quarter touchdowns, and lost, 21-6.

Chicago and Washington battled on David R. Francis Field, which had been a venue for the 1904 Olympics. Attendance figures for the contest varied greatly – from 5,000 to 11,000 – but in nearly every newspaper account the presence of Chicago boosters was noted. Shaughnessy did not get his wish regarding the weather. Under a clear sky, the temperature reached 72 degrees – average for a mid-October afternoon in St. Louis, but warm for a football game. Shaughnessy also did not get his wish regarding getting through the day injury-free. Rainwater Wells, making the initial tackle of the game (and thus qualifying for the coach's box of candy), suffered a kick to the head. "Wells wandered around the field aimlessly for four minutes before he was removed and didn't recover his wits until six hours after the game," the student newspaper reported. When Zimmer was shaken up in the third quarter, Shaughnessy kept him on the bench. Otherwise, the Maroons had no problem with their hosts, rolling to a 40-0 victory. (A sportswriter or two apparently missed an extra point at some point and reported the score as 39-0.)

Berwanger couldn't be overlooked. He kicked off, ran, passed, punted, returned punts, kicked extra points, and keyed the defense. And, even if they missed his involvement in virtually every play, fans couldn't help but notice the player with the facemask on his helmet. After a scoreless first quarter, Berwanger put the Maroons on the board early in the second stanza with a five-yard touchdown run. Later in the quarter, Berwanger launched a pass 30 yards toward quarterback Vin Sahlin. The Washington defender was about to intercept or knock down the pass when he collided with the referee. Sahlin caught the ball and completed a 56-yard touchdown play. Chicago scored again on Zimmer's 60-yard interception return. With Chicago converting on one of three extra-point kicks in the half – Berwanger was either one-of-three or one-of-two – the Maroons took a 19-0 lead into intermission.

The only touchdown of the third quarter came on a 22-yard drive set up by Zimmer's 35-yard punt return. (After this play, Zimmer, slightly injured when bumped out of bounds, sat out the rest of the game.) Nyquist notched the touchdown on a three-yard run up the middle, and Berwanger connected for the point.

Washington threatened to score early in the fourth quarter, when Chicago reserves had taken over for Berwanger and most of the starters. The Bears advanced to the Chicago 8-yard line, and, as he did the previous week against Cornell, Shaughnessy sent in the first string. Again, the starters halted the drive. During the quarter, Washington sent in its substitute center to finish the game. However, after just a few plays, the sub suffered an injury. The Bears had only two centers on the team, and under the substitution rules in effect at the time, the starting center could not return in the same quarter. While Conzelman scanned his bench, trying to figure out who could play center, Sahlin hollered to Shaughnessy and suggested that the Maroons waive the rule and allow the Washington starter back in. Shaughnessy signaled his assent, and the game resumed. In the same quarter, Sahlin collected his second touchdown of the afternoon with a 67-yard run, with Berwanger kicking Chicago's 33rd point. Washington continued to try an aerial attack. Though their victory was assured, the Maroons nonetheless threw for their final touchdown, with back-up Keith Hatter connecting with Bill Langley. Bart Smith booted the 40th point.

In his bylined article in the student newspaper, Zimmer stated that the Maroons received several favorable breaks against Washington, which he noted were at a sartorial disadvantage. "The Washington gridders were attired in heavy wool uniforms and handicapped by the excess weight and heat, they tired easily," he said. "We had light silk and cotton uniforms, so the hot day did not bother us as much. Still we tired more quickly than usual, and everyone in the game had a pretty thorough workout." Shaughnessy was not impressed. "We weren't actually 40 points better than Washington," he said a few days afterward. "Our blocking was bad and our tackling was mediocre."

As for Washington, "It was difficult for the bruised Bears to see any bright side to their picture, as they peered over their lacerated noses and tied their shoes after the battle," St. Louis sportswriter J. Roy Stockton observed. "But as Coach Conzelman pointed out, the toughest opposition remaining on the schedule will be as child's play after the Zimmers and the Nyquists and the Berwangers."[70] (Against supposedly easier opponents, Washington split its final six games to finish 4-5.) However, for the 2-0 University of Chicago, the opposite would be true. Tougher opponents awaited.

CHAPTER 16

After an unimpressive start to what they hoped would be a championship season, the Purdue Boilermakers prepared for the Chicago game with uncharacteristic trepidation. Noble Kizer's squad, Big Ten runner-up in 1932, looked sluggish in beating Ohio University in the opener, 13-6. The next weekend in Minneapolis, the Boilermakers inserted their reserves as shock troops to rally for a 7-7 tie against the upset-minded Gophers. For Purdue boosters, the tie stung like a loss. Now the Boilermakers had to visit Chicago, where the Maroons' 2-0 start energized the campus. The atmosphere on the Midway was markedly different than previous run-ups to the Purdue match-up. Maroon fans were long familiar with the sentiment, stated in a headline-like phrase, "Stagg fears Purdue." *The Chicago Tribune* referred to "Stagg fears Purdue" being "a Midway idiom" as early as 1915. With Stagg departed and an improved team on the field, the Chicago faithful experienced a mood swing. "Stagg was always the fearer-in-chief of Purdue," wrote John P. Carmichael of the *Chicago Daily News*, who added that Stagg's successor, Clark Shaughnessy, "took a look at the holdovers from '32 and a newcomer named Jay Berwanger and announced: 'I fear no man, nor will I fear Purdue.'"

Tom Barton, writing in the student newspaper, observed, "During the past four or five years there has been a very noticeable absence of the good old college spirit among the undergraduates at Chicago. Maybe there haven't been any championship teams but the Maroons have occasionally played good football in the last few years. Now Chicago appears to have a team – perhaps a championship team – so let's get behind our football team at the Pep session tomorrow and BEAT PURDUE." An editorial in *The Daily Maroon* by editor-in-chief John P. Barden noted that the "usually serious, solemn, and sanctified" university community had jumped on the Maroon bandwagon. "Coach Clark Shaughnessy has managed to inspire a fighting spirit in his team that has somehow trickled out to the students." He concluded: "Some have asked, 'Will you feel foolish if the Maroons do not beat Purdue?' 'No' is our emphatic answer. *The Daily Maroon* will back the team and 'this man, Shaughnessy' to the last gasp or final cheer of the Dartmouth game. Besides, it is not our policy to feel foolish." To back up his statement, Barden's front page carried, in huge type, a screened message overprinting the articles: BEAT PURDUE. In between every article on the page, the message was repeated: BEAT PURDUE. Overnight, some students wrote the message in chalk on campus sidewalks and buildings. Even the revered "C" Bench was decorated. BEAT PURDUE.

Shaughnessy was doing all he could to make that happen. The Wednesday afternoon before the Boilermaker battle, he worked the team overtime, until 7 p.m. At dusk, the squad switched to white footballs to enhance visibility. When even those could not be seen, Shaughnessy took the players into the fieldhouse, where they continued to work on new formations and plays. Seven of the 11 starters would be getting their first taste of Big Ten competition.

The day before the battle, Chicago students staged a day of "pep" events, including burning a Purdue ogre in effigy, steam calliope music on the quadrangle, a parade, a rally, and a dance. The parade was barely over when rain began. For Berwanger and his coach, however, their evening was not over. Starting at some point in their three seasons as player and coach, they would get together and review the game plan. What was never publicized at the time was that their private meetings included a smoke and shot of whiskey.[71]

The Daily Maroon published the words to several of the songs and cheers that would be chanted at the Purdue game, including "Chicago Loyalty." Another song, "Alma Mater," had been heard at Stagg Field with disappointing frequency over the previous decade, as it was sung only after a Maroons loss.

> *Today we gladly sing the praise*
> *Of her whose daughters and whose sons*
> *Our loyal voices let us raise*
> *And bless her with our benisons.*
> *Of all fair mothers fairest she,*
> *Most wise of all that wisest be,*
> *Most true of all the true say we,*
> *Is our dear Alma Mater.*

The standard cheer of the Maroons' faithful was a slight variation of that created by A.A. Stagg himself in 1900:

> *Chica-go, Chica-go, Chica-go, Go,*
> *Go-Chica, Go-Chica, Go-Chica, Go!*
> *Team! Team! Team! YEA!*

Revival of the "Cheering C," a group that had gone dormant as Chicago's football fortunes faded, was engineered by player Ed Cullen and fellow student Charles Merrifield. Fans who entered the "C" section of Stagg Field were issued large cards of maroon and white and given assignments according to their position in the stadium. Upon the leader's signal, they displayed their cards in concert to create the desired images, usually the university's "C" logo.

School spirit and cheers and cards were one thing, actually beating Purdue would be another. The Boilermakers, undefeated in 19 of 20 games, including the previous 16, featured several weapons, starting with backs Duane Purvis and James Carter. Purvis, the defending national collegiate champion in the javelin, was in the first of his two first-team All-America seasons. The previous weekend against Minnesota, he amazed spectators when he heaved a pass that flew nearly 60 yards. Tackle William "Dutch" Fehring, an honorable mention All-America as a junior, captained the 1933 Boilermakers as a senior. (His younger brother Ted was the other tackle.)

The rain that had begun Friday evening continued overnight and all morning Saturday – some 14 straight hours before the 2 p.m. kickoff. Chicago's official weather reporting station happened to be on the Midway campus,

A defender wraps up Berwanger in the sophomore's first Big Ten game, a 14-0 Purdue victory. In this season, 1933, Berwanger was on the field for every play of all five conference games. (Special Collections Research Center, University of Chicago Library)

where 2.47 inches fell in a 24-hour period. However, the rain was significantly heavier in other parts of the city, where the storm downed power lines, flooded basements and viaducts, and claimed three lives – two in lightning strikes and the third in an automobile pedestrian collision.

Spectators arrived for the Chicago-Purdue battle prepared for a soaking. Arch Ward, sports editor of the *Chicago Tribune*, noting the sea of umbrellas in the north grandstand, said the section looked like a "field of toadstools." Prepared or not, fans suffered through a miserable afternoon. Only half of the 20,000-25,000 fans anticipated showed up. Others stayed dry and listened to the game on the radio. They had their choice of stations, as WBBM, KYW, and WJJD broadcast the game. The chronicler of countless sporting events during his long career, Ward declared, "No game ever was played under worse climatic conditions." Tragedy struck that afternoon, when spectator John A. Castino, a 45-year-old business owner, died of a heart attack. (That same day, two fans attending the Michigan-Ohio State game in Ann Arbor suffered similar fates.)

With the Stagg Field surface saturated and puddles dotting the gridiron, Chicago and Purdue players splashed to their positions. Before long, the darkness and the players' soaked and mud-covered uniforms made them virtually indistinguishable to spectators. With only a couple of minutes to play before halftime, Berwanger, whose quick kick on the previous play was blocked, unleashed a spectacular kick from his end zone. It rolled out of bounds on Purdue's 43. With streaks of lightning flashing in the distance, Purvis picked up four yards. Then Purdue ran what Ward described as a "perfect play," one first used by Notre Dame in 1911. The backfield shifted to the left, back Carter took the ball through the right tackle hole and broke through like a thunderbolt. Fullback Fred Hecker blocked Berwanger in the defensive backfield, and Carter cruised across the goal line for a 53-yard touchdown. Dan Toriello kicked the extra point. Purdue's second touchdown came on another 57-yard drive. In the third quarter, Purvis gained every inch, finishing the drive by wriggling free of four would-be tacklers until he fell across the goal line. "It was the most brilliant bit of individual work the game developed," Ward reported. Purvis then stepped up and booted the extra point.

The Maroons shelved many of the plays in their playbook. Those requiring open-field running and deception, which would have involved deft handling of a slippery pigskin, were out of the question. Berwanger and his backfield mates never got it going. The weather was not entirely to blame. "Simply because Purdue was so smooth and generated so much power the Maroons looked awkward and at times helpless," Ward reported. "Their fast back field never had a chance to operate. Their running plays were usually halted at the scrimmage line and their passes were slapped into the sod. Their kicks were rushed and they were kept so deep in their own territory most of the time they at no stage developed a serious scoring threat."

That the Boilermakers only scored two touchdowns reflected the spirited Chicago defense, the dreadful weather conditions, Berwanger's booming (but rushed) punts, and a scoring opportunity short-circuited by a major penalty. When the final gun sounded, amid torrents of rain and flashes of lightning, Purdue slogged off the field with a 14-0 victory. The game was not as close as the score might have suggested. Chicago gained only 61 yards from scrimmage, while Purdue racked up 283, all of it on running plays. The Boilermakers attempted only one pass all afternoon. The Maroons completed three of nine passes for just 18 yards. Chicago got no closer to scoring than the Purdue 40. Of the Maroons' 11 starters, only two did not leave for substitutes – tackle Bob Deem, one of the game's last players to *not* wear a helmet, and Berwanger, whose helmet sported a face guard.

The Maroons' ineffectiveness in their first Big Ten challenge of 1933 tempered Chicago fans' enthusiasm. Reality set in. "The results of the game proved that the team was sadly inexperienced," the university yearbook stated, "a defect which could be remedied only by more determined practice." Captain Pete Zimmer conceded nothing. In his post-game article, he attributed the loss to bad weather and ill fortune. "We do not alibi when we state a fact, and the truthful reality of the Maroon-Purdue game was that the Maroons did not get a single good break throughout the game." The captain praised the squad's sophomore star: "Berwanger again demonstrated his real football genius and ruggedness, taking plenty of punishment in his many plunging slashes and vicious tackles." Zimmer said, "We are confident that the team did not get a chance to show its actual ability. I wish to express our deep appreciation to the student body for the support they gave us for the Purdue game. I hope University students will not withdraw this support, because I feel that we will earn every cheer they will give next Saturday against Michigan."

CHAPTER 17

Chicago partisans had entertained thoughts of an upset victory over Purdue, but few held such illusions regarding undefeated Michigan. The Wolverines owned all or part of the past three Big Ten championships and aspired to be the nation's top-ranked team. Chicago's only hope was that Michigan might be overconfident or experience a letdown after a key 13-0 win over Ohio State. "Chicago, however, does not anticipate a victory," the *Chicago Tribune's* Wilfrid Smith stated. "If victory comes it will be all the more acceptable, and if it doesn't materialize, there will be no disappointment."

Chicago students' pep rally was held in the fieldhouse at 5 Friday evening. Shaughnessy had his athletes demonstrate a couple of plays. The advance article in the student newspaper added, "Individual players might even be urged to overcome their reticence and utter a few immortal sentences." Cheerleaders showed no shyness as the men demonstrated chants for fans to call out the following afternoon, including, "WHO'S AFRAID OF THE BIG BAD WOLVERINES!"

Even if they weren't afraid of the Wolverines, the Maroons on game day immediately had reason to feel inferior. Michigan scored its first touchdown in the opening two minutes, had its second within seven, and made the hosts look inept in all aspects of the game. The final score was 28-0, but the contest could not have been more lopsided. Michigan just missed scoring on two drives, one when the first half expired before the Wolverines could run a play from the Chicago 2 after a long pass completion. For the Chicago fans among the 24,000 spectators, the only positive was that, unlike the previous Saturday, they did not have to witness the drubbing in a downpour. The afternoon was dry and cool, with temperatures in the mid-40s.

The Maroons suffered two lost fumbles, two blocked punts, three interceptions, seven other incomplete passes, countless missed blocks, and even a penalty for taking one timeout too many. "Repeatedly, Chicago's ball carrier, at the conclusion of a line thrust, would be the only Maroon player on the ground, ample proof of inefficient blocking," Smith observed. Michigan never had to play defense in its own half of the field after the early second quarter. Late in the game, the Maroons, desperately trying to avert a shutout and their most lopsided loss to the Wolverines ever, switched to an aerial attack.[72] On one passing attempt, Jerry Ford batted the ball out of Pete Zimmer's hands and into those of Michigan defender Russell Oliver. Later, sophomore Steve Remias, the one-time Chicago recruit, picked off a Berwanger pass.

The interception was only part of Berwanger's worst performance of his collegiate career. In addition, he was smothered on virtually every rush attempt. He lost a fumble. He mishandled a kickoff reception. He had one punt blocked, another partially blocked, and had yet another net just six yards before shanking out of bounds. Berwanger was in the defensive backfield for all four of Michigan's touchdowns, one of which immediately followed the block of a Berwanger punt; it was scored by the man Berwanger was assigned to cover. Asked at the end of his playing days if he wished he could have a do-over of any game, Berwanger cited this one.[73] While Michigan coach Harry Kipke played 28 of the 33 players he brought to Chicago, Shaughnessy, saddled with a weak bench, used just 15.[74] While the drubbing was going on, Shaughnessy tried to figure out who could be the first-string quarterback. After starter Bart Smith, he used Tommy Flinn, Ed Cullen, and Vin Sahlin in the position.

A *Tribune* sportswriter noted that Berwanger was "tense and over-anxious, as befits a 19-year-old boy with a reputation to uphold." (The young man probably was embarrassed to learn a few weeks later that Dubuque's Orpheum Theater showed patrons a Pathe News newsreel of the Chicago-Michigan debacle.) Chicago and Detroit sportswriters differed in their statistical evidence of Chicago's offensive ineptitude. George Morgenstern of the *Chicago Herald-Examiner* and Smith credited the Maroons with about 60 yards of offense while the *Detroit News'* Lloyd Northard gave them 83, though all agreed that Michigan amassed 336 yards of offense. Most of Chicago's paltry total came on two plays in the final quarter, when the Wolverines were probably thinking about their next opponent – undefeated Illinois.

The Maroons (2-2 overall and 0-2 in the Big Ten) picked themselves up and prepared for their next contest – a winnable game against Clarence Spears' Wisconsin Badgers (1-3 and 0-3). Shaughnessy removed dozens of plays from the Chicago playbook in an attempt to simplify matters for his offense. Of the 86 plays from five formations, the coach planned to run only about a dozen against the visitors from Madison. Blocking became a point of emphasis. The coaches also worked with Berwanger on punting, whose booming kicks in practice were absent in game situations.

The November 4 game at Stagg Field, played in mid-40s temperatures, matched two inexperienced teams going nowhere in the Big Ten Conference race. Though it turned out to be a contest that showcased the ineptitude of Chicago and Wisconsin, it also featured more than its share of thrills. Both teams squandered scoring opportunities with fumbles, interceptions, and stalled drives. Berwanger showed up on both sides of the ledger. He threw an interception and made an interception. He coughed up a fumble. He ran and passed for several first downs.

The back-and-forth between the Maroons and Badgers continued through 3½ quarters, and the game remained scoreless. Then the thrills intensified. On fourth down, the Wisconsin punter got off a low kick to Cullen. He mishandled the ball, and wound up on his rump as the Badgers fell on the fumble at the Chicago 25. With time winding down and the Stagg Field crowd of 20,000 – fans of the Maroons and Badgers alike – shouting encouragement to their boys, Wisconsin started what had the makings of the game's only scoring drive. However, Berwanger proceeded to pick off a Tommy Fontaine pass at his own 7-yard line. As the Badgers immediately tackled Berwanger, the ball popped free. Chicago's Sahlin picked it up and ran up the south sideline to near midfield. Wisconsin claimed it was an incomplete pass, but the referee ruled that Berwanger had control of the ball long enough for the interception before fumbling. Sahlin's heroics continued. He hauled in a long pass from Zimmer to give Chicago a first down at the Wisconsin 12. A penalty moved the Maroons back five yards to the 17, and then the Badgers' defense stiffened.

On fourth down, the crowd hushed as Berwanger set up to attempt a 25-yard field goal to win the game. The center's snap reached the holder, who placed the ball for Berwanger's boot. The kick had plenty of height and distance. The uprights were 23 feet, 4 inches apart (since 1991, they have been 18½ feet apart), but that was not enough. The ball sailed barely outside the right upright. The game ended seconds later, a scoreless tie.

On other campuses in other eras, Berwanger might have been treated as the "goat" – the scorned player whose missed kick cost his team a victory. There was little or none of that talk regarding the Chicago sophomore. The student newspaper printed a brief feature headlined, "All-Around Athlete and Good Fellow – Jay Berwanger." After briefly summarizing Berwanger's accomplishments in high school, writer David H. Kutner continued, "He came to the University on a two-year honor scholarship and worked in the athletic department to defray his living expenses." Asked to state his greatest thrill and greatest disappointment, Berwanger pointed to the long punt he got off from his own end zone while Michigan Wolverines bore down on him. His disappointment was just hours old – the field-goal try against Wisconsin, a miss partially blamed on the wind. "He's going into the Law school but one of his chief ambitions is to do well in the decathlon next spring at Kansas where he will be sent by the University," the article continued. "He wastes a lot of time playing bridge at the Psi U house. Of course he hasn't a girl and 'isn't interested' – but we hear different." Kutner concluded his summary of Berwanger: "A very modest and a thoroughly likable fellow!"

Though in later years Berwanger suggested that his academic interest was always focused on business, there was a period when he considered becoming a lawyer. His transcript indicates that he transferred from Law to the School of Business in the Fall Quarter of his junior year. Scores on the transcript also suggest that earning a law degree might have been tougher than eluding those Michigan tacklers.

He now lived in the Psi Upsilon fraternity house, across University Avenue from Bartlett Gymnasium, which occupied the same block as Stagg Field. Berwanger was "rushed" into Psi Upsilon by Joe Temple, and so he was introduced to Jane Fulton, Temple's girlfriend and future wife. (The paths of Jay and Jane would cross decades later.) The fraternity's initiation fee was $75. Members who lived in the frat house paid $420 for room and board and $45 in dues each academic year. The Omega chapter of Psi Upsilon, whose roots traced to the predecessor institution also named University of Chicago, was a leading fraternity and especially popular among athletes. Though fraternity brothers boasted that their house "had a captain in every room," it was not much of an exaggeration.[75] When Berwanger was a senior, seven captains or co-captains lived in the Psi U house. While Psi U alumni included a Wimbledon champion and Olympians, it was not for jocks only. Other alumni included John Paul Stevens, a 1941 graduate and U.S. Supreme Court justice; and Robert Orville Anderson, Class of 1939 and founder of Atlantic Richfield Oil Company.

Discussion at the Psi U dining table during the second week of November 1933 no doubt included the Maroons' upcoming game against Indiana

University, another struggling member of the Big Ten. Coach Earle Hayes' Hoosiers (1-3-1 overall) had scored only 15 points in their first five games, including their 7-0 victory over Miami (Ohio) in the season opener. Meanwhile, despite having talented running backs in Zimmer and Berwanger, Chicago had yet to score a touchdown in three conference games. The teams were evenly matched, from their 0-2-1 conference records to their preference for the modified single-wing offense.

One of Chicago's pre-Indiana practices was disrupted by a snowstorm, which forced the squad to complete the session in the fieldhouse. Injuries and poor performance caused Shaughnessy to shuffle his starting lineup.

Sahlin became the quarterback and Cullen shifted from the backfield to center, his position in high school, to sub for the injured Ellmore Patterson. Though he was now playing center, Cullen continued to call the signals. John Baker replaced John Womer at end. Raymond Pokela moved to starting left guard in place of Bob Perretz. Indiana had its own personnel issues — some were mixed with intrigue. Hayes benched several underperforming starters and left acting captain Ed Anglemeyer at home. Team officials denied rumors that several Indiana players threatened to strike over the Anglemeyer situation,

When he assigned uniform numbers for 1933, the University of Chicago's new coach, Clark Shaughnessy, gave Berwanger Number 99, explaining that the sophomore was as close to a "perfect 100" as he had seen. (Special Collections Research Center, University of Chicago Library)

and everyone else made the trip to Chicago.

After three disappointing games at Stagg Field, Chicago boosters re-energized over the prospects of a victory over Indiana on Veterans Day 1933. "That old Midway enthusiasm, which has kept the band of faithful Maroon followers together during lean years, has begun to bubble up again, as it does about Wednesday every week," the *Tribune* observed.

Just a few minutes after the 2 p.m. kickoff, Indiana struck first. With the ball at midfield, fullback Lewis Walker tossed the ball 25 yards toward a pack of interception-hungry Chicago defenders. Somehow, Indiana end Ettore Antonini came out with the ball and, somehow, to the bewilderment and frustration of the 12,000 hometown fans in attendance, he outran the Maroons for the final 25 yards and a touchdown. Fitzhugh Lyons' kick put Chicago in a 7-0 hole.

Later in the period, Chicago started a drive on its own 20 after a touch-back on a Hoosiers punt. Berwanger ran around right end, followed a screen of blockers and picked up 33 yards. After an offensive holding penalty, Zimmer connected on a long pass to Sahlin, who reached the Indiana 12. Berwanger rushed for five yards and then Ewald Nyquist carried the ball to the 1. On the next play, Berwanger crashed through the middle of the Indiana line for Chicago's first conference touchdown of 1933. He booted the extra point to make it 7-7. Indiana staged the only scoring threat of the game's second quarter, and Berwanger contributed to the opportunity. On third down, he juggled the snap from center and suffered a 13-yard loss. His punt on the next play shanked out of bounds on the Chicago 28. However, Indiana could get no closer than Chicago's 15 before missing a field-goal attempt.

The Maroons started a third-quarter drive at their own 44. Though Berwanger notched a first down with a 12-yard run, Zimmer contributed the highlights and the officials provided the controversy. The captain had a 27-yard gain and, a few plays later, crossed the goal line standing up on an apparent 34-yard touchdown dash along the south sideline. However, the officials ruled that Zimmer stepped on the sideline at the 2 – a decision that incensed Chicago partisans. From the 2, Nyquist and Berwanger each chal-lenged the Hoosiers and advanced the ball to within an inch of the end zone. However, that's where the ball remained after two more rushes. On third down, Berwanger appeared to get the necessary distance to give Chicago the lead, but the officials ruled that he had been stuffed short of the goal. After that controversial decision, the Hoosiers completed their goal-line stand by stopping the fourth-down play.

The affair turned strange in the fourth quarter. Indiana attempted a 62-yard field goal, and the ball rolled out of bounds on the Chicago 3. The Maroons couldn't do anything offensively, and Berwanger's punt reached only his own 30. Indiana tried another field goal, which Baker blocked to give the Maroons time for one hurried drive from their 28. Berwanger was key. He rushed for 17 yards. Then he connected on a pass to Baker, who tossed a lateral to Tommy Flinn, who scampered to the Hoosiers' 23. With the game clock about to expire, Berwanger lined up to try a 40-yard field goal to win the game. After barely missing in similar circumstances against Wisconsin the week before, Berwanger had the opportunity to give Shaughnessy his first Big Ten victory. The snap reached the holder, who placed the ball in position at the 30. Berwanger stepped forward and powered his foot into the ball. But there would be no heroics on this afternoon. Berwanger topped the ball miserably. It never had a chance. The game ended 7-7. The final three quarters involved plenty of action but nary a point. Both teams remained winless in the conference.

The tie was especially disappointing for Chicago, which for the second straight Saturday outplayed its opponent but failed to win. In four conference games, the Maroons had racked up some 750 yards of offense but had only one touchdown to show for it. Still, the campus newspaper found a silver lining. "Zimmer, Sahlin, and Berwanger all played their heads off. Each of those gentlemen gave exhibitions of football that will live long as real examples of the up-turn in Chicago athletics."

CHAPTER 18

The University of Chicago Maroons had no time to dwell on their two close calls with victory. They had to prepare for their rivalry game against a talented University of Illinois squad, which had just posted a 3-0 win at Northwestern. The Illini, 2-1 in the Big Ten and 4-2 overall, stood to finish third in the conference if they could beat Chicago and then Ohio State. The battle in Champaign would be Chicago's second and final road game of 1933. The Illinois-Chicago series spanned more than four decades and stood nearly even. The *Chicago Tribune* calculated that Chicago held a 17-16 advantage, with three ties and a game or two in dispute – including the 1894 contest, which was overtaken by darkness while the teams argued whether Illinois coach Bucky Vail could take part in the action. To this day, both universities claim victory for November 21, 1894 – Chicago by the 10-6 lead it held when the altercation started, and Illinois by forfeit.[76]

During Bob Zuppke's 29 seasons of coaching the Illini (1913-41), he won national championships four times (1914, 1919, 1923, and 1927). A native of Germany and raised in Wisconsin, Zuppke was an innovator, credited with the "flea-flicker" play, screen pass, spiral snap from center and even the huddle. For his part, Zuppke accepted credit only for regular use of the huddle.[77] Now Zuppke would face Shaughnessy, another offensive innovator. Zuppke's preparation included having his defense scrimmage the freshman squad running the open-field plays expected from Chicago, which reinstated Ed Cullen as starting quarterback.

Zuppke expected another low-scoring affair, and that was all right with him. Surveyed along with his conference peers about possible rules changes, he opposed liberalizing the regulations to help offenses. Northwestern's Dick Hanley, for example, advocated allowing a forward pass to be thrown from anywhere behind the line of scrimmage and permitting the team recovering a fumble or blocked kick to advance the ball. The Wildcats' coach also wanted the goal posts returned to their former position – on the goal line instead of 10 yards back. Overall, seven of the conference's 10 coaches favored making few or no adjustments in the rules of engagement. (Hanley, Wisconsin's Clarence Spears, and Sam Willaman of Ohio State were in the minority.) Though considered experts in offense, Shaughnessy and Zuppke expressed no concern over low-scoring games. "Good teams will score regardless of the rules," Shaughnessy said. "Low scores are due, I think, to more evenly matched teams." Added Zuppke, "The rules are man-made and therefore not perfect. Low score games are interesting. Michigan beat Illinois only 7 to 6 (on November 4), but nobody went home."

With the Great Depression in full force, University of Chicago officials saved money on the rare road trip by not booking hotel rooms for the football team in Champaign, 140 miles south, the night before the game. Coaches, players, band and about 500 fans boarded their train in Chicago barely four hours before kickoff. As soon as they disembarked in Champaign, the Maroons and their entourage proceeded immediately to Memorial Stadium in time for the 2 o'clock kickoff against Jack Beynon, Dave Cook, and the rest of the Illini. Though it was Illinois' final home game of 1933 and the late-November weather forecast in central Illinois was mild – the day's high temperature was 48 – fans stayed away by the thousands. The official attendance was 8,135 – a far cry from 10 years earlier, when in the first game ever played in still-unfinished Memorial Stadium, 60,632 spectators tromped through the muddy construction site to see Illinois beat Chicago, 7-0.[78]

The 1933 battle got off to a slow start, with both teams playing conservatively. The scent of an upset filled the air all afternoon. A Chicago threat in the second quarter, powered by double-digit rushes by Zimmer and Berwanger, fizzled when the center snap flew into an open space in the confused backfield. Berwanger fell on the ball but soon had to punt. Illinois did not advance into Chicago territory until late in the second quarter. However, on Illinois' next drive, Beynon connected with Crain Portman for a 19-yard touchdown pass. The *Chicago Tribune's* Edward Burns described it as a "beautifully executed maneuver, which completely fooled the keyed-up Maroons." Cook kicked the extra point. By halftime, the Maroons had collected five first downs to Illinois' one and had rushed for 102 yards from scrimmage to the Illini's 28. Yet they trailed 7-0.

Instead of being discouraged by the developments, the Maroons seemed to become more determined. Midway through the third quarter, with the ball on the Chicago 43, Vin Sahlin broke through the left side of his line, cut right and dashed into open territory. He covered 54 yards before Portman pulled him down on the 3-yard line. On the next play, however, Berwanger fumbled and Illinois lineman Chuck Bennis recovered. Chicago mounted another scoring threat early in the fourth quarter, when Zimmer connected with Sahlin for 40 yards, to reach the Illinois 30. However, the Maroons lost another fumble when Ewald Nyquist coughed up the ball and sophomore lineman Charles Galbreath recovered.

Illinois committed a turnover of its own late in the game, when Frank Froschauer fumbled on the Chicago 39. One sportswriter credited the recovery to end Rainwater Wells and another gave it to helmet-less lineman Robert Deem. In any case, the Maroons suddenly had one last chance to forge a tie. Berwanger was a principal in every play. The drive started with a five-yard offside penalty against Illinois. Berwanger then passed to Nyquist for 15 yards. Zimmer tossed to Berwanger, who chewed up 31 yards before being brought down at the 8-yard line. On first down and goal, Berwanger penetrated the Illinois line for three yards. On second down, he did the same, gaining two. On third down from the 3, Nyquist caught Berwanger's short pass but was stopped just short of the goal line. Chicago was down to its final play. Would the Maroons earn the chance to tie? On fourth down, Number 99 got the call. That surprised no one inside cavernous Memorial Stadium – especially the Illinois defense. The Illini stopped Berwanger for virtually no gain. Sportswriters' estimates varied, but when Berwanger was brought down, they said the ball was no more than two feet from the goal line. Underdog Chicago came out on top in rushing yards (193 to 92), passing yards (134 to 88), and first downs (10 to six). But Illinois prevailed in points, 7 to 0.

Berwanger was the star in his best Big Ten game of the season. He carried the ball an exhausting 36 times, and his 95 yards rushing was more than the Illinois team combined; the total included a first-down run from punt formation. He passed with accuracy. He punted solidly. He was a factor on defense. And, as was the case during the previous four conference games, he played every minute of the game. However, he had miscues, including lost fumbles and a costly penalty for roughing the Illinois punter in his own end zone.

Feeling fortunate to escape with victory, Illinois' Zuppke praised his opponents – especially their runners. "Well, those backs are too much for me. They're the best I've seen all season." Despite his team's loss, the *Tribune's* Burns described Berwanger's efforts "as scintillating an all-around perfor-

mance as Maroon followers have seen in their behalf these many years." That
was true, but Berwanger also failed in late-game situations on three consecutive Saturdays. He missed field goals against Wisconsin and Indiana and
failed to make that final yard against Illinois. If negative sentiment existed
among Chicago partisans, Maroons captain Zimmer was having none of
it. "And now, as to the undying Maroons, Jay Berwanger, who has never
lost the absolute confidence of the entire team, played a magnificent game
against the Illini. Though he carried the ball for 36 substantial gains, he never
faltered throughout the game, finishing as strong as he began." The captain
added this prophecy: "I believe he will be prominent among the greatest
football men in the history of the University before he completes his varsity
competition." Even in the era when substitution rules made it necessary for
athletes to play both offense and defense, it was remarkable that Berwanger
was on the field for every play of all five Big Ten games, not once giving way
to a substitute.

Chicago closed conference play winless (0-3-2 and 2-3-2 overall) while
Illinois (3-1 and 5-2) kept alive its quest for third place. Those hopes died
a bitter and bizarre death the next Saturday in Columbus. Trailing 7-6, the
Illini staged a late drive. A long pass put them on the Ohio State 9 with
about a minute remaining on the scoreboard clock. After advancing a couple

*Dartmouth tacklers try to bring down Berwanger in their 1933 season finale. Berwanger scored
two touchdowns, and the host Chicago Maroons exploded for four touchdowns in an eight-
minute span of the fourth quarter to seal a 39-0 victory. (Special Collections Research Center,
University of Chicago Library)*

of yards on first down, the Illini prepared for their next play. Suddenly, the official's pistol sounded, apparently signaling the end of the game. Delighted hometown fans cheered, and the Ohio State team and marching band swarmed the field in celebration. Distraught and confused Illinois players, some in tears, pounded the field in frustration. The game officials, in a "panic," knew something was wrong. They quickly found out that a member of a high school band – the musicians were fill-ins for the Illinois contingent – standing near the visitors' sideline saw the officials' pistol. He picked up and fiddled with the pistol, and it accidentally discharged. After several chaotic minutes, the field was finally cleared, and the Illini, emotionally drained and rattled, resumed their drive. A couple of plays later, Illinois' Dave Cook, whose field goal had won the Northwestern game two weeks earlier, lined up to attempt a game-winning kick. His 25-yard boot missed by inches. Ohio State officially recorded its 7-6 victory and third place in the Big Ten. The heartbroken Illini fell to a fifth-place tie with Iowa.

Some observers might have considered Chicago's home game against Dartmouth College anti-climactic, but at least it allowed the Maroons the opportunity to end their season on a high note. Dartmouth was 4-3-1, but three of its wins came against minor opponents at the start of the campaign.

The Maroons' final game of 1933 was their Homecoming contest, and they worked hard to get ready for Dartmouth. Shaughnessy's brother Ed scouted the Big Green and reported that an aerial attack might be Chicago's best strategy against the visitors, whose defensive line averaged a hefty 195 pounds. Chicago's two-day Homecoming schedule included a pep session at 7:30 on Friday evening, a carillon recital, and a dance in Ida Noyes Hall. Gentlemen paid 25 cents to enter the dance, while ladies were admitted without charge. Among the Homecoming events was a halftime tug-of-war on the football field pitting freshmen against sophomores.

On the Saturday before Thanksgiving 1933, some 26,000 fans poured into Stagg Field for the season finale against the visitors from Hanover, New Hampshire. Mother Nature cooperated, keeping snow and rain away while delivering a warmer-than-average afternoon; the thermometer at kickoff read 51 degrees. The game would be the last for six seniors, including captain Pete Zimmer, Vin Sahlin, and right guard Walter Maneikis. It was also a special occasion for Cullen, who played with the Dartmouth freshmen team before transferring to Chicago.

The Maroons played as well as they had all season. The only negatives were Zimmer taking a hard knock in the first quarter and Berwanger's inaccurate kicks from placement. Chicago grabbed a 6-0 lead in the opening quarter. Sahlin, aided by a Berwanger block, returned a punt 15 yards to the Dartmouth 39. Nyquist and Berwanger teamed up for another first down. Berwanger broke out for about 15 yards to the 14-yard line. Berwanger kept the ball on the next three plays but was stopped at the 1 on the third rush. The teams lined up for the fourth-down play. Dartmouth, anticipating Berwanger would get the ball again, was surprised when it went to Nyquist, who crashed across the goal line. Berwanger's extra-point kick missed. Chicago added two points on a safety after John Baker blocked a Dartmouth punt and the ball bounded back and out of the end zone.

The best running play seen at Stagg Field in 1933 occurred three minutes into the second quarter. Berwanger rushed through right tackle, cut left and ran down the sideline. He sidestepped and dodged four would-be tacklers before breaking into the clear for a 61-yard touchdown. Berwanger connected on the extra point to make it 15-0. Dartmouth started to get its offense moving later in the quarter. The Big Green reached Chicago's 18, when Berwanger burst into the backfield and tackled Harry Deckert for a three-yard loss to stifle the drive.

Trailing 15-0, Coach Jackson Cannell tried to shake things up by sending out 11 reserves to start the second half. Dartmouth responded on defense but fumbled on its first offensive possession. After a scoreless third quarter, Chicago had an apparent touchdown – a 35-yard pass from Berwanger to Sahlin – called back when officials said that Berwanger's toss did not originate the required minimum of five yards behind the line of scrimmage. It soon didn't matter. The floodgates opened with eight minutes left in the game. The Maroons exploded and the Big Green imploded.

Cullen scored the third Chicago touchdown on a 68-yard interception. Berwanger then kicked off and recovered the Dartmouth returner's fumble. Passes to and from Berwanger, interspersed with penalties, gave the Maroons a first down on the Dartmouth 12. Sahlin ran wide and scampered across the goal line for the final touchdown of his career. During the rally, Shaughnessy sent in several reserves, including seniors marking their last game. Their presence did not slow down the scoring rush. Chicago intercepted a pass right away. Senior reserve Bob Wallace contributed a nine-yard run to set the table on the Dartmouth 6. Berwanger then rushed around right end, cast aside tacklers and dived into the corner of the end zone for his second touchdown of the afternoon. He missed the extra-point kick. For the first time since facing Washington University in his second game, Berwanger made way for a substitute. Chicago fans, seeing the team's future at his best, rewarded him with a huge ovation.

One of the senior reserves Shaughnessy sent onto the field was Bill Berg. Despite being on a team lacking numbers, Berg had not played one minute all season. He had barely reported into the game when a Dartmouth pass came into his vicinity. He snared it and dashed 60 yards, untouched, for a memory-making touchdown. Wallace fared no better than Berwanger on the extra-point attempt, missing the inconsequential kick. Final score: 39-0.

The flood of 24 points in eight minutes stunned and excited the Maroons' boosters. "This crowd did something that no other in all the losing years has done," the *Chicago Herald-Examiner's* George Morgenstern reported. "It stood and roared a tremendous ovation as every Maroon senior came out with glory enough for his years on defeated teams, and it took the great Maroon sophomore, Jay Berwanger, into its chant of victory as he left the game after a smashing performance such as few backs have accomplished this year." The fans didn't go home right away, instead "rising up to know what this sense of long-awaited triumph was like." The *American's* Jim Gallagher described the scene: "As this is written, the dusk is coming up out of the East, and only a faint red glow in the western clouds illuminates historic old Stagg Field. Down there, where the Maroons have just won their most important football victory in many a year, a joyous gang of students are tearing down the goal posts – aided by more than one alumnus of the lean football years since 1926." He added, "The Maroons really seem to have hit the turn in the road. Their team, which has shown gradual but noticeable improvement with each succeeding week of the season, today reached its peak, and demonstrated all the potential power that has been idle all these preceding weeks."

The loss turned up the heat on Dartmouth's Cannell, who was in his second stint as head coach of his alma mater. Despite a winning career record, his teams had just posted back-to-back .500 seasons, punctuated by the embarrassing collapse in Chicago. He returned to campus, read the student newspaper editorial calling for his ouster, and submitted a one-sentence letter of resignation. Shaughnessy also had a .500 season (3-3-2), but he was heralded as a hero on the Midway. With the new coach, and with Berwanger coming back for two more autumns, Chicago's future was bright.

CHAPTER 19

With his first season of varsity college football concluded, Jay Berwanger attended classes for a few days and then returned home to Dubuque for Thanksgiving weekend. The Great Depression surely tempered Americans' enthusiasm for giving thanks and celebrating, but the 1933 observance was an occasion to note some silver linings. George T. Hughes, writing for the North American Newspaper Alliance, offered an upbeat summary, highlighted by price rises for key common stocks and commodities since the previous Thanksgiving. He noted that steel manufacturing increased production over the past year – even though factories were still operating at only 28 percent of capacity. "There was plenty of anxiety about the future on Thanksgiving Day 1932, and there is much today," Hughes wrote, "but it is on different scores." In any case, while dealing with their own financial circumstances on the farm and in the city, the Berwangers no doubt were thankful for Jay's accomplishments on the national stage.

Meanwhile, postseason honors rolled in for Berwanger. He made the All Big Ten second teams, listed as a halfback, for both The Associated Press and United Press. No other University of Chicago player did better than Honorable Mention. Illinois star Jack Beynon ranked Berwanger as the hardest man to tackle in the Big Ten. The *Chicago American's* Leo Fischer, whose columns were syndicated to other U.S. papers, placed Berwanger on his all-conference first team. "At the start of the season, before he had played a single varsity game, another conference coach declared he'd trade any four of his sophomores for the Maroon youngster," Fischer wrote. "At the end of the season the same coach was willing to make it eight." Perhaps Berwanger's most gratifying honor for the 1933 football season was not bestowed by sportswriters but by his teammates. The Maroons voted him their Most Valuable Player. Despite running behind a below-average offensive line,

Berwanger ranked fifth among conference rushers. He carried the ball in 46 percent of the Maroons' rushing plays, scored 55 of his team's 118 points, and took care of business on defense. The university yearbook paid him this tribute: "A runner of All-Conference caliber; a kicker of unusual accuracy; a passer of precision and skill; a blocker of positive and certain effect; and a tackler of power and talent. The pivot man for important formations; the ground gaining line smasher at crucial moments; the kicker in tight spots; and the ball carrier so difficult to stop in open field running. In all, a player of real merit."

In addition to choosing Berwanger as their MVP, the Maroons elected lineman Ellmore Patterson as captain for 1934. The Chicago Alumni Club and the Order of the C, the lettermen's club, selected other honorees: Robert Deem, best tackler; Vinson Sahlin, best blocker; and Walter Maneikis, most under rated. They, along with Patterson and Berwanger, whose honors were determined the previous evening at a team meal, were recognized at the alumni club's annual football dinner at the University Club. President Hutchins was a speaker, and he tried to calm the unease about the possible merger with Northwestern, stating, "Whether or not there is a consolidation, the University of Chicago will never abandon the college on the Midway."

Each Big Ten team's individual MVP became eligible for the 10th annual *Chicago Tribune* Silver Football Award, presented to the 23 electors' choice as the conference's top player – officially, the player "of greatest value to his team." The inaugural recipient, in 1924, was Red Grange of Illinois. Iowa senior quarterback Joe Laws, who would later play 12 seasons with

Berwanger long had designs on competing in the 1936 Olympic decathlon, but injuries and university administration's pressure to graduate on time contributed to his absence from the Olympic trials. (Special Collections Research Center, University of Chicago Library)

Green Bay in the National Football League, won the 1933 award in a close vote (23-17) over Minnesota junior Francis "Pug" Lund, a future member of the College Football Hall of Fame. Berwanger finished third with eight votes – at that time the best finish by any sophomore. It might have helped Berwanger's standing that the award was intended for the player "of greatest value to his team," rather than the conference's best athlete – a small distinction, but a distinction nonetheless. One elector explained it this way: "I feel that the award should go to a player whose absence from the team affects the playing qualities of other players. Jay Berwanger played without substitution in most of (his) games ... and by his splendid running and clever dodging pulled the Chicago team up from a mental attitude they had acquired through years of beatings. Berwanger, my first choice, was a steady, reliable player who played the same sort of game each day."

Between his sophomore and junior football seasons, Berwanger earned induction into the University of Chicago's Skull and Crescent, the sophomore honor society, whose members were selected for academic achievement and excellence in a chosen activity. Considering that Berwanger was not a dean's list student, one must assume that the selection committee gave him plenty of credit for his excellence on the gridiron.

When Berwanger returned to campus after Thanksgiving break, the clay surface in the university fieldhouse was rolled, lined, and ready for indoor track season. Berwanger, a powerful runner with Olympic aspirations, concentrated his training on the field events while also competing in the hurdles and dashes. He did not ease up in his training before indoor meets, and occasionally he did not enter his strongest events. Berwanger's focus was on the Kansas Relays decathlon in April. Early in the season, his training was hampered by an arm injury suffered during pole-vault practice. In late January 1934, the varsity whipped a squad of freshmen and alumni. Berwanger won two events – the high hurdles and long jump – and finished second to alum John Brooks in the 60-yard dash and low hurdles. Brooks is the earliest African-American athlete enshrined in the University of Chicago's Hall of Fame. His best event was the long jump, in which he won the national collegiate championship in 1933, two Big Ten titles (1932 and 1933) and set a Drake Relays record (1932).[79] During a six-season span (1932-37) he placed second or third in the national open championships five times, including 1933, when he landed less than an inch behind Jesse Owens. Brooks placed seventh in the 1936 Olympic long jump (won by Owens). A week after the 1934 alumni meet, though injury kept Berwanger out of the pole vault and weight events, he scored 20½ points – four firsts and a third – in an exhibition against the freshmen.

Meanwhile, news out of Columbus no doubt raised concern among fans of University of Chicago football. Sam Willaman was out as coach at Ohio State, and Clark Shaughnessy's name emerged as a possible successor. The Associated Press reported that "gossip" rated the Chicago coach as Athletic Director L.W. St. John's leading choice. The *Chicago Tribune* said that St. John confirmed that he had his athletic board's permission to approach Shaughnessy about the job. Would Berwanger and the Maroons lose their coach after just one season? For his part, Shaughnessy admitted, "The whole situation interests me very much," but also shrugged off the speculation and said he was satisfied with his job in Chicago. Initial wire service reports of Willaman's resignation listed Shaughnessy, Illinois' Bob Zuppke, and four others as being considered by Ohio State. None of the six wound up with the job. After a month of speculation, the Buckeyes hired Francis A. Schmidt from Texas Christian University.

While events played out in Ohio, Berwanger engaged in his first intercollegiate competition in track and field. The Maroons hosted the nearby Armour Institute of Technology, whose coach was none other than Lonnie Stagg. University of Chicago officials permitted their head tennis and assistant football coach to oversee the Armour track team. Berwanger collected four firsts – in the 60, high hurdles, low hurdles, and long jump – as the Maroons dominated, 78-35. Against North Central College of suburban Naperville, Illinois, Berwanger won the low hurdles in near-record time and finished second in the high hurdles and 60 as the Maroons won, 51-44.

Later, Chicago registered a come-from-behind victory over Purdue. With one running event remaining, the Boilermakers held a 38-34 lead, thanks in part to a double win by distance ace Charley Popejoy. The final race was a relay at the unusual distance of three-fourths of a mile. The Maroons, with Berwanger running anchor, easily won and took a 39-38 lead with one field event remaining. Minutes later, John Roberts won the pole vault to assure Chicago's victory. (Popejoy would later win the 1934 outdoor conference title at two miles. Nearly 40 years later, his son Ken, representing Michigan State, became the first miler to break four minutes in the Big Ten championships.)

The next Saturday, the Maroons traveled a few miles north for a quadrangular in Northwestern's Patten Gymnasium. The venue was so small that the sprints and hurdles were contested over only 40 yards, compared to the 70 yards staged in the Chicago fieldhouse. Berwanger won the low hurdles in

5.1 seconds and, despite taking an early lead in the highs, finished third. The meet was close all evening. Ohio State won the final event, the mile relay, to gain a first-place tie with Northwestern (39½ points). Chicago scored 30 points and Wisconsin 23.[80] Three days later, Chicago's win over Loyola was a 71-24 runaway, and Berwanger dominated, winning three events – the 60-yard dash in 6.4 seconds, 70-yard low hurdles in 7.8, and shot put (43-10½) – and barely losing the high hurdles.

Between track meets, Berwanger and his fellow football players attended to their classwork. Shaughnessy was seeing to that. The football coach, concerned about losing players to academic ineligibility, in January started to require his athletes to submit weekly updates on their academic progress. During the winter, they learned that their college careers would remain under the University of Chicago banner alone. In late February 1934, officials of Northwestern University and Chicago announced that they had dropped consideration of a merger. *The Tribune* reported that the merger was virtually a done deal in November 1933, when Northwestern trustees were scheduled to vote on the proposal, but the universities backed away in response to strong opposition on both campuses and elsewhere in the Chicago community.

Berwanger was a force in smaller track meets, and consistently good in many events, but not outstanding enough to score well in larger competitions. In an early-March triangular meet against Michigan and Northwestern, he won the shot put (45-4), but otherwise the best he could do was fourth in the 60, third in the high hurdles, and fourth in the low hurdles. When the Big Ten staged its 1934 indoor championships in Chicago, Berwanger finished last in the preliminaries of both the 60 and highs, but finished fifth in the shot put (45-5¾).[81] Decades later classmate and friend Ernie Dix contended, "Jay could have been better in track if he had better coaching. He used to sit around between track events and get stiff." There is little to confirm or refute that, but Chicago head coach Ned Merriam and volunteer coach Austin Menaul were not newcomers to the sport. A quarter-century earlier, as a student on the Midway, Merriam was a world-class quarter-miler who won three consecutive Big Ten titles at 440 yards (1906-08) and was a semifinalist in the Olympic 400 meters of 1908. Menaul was a 1912 Olympian in the pentathlon and decathlon.

While Berwanger in later years liked to claim that he didn't have time for girls during his campus days, gossip items in the neighborhood *Hyde Park Herald* suggested otherwise. Six weeks after stating that they were "uh-huh," the *Herald* indicated that a relationship was heating up: "Rose Tieber and Jay Berwanger never have any time to listen to the Biology lecture because they prefer their own *tete-a-tete* to negative and positive ions." He also attended fraternity parties and dances. A favorite dance spot was the Trianon Ballroom, 62nd and Cottage Grove, and he frequented many of the restaurants along 63rd Street. Another entertainment option was the world's fair at the other end of the Midway, in its second and final season.

The sophomore's indoor track season concluded with three meets in eight days. At the Central Amateur Athletic Union meet, staged on a Friday night in the university fieldhouse, he took fourth in the long jump and third in the shot put. The next day he returned to the fieldhouse for the Armour Tech Relays and competed in seven events. He placed fourth in the low hurdles and shot put, but he was shut out in the 70, highs, pole vault, and long jump. Finally, he joined Pete Zimmer, Bart Smith, and Ed Cullen to easily win an unusual event on the schedule – the football lettermen's mile relay. A week later, Berwanger concluded his indoor season by failing to place in the shot put (43-6) at the Butler Relays in Indianapolis.

During the three-week break in between indoor and outdoor competitions, Berwanger trained for the Kansas Relays decathlon, participated in spring football practice (but limited his work to forward passes), and went home for Easter break, during which he gave pointers in the shot put to members of the Dubuque High team. His visit came on the heels of his selection as his high school's top athlete of the previous decade.

While the Maroons competed in an outdoor quadrangular meet at Monmouth College, in Western Illinois, Berwanger kept his date at the Kansas Relays for his first decathlon. The decathlon is a grueling competition – 10 running and field events divided over two days – to determine the best all-around athlete. The competition also served as the Missouri Valley Amateur Athletic Union championships. On a raw and blustery Friday in Lawrence, the seven athletes opened with the 100-meter dash. Clyde Coffman, of the host university, whose resume included a seventh-place finish in the 1932 Olympics, won the heat in 10.5 seconds, edging Berwanger and Wichita's Lorenzo McClain, who tied for second at 10.6. The Chicago sophomore's long jump of 21-3½ (6.495 meters) ranked him only fifth among the seven. He rebounded in the next field event, the shot put, topping the field with a toss of 44-6½ feet (13.58 meters). In the high jump, Berwanger finished in a three-way tie for third at 5-7 (1.7 meters). He placed third in the first day's final running event, the 400 meters (54.5seconds).

Halfway through the competition, Berwanger was in second place behind Pittsburg (Kansas) Teachers College's Delbert White, 4,084-3,994. Could he close the 90-point gap? Meanwhile, the Olympian Coffman lurked in fourth place.

The second day of competition opened with the 110-meter high hurdles. Berwanger finished second (16.0 seconds) to Roy Patterson of Iowa Wesley-an. Berwanger collected another second in the discus (120-6½) while White (136-5¾) extended his points lead. White and Berwanger then tied for third in the pole vault at 3.5 meters (11-6) as Coffman won to cut 238 points off his deficit to White. After eight events, Berwanger remained in second place. However, the final two events were Berwanger's weakest – the javelin and 1,500 meters. He lost ground in the javelin, coming in sixth with a throw of 147-3½. Berwanger, a sprint and field-event man, was out of his element in the 1,500. His 1,500 at Kansas apparently was his first official race longer than a quarter-mile. Patterson crossed the line first in 4:46.6. Berwanger came in sixth, more than a football-field behind in 5:11.6. His points in the final two events dropped him from second place to fourth overall (7,442 points). Pre-meet favorites Patterson and Coffman closed the gap on White, but they couldn't overtake the Pittsburg star (7,679), who edged Patterson by 48 points and Coffman by 84. Despite his results in the ninth and 10th events, it was a solid showing for the 20-year old, who ranked seventh among American decathletes for the year.[82]

The featured event at Kansas was the invitational mile, in which Kansas' Glenn Cunningham, the indoor world-record holder, and future Olympian Gene Venzke were expected to take a crack at Jack Lovelock's world record of 4:07.6. Though local fans were happy with Cunningham's convincing win over Venzke, of Pennsylvania, the Kansan did not come close to the world mark, running 4:12.7. Less than two months later, Cunningham scored his world record (4:06.8).

Coming off his achievement in Lawrence, Berwanger won five events and tied for first in a sixth at North Central College in suburban Naperville. Judges ruled that he and Vince Godfrey of the host college finished in a dead heat for first in the 120-yard high hurdles. The Chicago star won outright in the 220-yard low hurdles (25.3), shot put (47-5, a career best), javelin (154-7), discus (127-2) and long jump (21-10). His 5½ wins helped the Maroons prevail, 72-54.

After suffering a lopsided 84-47 loss at Purdue – Berwanger collected a first in the low hurdles, three seconds, and a third – the Maroons took it on the chin at Northwestern, 81-45. Berwanger's contribution was winning the shot put (46-4), collecting two seconds and notching two thirds. He slipped at the finish line and lost the 100-yard dash by inches. At the start of the 220-yard low hurdles, he slipped again and barely managed to place third. He struggled in the discus and failed to place. In the Big Ten championship meet at Northwestern's Dyche Stadium, Berwanger qualified for the finals in the low hurdles and the long jump. In the hurdles championship, he lost his stride but still managed to beat everyone in the field but Oliver Duggins of Northwestern. He also had trouble with his steps in the long jump, taking off far short of the board, yet he landed in a third-place tie at 22-11¼.

The Maroons closed their season at home, finishing a distant last in a quadrangular. Chicago had to contend with Northwestern, Ohio State, and Wisconsin without their Number 1 weapon. Berwanger missed the Saturday meet so he could take the English examination he needed to pass for the College Certificate. Over the first two weeks of June 1934, he took comprehensive exams in Humanities, Biological Science and Geography. The results would arrive during his summer break.[83]

The football team completed spring practice with Berwanger making only occasional appearances. Shaughnessy, still concerned that he might lose some valuable members of his short-handed team to injury and academic ineligibility, tried various players at different positions. If he were to have gaps to fill in the fall, he wanted his athletes at least exposed to their new assignments. "Berwanger did not attend many of the practice sessions," the student newspaper noted, adding the understatement, "but rumor has it that not many of the players are thinking too seriously of copping the Iowan's berth." Indeed.

CHAPTER 20

After working two summers (1932 and 1933) in Ira Davenport's Dubuque Boat and Boiler Works, Berwanger worked the next two as a counselor at Camp Highlands for Boys near Sayner, Wisconsin. The lakeside site, deep in the woods of northern Wisconsin, provided an extreme contrast from the bustle of Chicago and the steady pace of Dubuque. His connection to the job was Walter J. "Doc" Monilaw, athletic director of University of Chicago High School, who was also the camp's long-time director. He also officiated sports, including track, and most likely worked at many of Berwanger's meets on the Midway. Earlier in his career, Monilaw, a physician and educator, helped establish the Missouri Valley Conference and co-founded the Drake Relays. A graduate of the Drake medical school and a pioneer in developing recreation programs, Monilaw directed Camp Highlands from 1914 to 1959. Started in 1904 by Monilaw's boss at the lab school, Harry O. Gillette, Camp Highlands remains one of the nation's oldest programs of its kind.[84] It is likely the only camp whose roster of former counselors includes two future Heisman Trophy winners – Berwanger and Iowa's Nile Kinnick (1939).

It didn't require the heavy lifting and manual labor of the factory, but Berwanger's new job afforded him a summer full of conditioning, sunshine, sports, fresh air, and good meals. Further, it pushed him into a strict routine. "I felt the conditioning I did at the boys camp was better than the physical labor" (at the boatyards) – for two or three reasons," Berwanger said decades later. "It was a regular life. Regular hours. Three meals a day. Exercise on canoe trips, running, and so forth." On evenings after working his previous summer job at the boatyards, Berwanger admitted, he occasionally stayed out "a little late."[85] The summer camp routine was good for the athlete, and he was good for the camp. Berwanger's talent and personality helped him connect well with the boys, and together they earned a Best Cabin Award in

1934.[86]

While at camp in 1934, Berwanger received word that he had passed his three comprehensive exams and thus was eligible for his junior season of football. However, a major eligibility problem hit Chicago's talent-strapped football team. The Big Ten ruled that both starting tackles, Bob Deem and John Rice, had used up their eligibility. The conference treated competition involving junior colleges the same as competition against regular colleges. Deem played on a junior college team before transferring to Chicago, and Rice's high school team, needing competition in its remote part of Texas, had played against some junior colleges. Not all conferences had such a strict rule. Some of Rice's prep teammates attended four-year colleges outside the Big Ten and remained eligible for their third year of varsity competition.

Fall workouts allowed players to get accustomed to the new, slimmer football that would be introduced in 1934 games. The easier-to-grip ball – the short-axis circumference lost about an inch – was expected to result in longer and more accurate passes and kicks and complement rules changes

In 1934, when Gerald Ford, Michigan's center and team captain, tried to tackle Berwanger, he suffered a deep gash to the cheek from Berwanger's cleat. Forty years later, Ford became president of the United States. Ford said he thought of Berwanger every day – when he looked into the shaving mirror and saw his scar. (Courtesy Gerald R. Ford Library)

expected to inject more excitement into the game. National rulesmakers dropped the five-yard penalty for consecutive incomplete forward passes as well as the automatic touchback for any incomplete forward pass crossing the goal line. (Consecutive incompletions across the goal line, as well as failed fourth-down passes that crossed the line, still meant a touchback.) Raymond "Ducky" Pond, the new coach of Yale, supported dropping the automatic touchback rule. "It will make the defense stay back and give the offensive team a better scoring chance inside the 20-yard line, which I had felt was one of the needs of the game." Most coaches believed that dropping the penalty for consecutive incompletions would stop the defense's practice, on the play after an incompletion, of massing at the line of scrimmage in anticipation of a run. "This change will affect goal line defense or last ditch stands particularly," Arch Ward of the *Chicago Tribune* explained. "Since the first incompleted pass into the end zone no longer causes a touchback and loss of the ball, field generals will give the pass even more action in that territory. Consequently the defense must spread to meet it or run the risk of a completed pass for a touchdown. With the defense spread, there will be more opportunities to cross the opposition with end runs or line thrusts. That decidedly is a step in the right direction." Rulesmakers rejected proposals to allow forward passes from anywhere behind the line of scrimmage – passers still had to release the ball from at least five yards back – and to start plays from scrimmage with the ball at least 15 yards (instead of 10) from the nearest sideline.

With the new rules and the new ball, Berwanger and the Maroons went to work. In his first season as Chicago coach, Clark Shaughnessy rarely conducted scrimmages because he wanted to minimize injuries to his shallow roster. He probably second-guessed himself in his second season after reserve quarterback Tommy Flinn, who weighed less than 150 pounds, wrenched his shoulder in a preseason scrimmage while trying to tackle the 190-pound Berwanger. (Shaughnessy rarely allowed Berwanger to engage in contact drills. He worried as much about injuries his powerful star might inflict on his teammates as he was injury to Berwanger himself.) Meanwhile, John Baker suffered a bruised shin and sophomore end Bill Gillerlain broke a finger.

Though hobbled, the Maroons expected an easy time of it in their 1934 season opener against Carroll College, the two-time defending Wisconsin intercollegiate champion. And they got it, barely breaking a sweat in a workmanlike 19-0 victory. Carroll's first-year coach, Elmer Lampe, played end for

Chicago in the mid-1920s. Though Carroll was undefeated in 1933, Lampe had little to work with for 1934. His preseason roster included only 26 players – and only one Pioneer starter weighed more than Berwanger. Carroll beat Milwaukee Teachers College in their opener, 6-0, but knew it would have its hands full in Chicago, where the newspapers referred to the contest as Pushover Day. At Friday practice, Shaughnessy introduced a half-dozen new plays, and those were the only plays his team ran against Carroll. The more complicated plays would wait for Michigan two weeks later; Shaughnessy even kept the new uniforms locked away until the Wolverines came to town.

About 25,000 fans, including some 17,000 Boy Scouts who received free admission, converged on Stagg Field the final Saturday of September 1934. Soon after the 2:30 p.m. kickoff, Chicago took control, thanks to Carroll miscues. The Pioneers fumbled while attempting to punt, and the Maroons recovered on the Carroll 25. Berwanger navigated all 25 of those yards, running around left end, for the first touchdown. In the second quarter, Carroll's Frank Turner fumbled Berwanger's punt, and the Maroons gained field position as the teams traded punts. Berwanger then covered 32 yards in two rushes for a touchdown and kicked the extra point to make the score 13-0.

Chicago's final touchdown came in the third quarter, and again Berwanger was central to the drive. He rushed for a dozen yards and, after a 15-yard roughing penalty against Carroll, passed to John Baker on a 24-yard touchdown play. "The game proved several things," the *Chicago Tribune* observed afterward: "1. Chicago has some excellent talent. 2. The Maroons have much to learn on such matters as offensive line play. 3. Carroll has a spirited, courageous team." Noted George Morgenstern of the *Herald-Examiner*, "The game demonstrated that Jay Berwanger still stands in the same relation to the Maroons that the Dean boys do to St. Louis; that Coach Clark Shaughnessy has at least one other good running back in Ned Bartlett, a sophomore; and that there is a good deal missing yet in the way of Maroon offensive blocking, particularly with reference to the ends. They got in the way of more ball carriers than they helped."

Carroll College, which would finish the season 2-3-2, was no challenge. The first real test would be Michigan, conference co-champion and national champion of 1933. Shaughnessy used the open Saturday on his schedule to scout Michigan's season-opening loss to Michigan State. After a scoreless half in Ann Arbor, Michigan State broke away for a 16-0 victory. The *Chicago Tribune's* Harvey Woodruff described it as a "humiliating" defeat for a Michigan team that had lost to State only twice in 29 games. The outcome surprised and worried Shaughnessy. "This (Michigan defeat) is the worst thing that could happen for our chances next Saturday," he said. "Michigan now will become fighting mad."[87] Michigan also dominated its series against Chicago, winning 16 of 23 games, including 10 of their last 12 meetings.

The respective coaches had different offensive philosophies. Harry Kipke preferred to play conservatively until Michigan advanced the ball close to midfield, while, as a Chicago sportswriter explained it, "Mr. Shaughnessy be-

For two summers, before his junior and senior seasons at Chicago, Berwanger (back row, center) was a counselor at Camp Highlands for Boys in northern Wisconsin. He and his son Butch, who worked at the camp for more than two decades, are in the Camp Highlands Hall of Fame. (Camp Highlands for Boys photo)

lieves that a first down is a first down wherever it is made." Usually matched against bigger, deeper teams, Shaughnessy built an offense around speed and deception. He built it around Berwanger.

Kipke knew he faced a rebuilding year after losing eight regulars from his 1933 champions. His task was made no easier when his best passer, William Renner, suffered a broken ankle during preseason workouts. Few observers expected the Wolverines to repeat as Big Ten champions – Minnesota, Illinois and Iowa were the preseason favorites – but Chicago partisans saw themselves as Davids preparing for a gridiron Goliath. The *Daily Maroon*, which came out three days a week, closed every article in its edition before the game with the tagline, "WHIP THE WOLVERINES." The first pep rally started at 10 Friday morning. All day, the figure of a Michigander was displayed inside a coffin loaned by a local funeral director. The day's final rally featured a torchlight parade that included at least 75 automobiles.

The next afternoon, an estimated 25,000 spectators poured into the Stagg Field stands for the battle, played under fair skies with temperatures in the high 50s. Chicago cheerleaders had little trouble whipping up enthusiasm among their partisans:

Go, Chicago.
Chi-ca-go, Chi-ca-go, Chi-ca-go, Go.
Chi-ca-go, Chi-ca-go, Chi-ca-go, Go.
Team, Team, Team.
Y-E-A!

The game started out as a chess match – a poorly played chess match. Michigan's Willis Ward shot the opening kickoff out of bounds – then did it again, giving Chicago the ball at its own 40. After that, Chicago and Michigan traded conventional plays and punts, with the Maroons gradually gaining field position. Berwanger lofted a punt that came to rest on the Michigan 5-yard line. The Wolverines' offense couldn't move the ball, and John Regeczi, kicking into the wind from his own end zone, got off a weak punt, which Tommy Flinn returned nine yards to the Michigan 26.

Berwanger then did something he had never done in a Big Ten football contest – he came out of the game. After playing every second of every conference game the previous season, the junior spent some time on the bench. To that point, Michigan defenders had bottled up Berwanger, who was replaced by Bartlett. After a four-yard rush to the 21, Chicago went to the air. Bartlett connected with Baker, who took in the throw at the intersection of the sideline and goal line. Seeing the players and officials head upfield and hearing the public address announcer declare a touchdown, the home team's fans started to celebrate. However, Baker had been ruled out of bounds on the 1. The people on the field were merely switching ends of the gridiron for the start of the second quarter. Shaughnessy sent Berwanger back into the game. Standing a few yards deep in the backfield, Berwanger took the snap from center Ellmore Patterson and charged toward the middle of the line, crashing through for a touchdown. Berwanger's kick for the extra point sailed wide to the right.

Even when they managed to stop Berwanger, Michigan defenders struggled. On one play, a Wolverines lineman dove at the Iowa native as he rushed past. A Berwanger cleat gashed his cheek, forcing Number 48 out of the game while a doctor stitched up the wound. That Berwanger left a lasting impression is an understatement. The former Wolverines star quipped that he thought of Jay Berwanger every single morning – when he looked in his shaving mirror and saw the scar. Some of those mornings were spent in the White House. He was Gerald Ford, Michigan's most valuable player of 1934, who 40 years later would become president of the United States.

After protecting its 6-0 lead through the second quarter, Chicago emerged from intermission and took control. Apparently concerned about the abilities of his defensive linemen, Kipke positioned two of his backs near the line; that opened big-play opportunities for the Maroons if they could get through the first wave of Wolverines. After an exchange of punts, Chicago got the ball on the Michigan 43. The Maroons immediately called upon Number 99, and Berwanger unleashed the best play of the afternoon – a 43-yard touchdown run around the left end. He was aided and abetted by several blockers, including Flinn, who provided the final block on the Michigan safety. Berwanger connected on the kick to notch his 13th point of the afternoon.

A Berwanger miscue then gave the Wolverines an opportunity to get back into the game. His punt sailed more up than out, advancing the ball only a dozen yards. However, Michigan squandered that chance on a trick play. A receiver caught a forward pass and then attempted to lateral the ball to a teammate. The result was a fumble, and Chicago recovered on its own 17-yard line, thus snuffing out Michigan's best scoring opportunity of the afternoon.

Berwanger shared the headlines with Bartlett. The sophomore re-entered the game for Chicago's first drive of the fourth quarter, which started on the Maroons' 40 after a Michigan punt. Bartlett ripped off a 30-yard rush before being pushed out of bounds. On the next play, Bartlett recovered an errant snap from center 10 yards behind the line of scrimmage but still managed to elude four Wolverine tacklers until he gained 10 yards to the Michigan 20. After an incomplete pass, Chicago went back to Bartlett, who slipped through the line and didn't stop until he crossed the goal line. Berwanger booted the extra point, and Chicago took a commanding lead, 20-0.

Desperation set in for Michigan, which switched to an aerial attack. The strategy blew up immediately. Chicago's Bob Perretz intercepted a Wolverine pass and returned it 20 yards to the Michigan 10. On third down from the 12-yard line, the Maroons again called on Bartlett, who initially fumbled the snap but then slipped through right tackle, rammed away would-be tacklers and easily scored a touchdown. Berwanger's kick ended the afternoon's scoring at 27-0.

Chicago fans cheered their team's most one-sided victory over Michigan ever. The university band struck up a different tune, free of the obligation to play "Alma Mater," the traditional dirge after a Maroons loss. The *Detroit News'* longtime sports editor, H.G. Salsinger opened his account: "Forgotten tonight are the heartaches of the yesteryears, the defeats, the humiliations, for tonight the Midway is ablaze with bonfires, bands parade the thoroughfare, torch processions light the byways and Chicago is happy for today." Later, he summarized the game simply: "When Michigan was

Berwanger makes a short gain against Indiana in 1933, his sophomore season. About 15,000 fans showed up at cavernous Stagg Field for the contest matching teams that failed to win a Big Ten game that season. The Maroons and Hoosiers tied, 7-7. (Special Collections Research Center, University of Chicago Library)

not chasing Berwanger she was chasing Bartlett, who is not quite as fast as Berwanger but more rugged." George Morgenstern of the *Chicago Herald-Examiner* reported, "When it ended – believe it or not – the golden lights of the scoreboard spelled out a legend that dazed the crowd of 25,000 and must have shocked the land, for this was it: Chicago 27, Michigan 0." Edward Burns of the *Chicago Tribune* noted, "It was something more than an upset. It certainly was a rout. The erstwhile lowly Maroons had everything they slyly hoped they had on offense and they had infinitely more than they thought they possessed on defense, as attested by the fact the Wolverines only once penetrated Chicago territory as deep as the 28-yard line." Chicago's victory was its first in the Big Ten for Shaughnessy. However, the Maroons' status as giant-killers diminished as the season progressed and Michigan's weakness became more evident. The Wolverines' only touchdown from scrimmage in 1934 came on a trick play in a 7-6 loss to Illinois, and they lost all six Big Ten games to finish the season 1-7.

Michigan's only victory of 1934 came against Georgia Tech in a contest steeped in controversy. Michigan gave in to the demand of their visitors from the South and did not play its two African-Americans, Willis Ward and Franklin Lett. Georgia Tech had long said it would not take the field in Ann Arbor if Michigan's black athletes played. The benching of Ward, the fastest runner on the squad, and Lett was an unpopular decision. Student organizations campaigned for Ward to play, and Ward's roommate on road trips, a white player, threatened to quit the team in protest. He relented only at Ward's insistence that he keep playing. The roommate who was willing to abort his playing career on principle was the future U.S. president, Ford. The University of Chicago faced no such controversy; the 1934 Maroons were all-white.

Segregationist views did not die easily. Two decades later, in 1955, Georgia Governor Marvin Griffin tried to prevent Georgia Tech from playing in the Sugar Bowl in New Orleans because the opponent, Pittsburgh, had a black player on the team. Tech students rioted. However, it was not a protest against racial intolerance but a reflection on the status of football. The students wanted Tech in the bowl game. Eventually, the state regents worked out a compromise and Tech made the trip. Immediately afterward, however, Georgia, Louisiana and Mississippi passed laws banning competition involving blacks and whites.[88]

CHAPTER 21

The University of Chicago campus was the site of a couple of rallies the day before the football team's home game against Indiana University. Only one concerned football. Four liberal organizations, including the Socialist Club, jointly staged a mid-afternoon demonstration to protest city police arresting three university students distributing handbills a dozen blocks north of campus and holding them incommunicado for 36 hours. At the noon-hour football rally, staged at the "C" Bench, the lettermen's hangout outside Cobb Hall, coach Clark Shaughnessy accepted an oversized "good luck" card signed by about 500 students. Also on the agenda were captain Ellmore Patterson, most of the players, and cheers led by Bob McIntosh.

In their first three games under first-year coach Alvin "Bo" McMillin, the Hoosiers whipped Ohio University, suffered a similar whipping from Ohio State, and then tied Temple, a Pop Warner-coached team that would finish the season 7-1-2. McMillin's offense, featuring running back Wendell Walker, posed an unusual challenge for opponents because it used five men in the backfield instead of the usual four.

The Maroons, though excited coming off their victory over Michigan, remained rooted in reality. The *Tribune's* Harvey Woodruff was allowed to watch Shaughnessy's closed practice. "So instead of finding a group of over-confident young fellows, (a) visit to the secret practice field for the final signal drills yesterday disclosed a group of earnest, enthusiastic boys. They have, as yet, no title illusions. They are content to take each game as it comes along." As well they should have. The Maroons were small in stature and limited in talent. Woodruff estimated that of the 47 players listed on Chicago's varsity roster, "perhaps 22 would be called football players at rival institutions where there is greater material." The majority, he said, would be classified as "just out for the team." Woodruff's article was accompanied by a four-column drawing of Berwanger in action. The drawing, taken from a publicity photo – Berwanger was not wearing his faceguard – appeared under the Tribune's headline, "ON YOUR GUARD, HOOSIERS!" The warning was prophetic.

Some 12,000-15,000 spectators took their seats in Stagg Field on a gray afternoon to see whether the Maroons could win consecutive Big Ten games for the first time since 1927. It had rained that morning, but the field had been covered and was dry for the 2 p.m. kickoff. The Hoosiers didn't need to see that morning's *Tribune* to know that containing Berwanger was their key to victory. Initially, they did just that. Toward the end of the first quarter, Berwanger fumbled on third down but Chicago retained possession. Indiana then blocked Berwanger's punt and took over on the Chicago 40. The Chicago defense stiffened, and the teams traded punts – the second being a Berwanger beauty that bounced out of bounds on the 1. Indiana couldn't make much progress, and its punt reached the 35, where Tommy Flinn ran it back to the 15-yard line. Runs up the middle by Berwanger and Ewald Nyquist advanced the ball to the 3. Berwanger took the ball on the next play and crossed the goal line just as the ball squirted loose. Flinn fell on the pigskin in the end zone, but the officials said it didn't matter: They ruled that Berwanger had advanced the ball to the goal line before losing possession and awarded a touchdown. Berwanger's kick for the extra point was low. On the final play of the first half, Berwanger put a charge into the crowd when he broke into the open, but he couldn't make his cuts and was brought down after an exciting 26-yard run. Chicago took its 6-0 lead into intermission.

Berwanger resumed making mayhem in the second half, but a long gain was called back. "The officials, who had been treating Chicago unkindly on suspected holding, chose to discover the Maroons guilty of that offense when Berwanger got away on a fine dodging run of 22 yards," George Morgenstern of the *Chicago Herald-Examiner* observed. "That must have made Jay sore, for the next time he got a chance, he repeated the same play for 34 yards, stopping at the Hoosier 26-yard line." On the next play, Berwanger lofted a touchdown pass to end John Baker. Berwanger kicked the point to make it a 13-0 game.

Indiana then took a gamble. For the post-touchdown kickoff, the Hoosiers elected to *kick* instead of receive, as was permitted under the rules, apparently hoping to gain scoring opportunities in the battle of field position and turnovers. Though they had seen Berwanger run and pass for touchdowns and explode for other long gains, the Hoosiers kicked off to him. Berwanger received the kick on his 3-yard line, started upfield deliberately – even "casually," sportswriter Morgenstern said – but jumped into high gear at about his 40, where he tucked behind some blockers. He then cut toward a sideline and broke into the clear with "the accumulated momentum of the Twentieth Century on straightaway track." Noted Harvey Woodruff of the *Tribune*, "It was a brilliant run made possible in part by perfect blocking." The touchdown extended Chicago's lead to 19-0. Still breathing heavily after zig-zagging to a 97-yard touchdown Berwanger missed the extra-point kick. With that, Shaughnessy removed his star for the balance of the game.

A downpour started in the fourth quarter, but the Maroons continued to move the ball until they missed a solid scoring opportunity on Bart Smith's fumble at the Indiana 10. The Hoosiers couldn't advance the ball, but they couldn't punt, either. They decided to kick on third down, but punter Bob Keck fumbled and fell on the ball on his 2. On his next attempt, Keck was forced to down the ball in his own end zone – but officials nullified the apparent safety because Chicago was offside. However, on his third consecutive punt attempt, Keck again fumbled the wet ball and recovered it in his own end zone. This time, the Maroons earned a safety and their 20th and 21st points of the soggy afternoon. Shaughnessy then felt comfortable pulling his remaining starters and inserting the young men who, according to the *Tribune*, were "just out for the team." Thirty-nine Chicago players saw game action.

Football fans read something unusual in their Sunday morning newspapers: "Chicago" on the top line of the Big Ten standings. The Maroons were 2-0 in conference action and 3-0 overall, with all three wins coming on shutouts. Iowa, Purdue, Illinois, and Ohio State were right behind at 1-0 while the favored Minnesota Gophers had yet to play a conference game. *The Christian Science Monitor* noted Chicago's early lead in the conference race, but added, "However, without J.J. Berwanger '36, halfback who begins to look like All-American material, Chicago did not go any place." Back in Bloomington, a sportswriter offered an original word to describe Indiana's fate in Chicago. The Hoosiers, he said, were "Berwangered."

After years of dormancy, University of Chicago football received greater attention in the city. The *Chicago Daily News* included a full page of Maroons photos in its color photogravure magazine. The *Daily News* took out an advertisement in the student newspaper to promote the magazine. The ad featured a publicity photo of Berwanger, who by this point was occasionally referred to by his nickname, "the Dutchman." That Berwanger was of German descent apparently made little difference to the nickname-makers. The rest of his life, Berwanger's friends called him "Dutch."[89]

An undefeated, unscored-upon football team gave students on the University of Chicago newspaper staff little to criticize. So they took after the cheerleaders. As was customary at the time, it was an all-male squad. "Our cheerleaders are vigorous enough in reviling us for not splitting an aorta or a shoelace or something on every syllable, but it never seems to occur to them that they have something to do with the disorganization of our organized rooting," complained Henry Reese, who went on to critique each Chicago cheerleader and lump them together as "a pretty uninspiring bunch." Colleague Tom Barton later opined, "Never having been accused of having an over-amount of collegiate exuberance, we can't account for this criticism … BUT … what ever happened to the Chicago rooters at various times during the game, usually when the going was toughest against the Maroons, and the ever-trying cheer directors tried to arouse some vocalizing from the stands. Next Saturday, let's STAND UP AND CHEER. For we have a real team."

However, readers of the *Daily Maroon* were probably less concerned about the cheer squad than the football team's game against Missouri of the Missouri Valley Intercollegiate Athletic Association, commonly known as the Big Six (forerunner of the Big Eight and then the Big Twelve). The Maroons were no powerhouse, but they expected an easy time of it when the Tigers came to town. Missouri had won only one game each of the previous two seasons and was 0-2-1 to that point in 1934, the "highlight" being a scoreless tie at Colorado in the season opener. In their previous seven games, including the final four contests of 1933, Missouri had scored a total of seven points. The team was coached by former Notre Dame star quarterback Frank Carideo, whose brother Angelo was the Mizzou quarterback. Not surprisingly, the Tigers ran the Notre Dame offense. Chicago's opponent after Missouri, Purdue, also ran the Notre Dame offense, and Shaughnessy figured he'd experiment against Missouri to prepare for Purdue.

On game day, the Chicago coach was so confident of victory over Missouri that he started mostly second-stringers. For the first time in his varsity career, Berwanger watched the opening kickoff from the sidelines. However, Shaughnessy's plan to make the game a dress rehearsal for Purdue blew up. The visitors from Columbia put up a surprising fight and the Chicago reserves struggled. After recovering a Maroons fumble, the Tigers drove to the 19-yard line. Shaughnessy couldn't stand it any longer. In what the 10,000 fans assembled saw as a dramatic entrance, Berwanger and six other first-stringers ran onto the field. They stopped the drive. However, the combination of stout defense by Missouri and mistakes by the Chicagoans – they lost six fumbles – kept the game scoreless into the second quarter, when Missouri punted deep into Chicago territory. Returner Tommy Flinn touched the ball at the 1 before it bounced into the end zone, where Missouri guard Dale Ream fell on it for six points. Missouri's touchdown was only its second in a calendar year. Chicago blocked the kick for the extra point. The Maroons raced the clock to tie the game at halftime. After a Missouri punt, they started a drive on their own 44. "From there on to the 3-yard line, it was Berwanger this and Berwanger that, with an occasional smash by Nyquist," the *Tribune* reported. With 15 seconds left in the half, Flinn scooted around left end to pull Chicago into a 6-6 tie. Berwanger had the opportunity to give his team the lead, but his kick for the extra point failed. After halftime, the Tigers thought they had taken the lead after Angelo Carideo appeared to catch a Berwanger fumble out of the air. He dashed 35 yards into the end zone. However, officials nullified the touchdown, ruling the ball bounced before Carideo gained possession – meaning that, under the rules of the day, the fumble could not be advanced. Missouri could not take advantage of Berwanger's fumble after that, and neither team scored in the third period. Nonetheless, Missouri was one quarter from an upset in what Chicago anticipated to be an easy game.

Berwanger, then a Chicago sophomore outfitted in his "iron mask," applies a stiff-arm to Michigan's William Renner in 1933. Asked whether there was any game he wished he could play over, Berwanger cited this one, a 28-0 loss to the visiting Wolverines. Note that two of Berwanger's teammates have faceguards on their helmets. (Special Collections Research Center, University of Chicago Library)

The Maroons got the momentum in the fourth quarter when Patterson blocked a punt and John Baker recovered the ball on the Missouri 21. From there, Berwanger and Nyquist alternated in carrying the ball, with Berwanger barely crossing the goal line from two yards out. His kick for the extra point sailed wide, but Chicago had its first lead of the afternoon, 12-6. On their next possession, three minutes later, the Maroons again featured Berwanger and Nyquist in a ground attack. With the ball on the Missouri 40, Berwanger started on what was shaping up to be an end run when he stopped, twirled and heaved the ball to Flinn, who was all by himself. Flinn made the catch and covered the final five yards into the end zone. It was a play that Chicago had run successfully in every game to that point in the season. After missing his first two extra-point attempts, Berwanger connected on the kick to complete the scoring in the Maroons' 19-6 victory.

The Chicago contest represented Missouri's 12th straight game without a victory. The 0-8-1 campaign of 1934 was the final season for 26-year-old Frank Carideo, whose three-year coaching record at Missouri was 2-23-2.[90] Twenty years after their meeting in Chicago, Cariedo and Berwanger entered the College Football Hall of Fame together as members of the Class of 1954.

CHAPTER 22

Not only would the Purdue-Chicago game of 1934 determine which team stayed tied for first place in the Big Ten, it would become the centerpiece for reinvigorated Homecoming festivities on the Midway. Even the university president, Robert M. Hutchins, no fan of big-time football, gave the Maroon gridders their due. His message appeared on the front page of the campus newspaper: "The Alumni have consistently maintained through the years an enlightened interest in the University, based on its educational objectives and achievements, that has been heartening to the faculty and to the administration. That loyalty has been so firmly based that the late football depression had no effect on the allegiance of the graduates. That particular depression seems to be at an end, so that the homecoming alumni today find the combination of a strong university and strong football team. In the achievement of that team all of us take a pardonable pride. I hope that tomorrow another achievement will contribute to the satisfaction of your return to the Midway."

A few days before the game, a half-dozen miles north of the Midway, the Century of Progress Exposition closed its two-season run in record-breaking style. People by the hundreds of thousands descended upon the campus of Chicago's world's fair to get their last look at the spectacle. On the final day, which fell on Halloween, 372,127 visitors passed through the gates – the most ever in a single day. The throng strained public transportation, outstripped parking capacity and caused vehicular and human gridlock. Despite adding coaches and trips, operators of streetcars, elevated trains, buses and commuter trains could not keep up with the demand. All the parking lots anywhere near the fairgrounds, were jammed by early evening, forcing late-arriving drivers to "cruise aimlessly" and add to the traffic congestion. Fortunately, most fairgoers were patient and in the "carnival spirit," and police were called to fewer altercations than expected. People formed lines up to 2½ blocks long just to purchase their 50-cent admission tickets; that process took up to 90 minutes. Among them was Chicagoan Helen Reid, a 65-year-old grandmother making her 50th visit to the exposition. In the early afternoon, after she presented her admission ticket – it might have been a season pass, good for 50 admissions – fair officials pulled her out of the line and declared her to be the 16 millionth visitor to the fair's 1934 season.[91]

Dubuque's Own

Here is Jay Berwanger, Dubuque's own son, who is making a name not only for himself but the community as well because of his spectacular work on the various college gridirons this season. Berwanger will be the honored guest Saturday, Nov. 3 when Chicago tackles Purdue in a Big Ten battle at Stagg field in Chicago.

After Berwanger matriculated to the University of Chicago, the Dubuque newspaper, the Telegraph Herald, regularly reported on his exploits on the Midway. Here, the paper is promoting a 1934 excursion from Dubuque to the Purdue game in Chicago. (Courtesy of the Telegraph Herald)

She was showered with gifts, including a deed to a five-acre lodge site in Michigan, perfume, clocks, dinnerware, and even cigars.

It is likely that Mrs. Reid was safely in her bed when bedlam hit the fairgrounds. As Halloween night progressed and the closing hour approached, patrons became increasingly unruly and bold. What started out as souvenir-harvesting – removing signs, sod, and even parts from an airplane displayed outside the Pantheon le Guerre – turned into brazen acts of vandalism. Rioters tossed chairs into the lagoons, broke windows, climbed light poles, and hurled the bulbs onto the ground. Though greatly outnumbered, police massed at the gates and prevented – by force when necessary – thieves from getting out with their souvenirs. Fair officials were not terribly concerned about the damage, noting that most of the buildings were to be razed anyway. (The fairgrounds later became the site of McCormick Place exhibition complex and Meigs Field airport.) The fair was a huge success: Total attendance for both seasons was 48.8 million, and the Chicago exposition was able to cover all its financial obligations.[92]

As the official tear-down of the Century of Progress began, the build-up for the University of Chicago-Purdue University football game continued. Back in Iowa, Berwanger's hometown newspaper, the *Dubuque Telegraph-Herald* and *Times-Journal,* promoted a trip to the Purdue game. The paper set a goal of having 250 Dubuque boosters at Stagg Field. Tickets cost $2.20 each. Dubuque organizers received Chicago administrators' permission to bring the American Legion drum and bugle corps, whose 37 members were allowed to perform and to sit near the Chicago sideline. Dubuque boosters' donations covered the band's expenses, and Chicago-Dubuque Motor Transport Company hauled their instruments free of charge. All the Dubuque tickets were sold, and the Iowa contingent occupied a section at a 30-yard line, behind the Maroons' bench. Among the Dubuquers was a Berwanger fan who had yet to see him play a college game – his own father. Accompanying John Berwanger was Ira Davenport.

As he prepared his Maroons for the battle, Shaughnessy shrouded daily practices in secrecy and moved them inside the university fieldhouse. Meanwhile, in Lafayette, Indiana, Purdue coach Noble Kizer cancelled his starters' usual Monday day off and conducted a full practice. The 2-2 Boilermakers again featured their "touchdown twins," James Carter and Duane Purvis, who a year ago played key roles in Purdue's 14-0 victory in a rain-drenched Chicago. The Maroons had Berwanger and Ned Bartlett, but would they be enough? Assistant coach Marchmont Schwartz scouted Purdue's 20-0 win over Carnegie Tech in Pittsburgh the previous weekend, and he warned the Maroons that they faced a stiff test, especially from Purdue's passing game. The task was made tougher with tackle Clarence Wright unavailable and Prescott Jordan expected to see only limited duty after both were banged-up in the Missouri game.

Chicago's 48-man varsity roster – one player dropped during the season – included 26 players from the Chicago metropolitan area; three from other Illinois communities; nine from California (including brothers Bart and Gordon Petersen, whose brother Kendall was on the freshman squad); Berwanger and two others from Iowa; two from Texas; and one each from Florida, Indiana, Ohio, Minnesota, and Michigan. It was a young squad, with 27 sophomores, 15 juniors, and six seniors. The roster included two young men whose fathers played for Amos Alonzo Stagg: Harmon Meigs, whose father, Merrill, was publisher of the *Chicago Herald-Examiner* and an aviation pioneer for whom Meigs Field would be named; and back-up punter Jack Scruby, son of Horace Scruby, who was also a punter at the Midway.

To keep his players' emotions in check before the big game, Shaughnessy withheld them from the Homecoming pep rally Friday night. "Coach Clark Shaughnessy, of the University of Chicago's Maroons, a most taciturn man who rarely commits himself even when asked what time it is, or does he like his steak rare or medium, came right out in the open yesterday and opined that the 30,000 customers who plan to see Chicago play Purdue tomorrow are destined to see a fine, exciting game of football," Edward Burns of the *Tribune* wrote. "In this statement Mr. Shaughnessy didn't exactly scoop that part of the world which has heard of Jay Berwanger and Ned Bartlett of the Maroons and Duane Purvis and Jim Carter of the Boilermakers, but just the same it is nice to have the Midway football boss forecast another stirring act in the renaissance drama the U. of C. valiants have been putting on out south this season."

Despite forecasters' prediction of rain, the University of Chicago expected its biggest home crowd since the Maroons' won the conference championship a decade earlier. Still, if all 30,000 anticipated show up, they would occupy barely half the seats if Stagg Field were configured to capacity. Built in 1892 and named Marshall Field, the facility in 1913 underwent a major renovation and expansion. The *Chicago Tribune* campaigned to rename it Stagg Field, during which the paper used its own suggestion as if it were a *fait accompli*. In 1914, the university did make the name change in honor of its incumbent coach.[93] Stagg Field, like many campus structures, had a castle-like design, with parapets along the ivy-adorned gray stone walls and corner towers. In the 1920s, when college football's national popularity soared, all but two Big Ten schools built new stadiums.[94] One, Wisconsin, already had Camp Randall Stadium, built in 1917. The other was Chicago, where Stagg and his backers had lobbied for a $3 million stadium at the south edge of campus. However, the most they could get from trustees was additional seating at the existing facility to increase its capacity to 50,000, plus the promise of a new fieldhouse (which was completed in 1931).[95] When the Chicago program was in decline, even in the Berwanger years, the university did not erect all its bleachers. Seating for about 30,000 was the norm in the early and mid-1930s, and that was plenty. While Chicago was stuck with the oldest football facility in the conference, it did offer fans a bargain: Game programs in 1934 cost a dime, compared to the quarter charged at other conference venues.

Fans who braved the rain for the Purdue-Chicago game might have saved their dimes for programs, because they only needed to know two uniform numbers – 42 for Purvis and 99 for Berwanger and Carter. Those three "fought it out practically among themselves to the bitter end," George Morgenstern told his *Herald-Examiner* readers. It was an epic battle.

Purdue threatened to score on its first possession. Purvis launched a 45-yard pass to Carter, who was tackled at the 10-yard line. Berwanger halted that drive with an interception. The Dubuque delegation was boisterous all afternoon, cheering Berwanger on every carry and every tackle. Chicago went nowhere in its first possession – and it got worse. Bartlett, a strong complement to Berwanger in the backfield, suffered a leg injury on his first carry and left the game. (He tried to return in the fourth quarter but lasted only one play.) Berwanger early in the game also took a hit, the significance of which would not become known until much later. On its next possession, Purdue marched down the field 55 yards, with Carter scoring on a two-yard sweep about right end. Dick Sandefur connected on the extra-point kick to make Purdue's lead 7-0. Chicago went three-and-out again, with Berwanger punting to the Boilermakers' 40. On the next play, Carter crashed through right tackle and appeared to be bottled up. But he reversed direction and broke into the clear for a 60-yard touchdown. Sandefur kicked the ball between the uprights, but the extra point was taken off the scoreboard, in accordance with the rules of the day, because of a holding penalty. Purdue 13, Chicago 0.

On the first play of the second quarter, Berwanger connected with Tommy Flinn for a 27-yard touchdown. Berwanger's kick cut the deficit to 13-7. Despite the rain, the teams continued to battle in exciting fashion. Chicago advanced to its own 32, where the Maroons ran a play that had worked in every game to this point in the season. It worked again. Berwanger started to run toward right end. As defenders closed in, he stopped, turned, and heaved the ball back across the field to Flinn, who made the catch at the Purdue 43, picked up some "savage" blocking from his teammates and scored one of the Maroons' most exciting touchdowns of the season. Berwanger's kick gave

Chicago a 14-13 lead.

The back-and-forth continued throughout what a sportswriter described as a "dreary rain." Purdue answered with a 68-yard drive, with Purvis providing some powerful runs until Carter lofted an 18-yard touchdown pass to end Frank Haas. Sandefur's kick sent Purdue back into the lead, 20-14.

On the first play of the fourth quarter, Purvis broke loose and splashed 73 yards for another touchdown. The extra-point attempt failed, but the Boilermakers extended their advantage to 26-14. After Chicago went nowhere on three plays from its own 15, Berwanger stepped back in punt formation. However, the Dutchman executed the fake and fired a pass to Flinn for a 16-yard gain and a first down. The drive continued, with Berwanger catching passes and making powerful runs. "The Chicago team, crazy as it might seem, took to the air in the driving rain and lurched up the field, unstoppable, with coordination gone, all finesse forgotten, and nothing left but a fighting heart that wouldn't take defeat," Morgenstern said. Berwanger capped the Maroons' exciting and dramatic 85-yard scoring drive when he caught Flinn's short pass and barreled the final five yards to the end zone. The extra-point try failed, but Chicago cut its deficit to 26-20. However, only two minutes remained. The Maroons ran out of time for any more miracles.

Performing in front of hundreds of fans from his hometown, Berwanger had played his heart out, persevering despite a yet-to-be-disclosed injury. Dubuque reporter John Fuhrman told his *Telegraph-Herald* readers, "Every play in which Berwanger figured drew hearty cheers from the stands with Dubuque's special section on the 30-yard line and the Legion boys supplying more than their share of the good old college yells. Throughout the entire game the name of Berwanger was shouted from all sections." The *Herald-Examiner's* Morgenstern said of the Maroons star, "His father, gray-haired, 55-year-old John Berwanger, former blacksmith of Dubuque, must have been the proudest man in all the crowd of 25,000 that sat in the rain, for it was the first time he had ever seen his boy in a college football game, and young Berwanger showed him the incentive for the Maroon stands to rise and cheer." Father and son had a brief post-game exchange – a handshake and a few words – before the Dutchman headed for the locker room. The Chicago star's efforts on the soggy afternoon were appreciated by all, as even Purdue fans joined in the applause for Berwanger as he left the field.

CHAPTER 23

After suffering a blow to their faint hopes of a Big Ten title, the Maroons had to travel on consecutive weekends in November 1934. Chicago boosters wanting to watch their favorites play in Ohio and Minnesota had their options. They could take the Pennsylvania or New York railroad lines to Columbus; for a trip to Minneapolis, they had their choice among the Milwaukee, the Northwestern or the Burlington railroads. Round-trip fares ranged from $8.45 to $15, with charges for Pullman berths ranging from $2 to $3.75.

Many fans already had their tickets to Columbus when they learned the demoralizing news: Berwanger would not play against Ohio State. During his heroic effort against Purdue a few days earlier, Boilermaker players kicked or, more likely, twisted his knee. Knee problems occasionally flared up the balance of his athletic career. Shaughnessy tried to keep the injury secret – at least for as long as possible – in hopes that the Dutchman's knee would come around and that the Buckeyes wouldn't know he was wounded. The coach abandoned that notion and disclosed that Berwanger would sit out against Ohio State in hopes that he could be ready for Minnesota the following weekend. Losing Berwanger was bad enough, but it followed the news that Ned Bartlett, a solid running back in his own right, was likely to miss the rest of the season with an injury suffered against Purdue. The Maroons also had to figure out who could fill in for Berwanger as punter and as primary passer; Keith Hatter got the nomination. Injuries would also cause lineman Clarence Wright and end Bart Petersen to miss the game in Columbus. The loss of those players, right before facing an Ohio State team that had just crushed Western Reserve by a 76-0 margin, shattered the Maroons' morale. (The coach of Western Reserve was Sam Willaman, who coached Ohio State the previous five seasons. Observers debated whether or why new Buckeyes coach Francis Schmidt ran up the score against his predecessor's team.)

Marshall Field & Company, the department store whose founder decades earlier donated the land for the Maroons' football field, advertised the "swellest possible substitute" to being in Ohio Stadium – the Grid Graph. The electronic board representing a football field allowed patrons to see a visual representation of every play and every movement of the ball. The board displayed the names of all the players, and an illuminated bulb indicated the ball carrier. Patrons in the facsimile stadium on the Fifth Floor of the store saw lots of ball movement that afternoon – almost all of it by Ohio State.

The Buckeyes whipped the shorthanded and underpowered Maroons, 33-0, and it was every bit as bad as the score indicated. Though the runaway was well under way at 20-0, Shaughnessy sent the hobbled Bartlett into the game to attempt a passing attack. Though he could barely walk, Bartlett gave it his best shot but couldn't get anything going. Meanwhile, a restless Berwanger watched from the sideline. The student newspaper quipped that the Dutchman fidgeted so much during the contest that he wore a smooth spot on the bench.

To prepare for Minnesota, Shaughnessy devised and drilled his team on trick plays. It would take treachery and an incredible amount of luck for Chicago to beat the heavily favored and undefeated Gophers. To that point, Minnesota had outscored its six opponents by a combined 201-31 margin. In their 30-0 loss in Minneapolis the previous Saturday, Indiana registered exactly zero yards of offense, including minus-10 yards rushing. Foremost among Minnesota's stars was Francis "Pug" Lund, soon to receive the *Chicago Tribune's* Silver Football Trophy as the Big Ten player considered most valuable to his team. Though far from 100 percent physically, Berwanger and Bartlett had recovered enough to play. However, end John Baker, who suffered a smashed nose at Ohio State, was unavailable. The contest would be a homecoming and a reunion for Shaughnessy, who starred at Minnesota. Gophers coach Bernie Bierman was Shaughnessy's former teammate and later his Tulane assistant coach. Bierman is remembered as "the epitome of a taciturn, I'll-let-my-boys-do-the-talking-on-the-field coach. His were superbly disciplined and superbly conditioned teams."[96] The Maroons' line was so much smaller than Minnesota's that observers speculated that Gopher defenders might crash through and swarm Berwanger before he could get going. A Chicago sportswriter pointed out that the Maroons had a winnable game against Illinois the Saturday after the expected shellacking by Minnesota. "Under the circumstances, the politic thing to do would be to keep Jay

Berwanger, Captain Ell Patterson, Ned Bartlett, and all the other key men on the team safely at home, and send the third string in with the instructions to duck. But college football is an amateur sport with a well recognized, though unwritten, code of duty, and so every able hand will be tossed into the Gopher chopping bowl …" Nonetheless, the writer noted that, with the return of Berwanger and Bartlett, Maroons players held a "quiet expectation" that they could give Minnesota a tougher fight than anyone expected.

Shaughnessy expanded his travel roster to 34 players, but with expense money scarce – his program spent $2,000 all season – he left all his assistant coaches at home. The team rode the Northwestern rails overnight Thursday and checked into Minneapolis' Curtis Hotel. Advertised as the "largest in the Northwest," the Curtis had a private bath in every room, with rates starting at $2 a night.[97] The Maroons didn't get much rest. By late morning, Shaughnessy assembled the squad in the hotel's grand ballroom, where he walked them through signals.

With unseasonably warm weather and Berwanger in town, Minnesota officials expected more than 40,000 spectators in Memorial Stadium. "The natives have expressed a sort of polite curiosity about seeing Jay Berwanger, not that they expect him to do anything that Lund, (Stan) Kostka, (Julius) Alfonse, (Sheldon) Beise, (George) Roscoe and a few more of the Gophers will not do earlier and more often. But just because they have heard a lot about him." University of Chicago public relations man Will Morgenstern, looking ahead to the Illinois game, quipped that Shaughnessy should have Berwanger run a pre-game lap around the field, wave to the crowd so that fans might see him, call off all bets, and then rest the Dutchman for the Illini. Regarding those bets: Minnesota fans wagered on whether Chicago could finish within 30 points of the Gophers. The *Chicago Tribune's* Charles Bartlett noted that Berwanger made bettors a bit nervous about that point spread. "The leg bruise which he sustained in the opening minutes of the Purdue game is not entirely healed yet, but wild horses probably could not hold Jay on the bench tomorrow," Bartlett wrote, adding that Shaughnessy indicated that Berwanger would play most of the game.

The underdogs started out by challenging the Gophers. On their first possession, they advanced to the Minnesota 34, but Lund's interception halted the drive. Not only did the two head coaches know each other, they used the same offensive formations. "When Minnesota would start running a play we would call our signal for the play," Berwanger recalled. "You could see what was developing."[98] The Maroons knew what was coming, but they still could not stop it. On its second possession, Minnesota drove to the Chicago 26. Lund lofted a pass to the goal line, where Flinn defended against All-America end Bob Tenner. Chicago partisans were relieved when the ball hit the ground – but then stunned when an official called a penalty. Flinn was flagged for pass interference. Two of the Chicago sportswriters present said the official was the only person among the 46,000 in Memorial Stadium who

Contrary to some reports, the figure on the Heisman Trophy was not of Berwanger – or was it? The statue design was approved by the Downtown Athletic Club a month before Berwanger won the balloting. Berwanger in 1979 told a Dubuque sportswriter that sculptor Frank Eliscu asked his model to strike a pose like that he had seen in this photo of Berwanger. (Chicago Tribune photo. Reprinted with permission)

saw a foul. But his opinion was the only one that counted. Beise then rushed through left guard for a Minnesota touchdown and consensus All-America guard Bill Bevan kicked the extra point to make it a 7-0 game.

Chicago received its own lucky break when Lund fumbled a Berwanger punt and Wright recovered on the Gophers' 17. Berwanger's bid for a touchdown pass barely missed and Minnesota's defense held. However, the Maroons, taking all the Gophers could throw at them, were still in the game, trailing by only seven points at intermission. Berwanger recorded 14 tackles just in the first half.

However, Minnesota broke open the game early in the second half with two long touchdown drives, scoring on rushes by Lund and then Alfonse. Bevan made both point-after kicks to extend the hosts' lead to 21-0. At this point, Shaughnessy pulled Berwanger and a few other starters. Bierman likewise started sending in reserves. The only questions were the final score and whether the Maroons could beat bettors' 30-point spread.

Early in the final quarter, backed up to their own 10, the Maroons had to punt from their end zone. Maurice Johnson broke through the line to block the punt by Berwanger's understudy, Keith Hatter. Bevan jumped on the ball for a touchdown and then kicked the extra point to make it 28-0. A 19-yard end-around by Arthur Clarkson and the extra-point kick by Bud Wilkinson (a future coach of national powerhouse Oklahoma) extended the lead to 35-0, causing some bettors to breathe easier. Their sense of relief disappeared in the game's closing moments. As sportswriter Warren Brown described it, "Minnesota had an organization composed of players who had probably figured they were there to watch and not to perform themselves." One of those Gopher reserves for some reason threw a pass. Bart Smith intercepted it at the Maroons' 40 and started running. "It was getting rather dark, and the chances are that the Gophers didn't see him very plainly," Brown quipped, "or they never would have let a thing like that happen." After notching the touchdown, Smith kicked the final point to reduce Minnesota's margin of victory to 28 points, 35-7. Those were the only points Minnesota allowed in the final four games of its national championship campaign. (Despite losing five players, including Bevan and Kostka, to the Big Ten rule regarding transfer students and eligibility, Minnesota posted another 8-0 campaign in 1935. The Gophers went 28 straight games without loss until falling at third-ranked Northwestern on Halloween 1936.)

Berwanger and Bartlett got out of Minneapolis without aggravating their injuries, and the Maroons turned their attention to what they considered a winnable game, the season finale against Illinois. The Illini had just fallen out of a three-way tie for the conference lead (with Minnesota and Purdue) by losing to lowly Wisconsin in the Badgers' Homecoming game, 7-3. The winning score occurred when Badger center Allen Mahnke snatched a fumble out of the air and rumbled 25 yards for a touchdown.

Illinois coach Bob Zuppke's pass-happy offense, headed by quarterback Jack Beynon, featured a trick play sportswriters called the "Flying Trapeze," in which two players in the backfield tossed laterals back and forth until one spotted an open receiver downfield for a forward pass. Opponents struggled all season to defend the play. In their conference opener, the Illini worked the Flying Trapeze for the winning touchdown in their 14-13 win over Ohio State. In the days before the Chicago game, Zuppke drilled his players on stopping Berwanger, an opponent bigger than most of his linemen. He had freshman Deane Frary "play Berwanger" in all their practice sessions.

Illinois had dominated the Chicago series (13-4-2), but the Maroons liked their chances. His leg injury apparently healed, Berwanger was ready to go at full speed. Anticipating a large crowd, Chicago officials brought additional bleachers out of storage – enough to accommodate 33,000 fans. Illinois sold its allotment of tickets and asked Chicago for more. The Illini marching band, advertised as the nation's largest, planned to make the trip and perform before the game and at intermission. Radio station WGN booked Quin Ryan to broadcast the battle. Set for 2 p.m. the Saturday before Thanksgiving, the game was the final competition for several Chicago players, starting with center and captain Ellmore Patterson and including Tommy Flinn, Ed Cullen, John Baker, John Womer, and two juniors whose eligibility would expire under the conference's transfer rule, ends Bart Petersen and Bill Langley.

While those departing Maroons received their due, everyone knew that Berwanger, a junior, was pivotal to the team's success. A Chicago alumnus, James R. Couplin, eagerly anticipating the game against the Orange and Blue of Illinois, submitted his inspired verse to the campus newspaper:

Of soldiers bold we've all been told
Before Hector had his fame,
But a man of men, worth easily ten,
Jay Berwanger is his name.

When the spot is tight, he gathers might,
Punts 60 yards or more
"American-All" he gets the call,

Chicago to the fore.

Of him I have not told you,
Try not to hold the sack,
For when he hits that Orange line,
It's surely going to crack.

The Illini and Maroons had battled about 10 minutes when an Illinois defender deflected a Berwanger punt, which Les "Swede" Lindberg picked up and returned to the Chicago 20. On the drive's first play, Lindberg passed to Beynon for eight yards. The Maroons knocked down the next pass. On third down from the 12, Beynon's pass was deflected into the air. The ball fell into the arms of Illinois tackle Charles Galbreath. The lineman lumbered toward the end zone, fighting off Chicago tacklers to score an unusual touchdown – the same type of play that had just cost Illinois the Wisconsin game. Lindberg, who had converted all his point-after kicks in every conference game this season, finally missed. Chicago had three quarters to make up the 6-0 deficit.

The Maroons had their chances. In the second quarter alone, Chicago advanced to the Illinois 29 on one drive and blocked a punt at the visitors' 35 to start another. Both times they came away empty. Berwanger was a marked man, and the Illinois crashed through his blockers to bottle up the Man in the Iron Mask.

Illinois missed its own opportunities. Late in the third quarter, on a first-and-goal play from the Chicago 8, the Illini attempted the Flying Trapeze. Beynon tossed a lateral to Lindberg, who returned a lateral to Beynon, who threw a forward pass to Lindberg. This time, however, the play failed.

With time ebbing away, Chicago forged another drive. Berwanger, Nyquist and Smith pounded at the Illinois defense and made headway. They advanced to the Illinois 22. On fourth down, the Maroons called upon Number 99 to throw a pass and keep the drive alive; to that point they had completed only two of seven attempts for seven yards and an interception. The 31,000 fans knew the next play would likely determine the victor. Berwanger looked downfield and tossed a pass. The ball fell to ground, harmlessly incomplete. Illinois took over on downs with five minutes to play and ran out the clock, denying the Chicago offense another chance. Illinois' fluke touchdown in the first quarter stood up all afternoon. The Maroons came that close to a team that wound up fourth in a national ranking based under the system developed by Illinois economics professor Frank G. Dickinson.

That evening, the Illini Club of Chicago hosted the team at its annual football dinner. Of course, the victory at Stagg Field fueled the celebratory mood. Called to the dais, Zuppke gave a rambling review of the season, speaking directly to his players. When he began to discuss the game of that afternoon, he said them, "And that fellow we stopped today – what was his name? I'm not good at names." In unison, his players replied, "Berwanger." The dean of Big Ten coaches continued, "Well, he's a great football player, and it took good work to stop him, for which you deserve credit." Continuing to address his squad, he added, "And there's another thing I want to say about those Maroons. You played against gentlemen. Not once, but several times, I saw Maroon players come charging up as a play was stopped and they stepped over you boys who were on the ground and did not fall on you with their knees. And I'm proud to say you did the same thing. Chicago played like sportsmen, and I don't say this just because we beat them, because there will be other years when they may beat us, though I hope not. But we appreciate a rivalry of that kind against boys who surely reflect the teaching of Clark Shaughnessy, their coach." Illinois end Bill Waller agreed. "I've never been in such a hard-played game where such good feeling prevailed between the players," he said. "There was absolutely no unnecessary roughness, none of the bickering and calling of names which sometimes occurs."

The opposing coach's kind words did little to soothe the Maroons' feelings after their closest and most frustrating loss of the season. Disappointment filled their locker room, the *Tribune* reported, "But there were no complaints, just regrets that marches which might have yielded the knotting points were stopped short of their objective." As Zuppke noted, Berwanger never broke loose. He was held to just 55 yards rushing on 23 carries. The University of Chicago opened the season with four straight wins and finished with four straight losses. Their 2-4 mark in the Big Ten dropped them to seventh place. Of the conference teams they defeated, Michigan was winless and Indiana had just one win, spoiling in-state rival Purdue's bid for a share of the conference championship.

Though it was no substitute for team victories, postseason recognition for Jay Berwanger would ease some of the sting felt by the Maroons and their followers.

CHAPTER 24

Sportswriters and football coaches selecting postseason honors in 1934 had their hands full. "Halting Minnesota's powerhouse without a point, getting a soul-satisfying interview from Kenesaw Mountain Landis or meeting Greta Garbo are simple problems compared with the hapless task of choosing an all-state Big Ten football team that will please a majority of the campus enthusiasts this fall," Paul Mickelson of The Associated Press wrote, claiming that some unnamed electors were opting to sit out the process. Though he did not give his reasons, Shaughnessy did not cast a ballot for The AP's Big Ten team. The electors' challenge was particularly acute regarding the backfield. Most everyone considered Berwanger a leading candidate. Other contenders included Minnesota's quartet of Pug Lund, Glenn Seidel, Stan Kostka, and Julius Alfonse; Jack Beynon and Les Lindberg of Illinois; Duane Purvis and Jim Carter of Purdue; Richard Heekin of Ohio State; and Dick Crayne of Iowa.

When the selections started hitting the newspapers, Berwanger made everybody's first team – or nearly so. He landed on the Big Ten teams announced by The AP and United Press. Nine of the 10 conference coaches voted for him on the UP team; the 10th was Ossie Solem of Iowa. Chicago and Iowa did not meet on the gridiron during Berwanger's career. During Berwanger's senior year of high school, Solem came to Dubuque and declared that an Iowa athlete who left the state for college was a traitor. Were hard feelings involved? Perhaps Solem felt he couldn't vote for someone he had not seen play, or perhaps he favored his own running back, the Iowa native Crayne.

A poll by *Liberty Magazine* placed a Chicago standout on its first team, but it was not Berwanger, who made the second team. The Maroons' *Liberty* first-teamer was center Ellmore Patterson. Grantland Rice, aided by his own

Bonnie Rockne, the widow of famed coach Knute Rockne, and sportswriter Christy Walsh congrat-ulate Berwanger, a junior, on his selection as captain of Walsh's 1934 All-America football team. (Special Collections Research Center, University of Chicago Library)

advisory board, announced his All-America picks in *Collier's*. Berwanger was among the 12 backs rated All-America, but he fell short of making the first team. That honor went to Stanford's Robert Grayson at quarterback, Rice's William Wallace and Navy's Fred Borries at halfback, and Lund at fullback. Two other Minnesota Gophers joined Lund on the first team: guard Bill Bevan and end Frank Larson.[99]

Amid announcement of football honors, The AP also revealed its second annual award for the Big Ten's best all-around athlete – and Berwanger won that. The football star and track athlete received 22 votes from the electors – coaches, officials and sportswriters – to outpoint Purvis (14) and Michigan's Willis Ward (12).

Elmer Layden, Notre Dame coach and member of the All-America Football Board, described Berwanger as "the outstanding all-around back of the Middle West in 1934," with Purvis, Lund and his own George Melinkovich "just behind" the Dutchman. The regional honor was a prelude to the big prize: all-America status. Sportswriter and sports agent Christy Walsh announced that his All-America Football Board picked Berwanger for first-team honors. Walsh wrote of Berwanger: "In his sophomore year, this broad-shouldered blond boy from Iowa became the hope of football enthusiasts on the Midway and, during his junior year, he justified every hope and brought the first All-America certificate to the University of Chicago in eleven years. Coach Bob Zuppke recently called Berwanger the best all-around backfield man in the Big Ten circuit. And considering the class which that embraces, the Chicago back should hold his own in any company. His powerful physique and his capacity for rough going make him a defensive backfield all by himself – and he has been just that to Chicago. Berwanger is an exceptionally fine kicker and has added many points to the Maroon score through his placement shots." Joining Walsh on the selection board were Layden; Glenn "Pop" Warner, Temple; W.A. Alexander, Georgia Tech; Edward L. Casey, Harvard; and Howard H.

In 1934, after his junior season, Berwanger was named to sportswriter Christy Walsh's All-America team. His fellow first-teamers elected him the honorary captain. (Author's photo)

Jones, Southern California.

As national honors came Berwanger's way, his University of Chicago teammates made a surprising decision. In selecting their Most Valuable Player of 1934, they chose Patterson. The election of their senior captain, over Berwanger, a junior and last year's MVP, required two rounds of balloting. The first time around, the vote was divided among Patterson, Berwanger and Tommy Flinn. Patterson edged Berwanger on the second ballot. It is unlikely that any of the Maroons saw Patterson as the most talented on game day. But, in addition to providing reliable center snaps and throwing blocks that helped Berwanger make his highlight-reel gains, Patterson put extra effort into his responsibilities as team leader. "Shortly after his selection as captain he voluntarily undertook to keep in constant touch with all the candidates for the squad and with their instructors," the *Chicago Tribune* noted. "As a result of his efforts there was only one serious ineligibility on the squad. Patterson was known to the players as 'Father Ellmore' because of his serious mien." Shaughnessy described Patterson, president of his University of Chicago senior class and also a tennis letterman, as "the finest captain in the United States." Though they did not name him their Most Valuable Player, his teammates elected Berwanger team captain for the 1935 season

Back home in Dubuque for Christmas after an All-America season, Berwanger poses with a few of his awards. He made several All-America teams in 1934 and even more in 1935, when he was a consensus All-America. He was a first-time pick on no fewer than 14 All-America squads, more than any other collegian that season. (Berwanger family collection)

and gave him the "best blocker" award.

Despite the rationale presented, the choice of Patterson over Berwanger as MVP surprised many observers. The newspapers did not report comments from any of the principals, but, considering Berwanger's reputation for modesty, he probably would have only congratulated and praised Patterson. As his team's MVP, Patterson became eligible for the *Chicago Tribune's* Silver Football, awarded to the Big Ten player deemed the "most indispensable player" to his team. An unidentified Chicago alumnus, writing to the Tribune, understood the distinction. "Jay Berwanger, one of the greatest players in the

Though he received national acclaim throughout his college career, teammates and coaches said Berwanger remained humble and modest – qualities he retained throughout his life. (Special Collections Research Center, University of Chicago Library)

country, has received the publicity because his kicking, passing, and running are visible. The fellow down there encouraging his men and making about half the tackles for his team was Patterson. ... To see this type of player honored convinces me of the soundness of conditions for the Silver Football." After graduating from Chicago, Patterson continued to exhibit leadership. He entered the banking business and ascended to chairman and chief executive officer of J.P. Morgan & Company and its subsidiary Morgan Guaranty Trust Company of New York. Patterson also served on the boards of several large corporations, on the President's Commission of Financial Structure and Regulation, and on the board of the Federal Reserve Bank of New York. In the mid-1970s, he chaired an ad hoc committee to help New York City work out of its financial crisis.

Including Patterson, half of the Silver Football nominees were linemen. Candidates from the other conference schools were Don Veller, Indiana; Dick Crayne, Iowa; Les Lindberg, Illinois; Ed Whalen, Northwestern; Gomer Jones, Ohio State; Duane Purvis, Purdue; Pug Lund, Minnesota; Milt Kummer, Wisconsin; and the future U.S. president, Gerald Ford of Michigan. The award wound up going to a back, Lund.

Toward the end of the postseason awards period, Berwanger received a huge national honor: His fellow all-America first-teamers elected him the captain of Walsh's all-America team. It was a nice consolation prize for an athlete who was not elected MVP of his own team.[100]

Between Christmas 1934 and New Year's Day, speculation flared that Berwanger would lose his coach for his senior season. As was the case a year earlier, Shaughnessy was under consideration for another job, head coach at Harvard. Shaughnessy interviewed with Harvard athletic director William J. Bingham during a coaches convention in New York, and the *Tribune* said Chicago Vice President Frederic C. Woodward met with the coach in the president's office the evening before Harvard's board was to meet. The *Tribune* noted that a college rarely mentions the names of possible coaches without some assurance that the candidate was interested in the position: "The Harvard job, it seems, is Shaughnessy's job if he wants it." Newspapers reported that Shaughnessy would receive $8,000 a year to coach football and, to sweeten the pot, another $2,000 to serve as assistant athletic director.[101] However, Bingham wouldn't confirm those stories, stating he intended to submit at least 10 names to the university's athletic board. Shaughnessy was silent on the situation, and sportswriters speculated that either he had not been offered the job or that he had not decided whether to leave Chicago. A little more than a week later, Harvard hired Dick Harlow of Western Maryland. He coached the Crimson 11 of the next 13 years, during which the Crimson twice trounced Shaughnessy and the post-Berwanger Maroons (1938-39). It was never disclosed whether Shaughnessy turned down the Harvard job or whether he not been Harvard's first pick after all. In any case, he prepared for his third football season at Chicago – his last with star Jay Berwanger on his roster.

CHAPTER 25

As his various postseason honors arrived, Berwanger worked out with the track team, running sprints and hurdles and competing in virtually all the field events. However, while running the hurdles in a mid-January practice, he re-injured the knee that he hurt during the Purdue football game 2½ months earlier. The gimpy knee caused him to scratch from early meets and limit himself to the shot put for the balance of the indoor season.

Berwanger was not so hobbled that he couldn't socialize. The campus newspaper noted that he showed up at a Maroons basketball game "with a new Northwestern dollie." The gossip columnist, writing under the pen name Rabelais, conducted a campus poll to identify the most beautiful woman and most handsome man on the Chicago campus. Berwanger finished 10th, while top honors went to teammate Ned Bartlett. Academically, as the winter quarter began, Berwanger dropped law as his major and transferred to the College of Business.[102]

The second weekend of March, Chicago hosted the Big Ten Conference indoor championships. With his knee still bothering him, Berwanger scratched from the 60-yard dash (won by Ohio State sophomore Jesse Owens in a world-best 6.1 seconds) and managed only eighth in the shot put; his mark of 42-10½ was five feet short of his personal best. The Maroons scored only 3½ points all weekend, narrowly avoiding a last-place finish, far behind champion Michigan (49½) and runner-up Ohio State (22½).

A couple of weeks later, Clark Shaughnessy convened the football team for five weeks of spring practice. Fifty-three players reported. As he did the previous year, Berwanger stayed on the track team, but he also worked out with the football team as much as he could. On the second day of spring practice, Berwanger welcomed a couple of visitors – Bonnie Rockne, widow of legendary coach Knute Rockne, and sportswriter Christy Walsh, chairman of his All-America Football Board. They came to campus to present him the trophy recognizing his selection as captain of the 1934 All-America football team. He no doubt accepted the award with modesty, as the *Daily Maroon* noted that Berwanger possessed the "prowess of Red Grange with the publicity-shyness of Greta Garbo."

In other sports news, Amos Alonzo Stagg Junior, son of the Grand Old Man, disclosed plans to leave the University of Chicago. An assistant football coach under his legendary father who continued to coach the Maroons' championship tennis program, Lonnie Stagg accepted a position at Susquehanna College, of Selinsgrove, Pennsylvania. The younger Stagg was to serve as athletic director; intramural director; and coach of football, basketball, and track. Thus, for the first time in its entire 43-year history, the University of Chicago would not have a Stagg on the payroll. Lonnie enjoyed a successful and long tenure at Susquehanna, coaching football through the 1954 campaign. In 1947, his 85-year-old father joined Lonnie, then 48, at Susquehanna. They operated as "co-coaches" of the football team for six seasons, through 1952, when the elder Stagg marked his 90th birthday.

Shaughnessy planned a rigorous spring program divided between practicing fundamentals and learning his innovative offense. Rainwater Wells, the speedy end from California, emerged as the first-string quarterback for 1935. He was to succeed the graduating Tommy Flinn, whom Shaughnessy hired as an assistant coach for the 1935 freshman team. Shaughnessy also secured the coaching services of Robert Jerome "Duke" Dunne, captain of the 1921 Michigan Wolverines. Dunne, who had been an assistant coach at Northwestern (1923-25) and Harvard (1926-30), was a municipal court judge in Chicago. He arranged a leave of absence from the courtroom so that he could assist Shaughnessy. Other coaches were Otto Strohmeier, ends; Julian Lopez, backs; Nelson Norgren, freshman head coach; and recent grads John Baker and Robert Deem, freshman assistants. The captain of the 1934 Maroons, center Ellmore Patterson, coached candidates for his former position in the spring, but he resigned before fall practices. Patterson, who the student newspaper once described as "a success story who is a little bewildered by it all," left for New York to take a job with J.P. Morgan and Company, the banking behemoth he would one day head.

Berwanger nursed his knee through the spring, and Shaughnessy kept him out of the annual spring game in early May. A few days later, Berwanger might have made it a point to get inside the fieldhouse to get a glimpse of some special visitors. Baseball's New York Yankees, including Lou Gehrig, used the facility for a workout after rain washed out their game against the White Sox.

Throughout the outdoor track season, Berwanger's knee problem limited him to three field events: javelin, shot put and discus. In late May, he scored Chicago's lone point – for fifth place in the javelin – in the Big Ten championships. Berwanger was in the house when Ohio State's Owens shocked the sports world by breaking three world records and tying a fourth in just a 45-minute span. He tied the 100-yard record (9.4 seconds) and then set world marks in the long jump (26-8¼), 220-yard dash (20.3) and 220 low hurdles (22.6).

College campuses have long had the reputation of having a liberal bent, but the University of Chicago was considered extremely so. Critics considered it a breeding ground for, in the vocabulary of the day, "reds" – communists and socialists. Indeed, the campus did host student organizations such as the Socialist Club and National Student League, and several professors espoused sympathetic positions. The simmer turned into a boil in the winter and spring of 1935. During the winter quarter, a group of students, apparently based in the basement of the Sigma Chi house and headed by Hulen "Tex" Carroll, formed the Public Policy Association to combat the "red menace." *The Daily Maroon* let Carroll have it, taunting him and comparing his tactics to those of the chancellor of Germany, Adolf Hitler. Shortly after the PPA formed, someone nearly convinced Berwanger to pose for a photographer while ripping up a copy of *Upsurge*, the National Student League publication, but at the last moment the football star thought better of it.

The PPA invited the American Legion to hold a mid-April rally on campus, and some 1,200 brass-helmeted members, fortified by four brass bands, assembled in the fieldhouse. Edward Hayes, Legion past national commander, denounced the university as the "reddest" in the nation and worked the crowd into a fever. "The University of Chicago has the worst record in the United States in the *Literary Digest* peace poll," Hayes declared, claiming that nearly one-third of respondents from the university said they would not take up arms in an invasion. "Develop men for war, as you develop men for football. Radicalism is a blind alley of thought!"

Taking this in were several dozen students and John Barden, past editor of the *Daily Maroon*, a publication oft-criticized for fomenting radicalism. Ironically, Barden now wrote for the *Chicago Tribune*, whose owner and publisher, Robert McCormick, regularly criticized the University of Chicago for leftist leanings. After listening to several anti-UC speeches, a few of the undergraduates asked to present a rebuttal but were rebuffed. Carroll, seeing Barden on the platform and thinking the journalist also wanted to speak, confronted Barden. The two exchanged words, Carroll slugged Barden, and a ruckus ensued. The outnumbered students got the worst of the Legionnaires' fists and trumpets. Fifteen policemen already assigned to the rally soon cleared the fieldhouse.

The dean of the university, George A. Works, announced an immediate investigation of all radical groups on campus after disclosure of "pink" activities by one Virginia Ballance Bash, a 22-year-old student who edited *Upsurge*. Miss Bash had just testified at the trial of Jack Kling, a 22-year-old on trial for unlawful assembly after speaking at a League of Struggle for Negro Rights rally several blocks from campus. She was already on administrators' radar after an *Upsurge* article charged the university with injustices to black students. Miss Bash's activities would not have been of special concern except that her father happened to be Major General Louis H. Bash, quartermaster general of the U.S. Army. Understandably, General Bash was displeased with the university's apparent leftist influence over his daughter.

Another unhappy relative was drug store magnate Charles R. Walgreen, who pulled niece Lucille Norton out of the university, for the same reason. "I am unwilling to have her absorb the Communist influences to which she is assiduously exposed," Walgreen told President Hutchins. The businessman accused faculty member Frederick L. Schuman of espousing free love, pointed out that two university courses included Marxism, and demanded a public airing of his complaints. Initially, Hutchins shrugged off the complaint, made patronizing statements about academic freedom, and figured the matter would fade away. But Walgreen, supported and coached by William Randolph Hearst's red-hunting *Herald-Examiner*, had the power and prominence to keep the issue alive. The Illinois Legislature soon entered the fray with publicity-generating hearings. "In fact, Walgreen's charges were absurd," wrote retired faculty member William H. McNeill, a Chicago undergrad at the time, who added that nearly all the professors were actually conservatives. Further, the university's "offense" was respecting the First Amendment rights of left-leaning students, some of whom staged rallies against Walgreen and skewered him in the campus newspaper. Walgreen's claims suffered a blow when his own niece admitted that she never attended any of the socialist Schuman's classes. Meanwhile, Hutchins stepped up his defense of academic freedom and the need for a university to teach about and debate various political theories, including those considered unpopular and dangerous. Before long, state legislators dropped the matter and Walgreen, who came to realize that he had been manipulated by the *Herald-Examiner*, came around to be one of the university's most ardent supporters.[103]

While this was playing out, the university's athletic director offered an explanation why the varsity teams were falling farther behind their Big Ten rivals. In so many words, T. Nelson Metcalf cited Hutchins' academic creation known as the New Plan. Metcalf said high admission standards, academic standards and the all-or-nothing comprehensive exams made it increasingly difficult to attract and retain quality athletes. It was a familiar lament on the Midway – long preceding the arrival of Metcalf and Hutchins – but the competitive gap was clearly widening. Hutchins had already made his position clear: The University of Chicago will not stray from its principles in the pursuit of athletic victories. "It will not subsidize athletes; it will not discriminate against them," he told 600 alumni gathered in the Palmer House. "To the extent to which other institutions in this region adopt the principles of the University, this University will be more and more successful in intercollegiate competition. If other universities do not adopt these principles, the University can hope to be no more successful in the future than it has been in the past." On the same night they heard Hutchins argue against special treatment for athletes, the alumni called forward Berwanger to receive their "honorary degree," a so-called Master of Football Arts. Nonetheless, Hutchins' position had some support among academics. Faculty representatives of Big Ten members again rejected recommendations from athletic directors and football coaches to reinstate one subsidy, "training tables" for football players. The training table – quality food, provided in ample quantities in a team setting – was once common among big-time college programs; during the reform movement of the early 20th century, many schools eliminated the training table.

Meanwhile, student organizers launched a festival of spring called the Midway Fandango. The students went all-out for the three-night event, the proceeds of which were to fund scholarships. It featured a parade, carnival rides, kids' games, a dance, Blackfriars show, queen contest, and games of chance. From the student perspective, Fandango was a great success – the first of what they expected would be an annual event. However, as Berwanger would come to discover, university administrators held another opinion.

Though his participation in track was significantly curtailed, Berwanger received another varsity letter and was elected to share 1936 co-captain duties with Quentin Johnstone, a quarter-miler and long-jumper. Another honor that came his way was induction into the Owl and Serpent, the honor society for senior men. Berwanger also became a college marshal and aide, one of a dozen hand-picked students to assist at convocations and other university activities; these events no doubt included those for prospective undergraduates. A friendly welcome from an All-America football player surely could not hurt University of Chicago recruitment efforts.

For the second consecutive summer, Berwanger worked as a counselor at Camp Highlands for Boys in northern Wisconsin. He had to work harder than usual that summer after failing a business law course during the spring quarter. He needed that credit to be eligible for his final season of football. His buddy Ernie Dix failed it, too, and they committed to passing the re-take at the end of the summer. Dix recalled receiving regular phone calls from Berwanger giving "all kinds of instructions to get people's notes, books and whatever." When Berwanger's camp job concluded, he and Dix made a call on the business law professor, who was not enjoying a summer of static because the football star had not received a passing grade. "He gave us each a sheet with 20 questions, saying that if we knew the answers we would pass the test," Dix said decades later. Berwanger didn't trust the profes-

The physique of a star athlete: Berwanger during his collegiate days. (Berwanger family collection)

sor. "We not only knew the answers but we went over the whole work of the course," Dix said. "Wouldn't you know, not one of those questions appeared on the exam. However, out of 17 taking the exam, we ended up Number 1 and Number 2." Their places on the football team were assured – Berwanger in the spotlight and Dix on the bench.[104]

Even before the Maroons assembled for their first fall practice of 1935, Shaughnessy had to shuffle the lineup. During the summer, Rainwater Wells, the starting quarterback on the depth chart, dropped out of school after it was revealed that he had secretly married Caroline Fickinger in March. As a result, Ewald Nyquist, who had spent the spring learning the end position, returned to the backfield and Berwanger assumed responsibility for calling signals. Even with the All-America captain, the Maroons faced a tough season. Shaughnessy said as much in the outlook he wrote for the campus newspaper:

"By tradition and temperament football coaches are long-faced fellows. As a great respecter of tradition, and, at this season of the year, a great warrior, the most I can say about Chicago's football prospects is that we shall have a spirited team that will play an interesting and at times a lively game. We have a starting team which has fair size and speed and some experience. Our line reserves are not what a coach would wish, and our backfield replacements are mostly a problem. On the other hand, we still have Jay Berwanger and the right to hope for good health and our share of the breaks."

In its first 43 seasons of varsity football, the University of Chicago had lost only a handful of season openers. Stagg, like many of his peers, typically scheduled pushover opponents for the first game or two. Easy games allowed his charges to fine-tune their play before battling conference opponents. Now in charge of his schedule in his third season, Shaughnessy pulled a two-pronged surprise. He agreed to open the 1935 campaign with a road game. The Maroons had played a season opener away from home only once before – in 1915, and that was just a few miles up the road at Northwestern. The second surprise was the quality of the opponent. It was no Lombard, Lawrence or Monmouth. The Maroons would visit the Nebraska Cornhuskers. Coach Dana X. Bible's team was coming off what was, by Nebraska standards, a disappointing year – 6-3 in 1934 after going a combined 29-7-1 the previous four seasons.

Forty players, Shaughnessy, and Athletic Director Metcalf arrived in Lincoln mid-morning Friday after riding the rails overnight. The players spent an hour looking around the campus and town, where the streets were adorned with red-and-white banners. The Nebraskans were hospitable to their guests from the Windy City, and many planned to attend the game just to see Berwanger. The *Chicago Tribune's* Wilfrid Smith described the match-up as "a November contest moved up to opening day." Still, Smith noted, local observers predicted a convincing victory for the Cornhuskers, who featured halfback Lloyd Cardwell and quarterback Jerry LaNoue. No Chicago radio station planned to air the Nebraska game, but the department store Marshall Field & Company reminded fans that it would operate its

"Grid-Graph" – a light board simulation of the game – in the Sportsman's Department.

Some 30,000 fans – then a record for a Nebraska home opener – jammed Memorial Stadium. Not long after the 3 o'clock kickoff, Cardwell gave the Cornhuskers their first touchdown after runs of 13, 31, and finally seven yards. The junior was virtually unstoppable, taking advantage of large holes opened by his husky line. In the first half alone, he racked up 161 yards in only a half-dozen carries. Berwanger made many tackles that afternoon while playing safety instead of his usual defensive cornerback post. Berwanger answered with a touchdown of his own following recovery of a LaNoue fumble at the hosts' 23-yard line. After Duke Skoning rushed for four yards, the Dutchman gave the crowd an example of why he was the captain of the 1934 All-America team. He crashed through left tackle and powered across the goal line virtually untouched. After his 19-yard touchdown run, Berwanger kicked the extra point to tie the game at 7.

The Cornhuskers made the most of their size advantage and started to wear down the Maroons. A bit of trickery didn't hurt, either. Immediately after his touchdown and extra point, Berwanger kicked off to Henry Bauer

Trimming the family Christmas tree in Dubuque, 1934 or 1935. (Berwanger family collection)

at the 10. Bauer ran diagonally and reached the 20, where, to the Maroons' surprise, he handed off to Cardwell. The reverse put the 6-foot-3, 190-pound Cardwell in the clear. A diving attempt by Ned Bartlett did little besides cause Cardwell, nicknamed "The Wild Hoss of the Plains," to stagger as he crossed the goal line for the go-ahead touchdown. After that, the Cornhuskers kept the lead.

Nebraska scored touchdowns in each quarter, and Cardwell carded his third of the day on a nine-yard pass play in the third period. After that, Coach Bible gave him the rest of the afternoon off. From the Chicago perspective, Shaughnessy later said Cardwell was the fastest back he had ever seen. The final touchdown drive came courtesy of Sam Francis. He intercepted a Berwanger pass and advanced it a couple of yards to the Chicago 38. A fullback, Francis then rumbled upfield until Berwanger brought him down at the 20. Backup Bob Bensen gained 19 on the next play, after which Francis broke through the tired Chicago line for a one-yard touchdown. Final score: Nebraska 28, Chicago 7.

On paper, Cardwell, who would go on to star with the Detroit Lions in seven professional seasons, outplayed Berwanger. However, the *Tribune's* Smith said such a comparison would be unfair, "for Cardwell was superior because he was given better support from his teammates than that which Berwanger enjoyed. So, by analysis, Nebraska's scarlet jerseyed men, who became stronger, apparently, as the game advanced, and battered the Maroons unmercifully in the closing minutes, are the lads to whom Cardwell should return thanks." The Nebraskans recognized Berwanger's special talents. The sports editor of the campus newspaper took some pity on Berwanger, calling him a "great player on a mediocre team." Arnold Levin of the *Daily Nebraskan* observed that Berwanger was "visibly worn out" by halftime, after which he was "whittled down to Cornhusker size and then taken for a ride." He continued, "The burden falls on him and him alone. He runs like a demon; his passing is good, but nothing extraordinary; his punting is excellent; and his blocking superb, but he doesn't have teammates of fine enough caliber to maintain his pace." That was the story throughout Berwanger's college career.

CHAPTER 26

After being dominated at Nebraska to open the 1935 season, Chicago hosted two lesser opponents: Carroll College and Western State Teachers College (later Western Michigan University). Former Maroon Elmer Lampe was in his second season as head coach of Carroll, which went 2-3-2 in 1934 and lost its 1935 season opener to Milwaukee Teachers College, 7-6. No one expected Carroll to win – not even the visitors from Waukesha, Wisconsin. Shaughnessy did not let up on his team throughout the week of practice, shuffling the lineup – Bartlett dropped to the second string for what the *Tribune* described as "indifferent play" against Nebraska – and conducting a full scrimmage as late as Friday afternoon. The Maroons' lack of depth, a long-standing deficiency, was evident when Shaughnessy needed a left end to replace Bob Perretz, who sprained his left ankle in Lincoln: He settled on Ernie Dix, who just three years earlier needed Berwanger's help in figuring out how to put on his equipment and who wasn't on the team in 1934 when he worked a part-time job to cover his college expenses.

Prognosticators set the point spread for Chicago's victory at 30. They missed it by only one point. In their home opener, the Maroons dominated Carroll, 31-0. Berwanger played parts of the first and third quarters only, and played well – his 30-yard return of the second-half kickoff was a highlight – but he scored no touchdowns. Wearing a white helmet with his trademark face guard, the Dutchman contributed one extra-point kick to the scoring summary.

"Saturday's game with Carroll topped off a hard week of practice for us, as Coach Shaughnessy has been trying to remove some of the bad points of our game that were evident at Nebraska," stated an article in the campus newspaper under Berwanger's byline. "The Carroll team was not stiff competition by any means, but it did give the coaches an opportunity get a line on the reserves." (Asked 50 years later about his weekly column in the *Maroon*, Berwanger laughed, "I didn't write it, that's for sure."[105]) Though Berwanger – or at least his ghost-writer – was understandably complimentary, the coaches were not pleased. Shaughnessy railed about what he considered sloppy play, and he scheduled more scrimmages and full-contact drills. Berwanger probably saw limited or no duty in those "in order to protect our freshmen and substitutes who would have opposed him," Shaughnessy said. "The boy is just too strong for the others." The team was so short-handed that it added to its roster another one of Berwanger's friends and Psi Upsilon brothers: all-conference basketball player Bill Haarlow.

Though it had won nine straight games and 11 of its previous 12 contests, dating back 1933, Western State Teachers College was easy pickings for the Maroons. "The early portion of the first quarter might very easily be summarized in one word: Berwanger, with a bow to (Duke) Skoning," the *Tribune's* Charles Bartlett reported. After cracking off some solid runs, booming a few punts, connecting on a pass, and making some defensive stops, the Dutchman cut through right guard for four yards and Chicago's second touchdown. His kick for the extra point sailed wide, but the Maroons were up 12-0 early in the second quarter. The third touchdown came on a 14-yard pass play, Berwanger to Merritt Bush, a tackle who had lined up at end. Berwanger called it "the highlight of the game," noting that it was Bush's first touchdown in his Chicago career "and he got a kick out of it." Regarding kicks, Berwanger missed his attempt for the extra point.

Chicago scored again quickly, and again it involved a Berwanger pass. He fired into the left back corner of the end zone, where Bob Fitzgerald, better known as a basketball letterman, snagged the ball for an 18-yard touchdown in his first football game as a regular. Shaughnessy tried another placekicker for the extra point, and Adolph Schuessler barely got the ball over the crossbar. With the Maroons in control, 25-0, Berwanger spent the rest of the afternoon watching from the sidelines. After Chicago recovered a blocked punt in the end zone for its final touchdown, Shaughnessy let another basketball player, Haarlow, take a crack at the point-after kick. He missed. Western State averted a shutout with a late touchdown to make the final score 31-6.

"Western State proved to be a fair test for us, although it did not appear to be as strong as its record would indicate," Berwanger wrote in the *Maroon*. "Their passes kept us on our toes, and I think that we showed Coach that his hard work on pass defense last week was to good advantage." The captain

As a junior in 1934, Berwanger was named honorary captain of an All-America team – but lost his own team's vote as Most Valuable Player. (Special Collections Research Center, University of Chicago Library)

concluded, "The whole team played better than they have done so far this season, and more cooperation was apparent. Right now, however, last week's game is a thing of the past and we have to think about what we will be able to do against the Purdue team Saturday. They have showed that they have an especially good set of backs, and it will be up to us to find out some way to stop them." Would the LaSalle Street Coaching Staff have some ideas?

The LaSalle Street group, an assembly of Chicago alumni and other boosters who made second-guessing an art form, hosted Athletic Director T. Nelson Metcalf, Shaughnessy, and his coaching staff for their annual get-together. "Charles Higgins, president of the Chicago Alumni Club, will present a scholarly blackboard demonstration of several bomb-proof plays, which are guaranteed to mystify the opposing team, to say nothing of Maroon coaches and players," the campus paper quipped, reminding readers that Higgins is remembered "for his astounding dash for cover when rain interrupted last year's tilt with Purdue."

However, the Maroons would need more than trick plays from second-guessers to beat Noble Kizer's Boilermakers, victors over Chicago seven straight times. Purdue had already won its first two games, shutouts on the road against Northwestern and Fordham. Purdue was used to donning the visitors' uniforms. The Boilermakers often had more away games than home contests, but the 1935 schedule was particularly lopsided, with six of eight games on the road.

Shaughnessy's brother Ed, who Berwanger later described as "the most remarkable scout I have ever seen," watched Purdue and came back with tips. He told Berwanger that when Purdue's left halfback ran around end, he threw his head one way and ran the other. "If you go opposite to the way he throws his head you will able to tackle him every time," he said. Ed Shaughnessy also noticed that, when leaving the huddle, the Purdue signal-caller always looked in the direction of the upcoming play. He reported that when the running guard was going to pull out, he lined up with one foot slightly behind the other; if he was going to hold position and block, the guard would line up with his feet even. The tips were helpful, but would they be enough?

On a perfect mid-October Saturday afternoon – the temperature at Stagg Field was 74 at the 2 p.m. kickoff – the game opened with both teams struggling to mount a drive. "Although the Maroons were holding their own, there was that indescribable something which left the impression that sooner or later Purdue would capitalize on its power," Harvey Woodruff of the *Chicago Tribune* said. The moment came midway in the second quarter, when John Drake reached the end zone unmolested on a two-yard run. After Dick Sandefur's kick, Purdue held a 7-0 lead. That was all the scoring the Boilermakers would need.

When his team was on defense, Kizer assigned hard-nosed Ed Skoronski to stick with Berwanger and only Berwanger. The team captain at age 25, Skoronski went wherever Berwanger went, recording plenty of hits on Chicago's 21-year-old star. "We never had anyone to block him," Berwanger recalled. "He didn't hurt me, but he bruised me." Though Skoronski and Purdue kept him out of the end zone all afternoon, Berwanger played an outstanding game. As was the case in last year's Purdue contest, Berwanger and the Maroons fought to the end. Chicago's best scoring threat started with Berwanger's kickoff return of 25 yards. The Dutchman soon connected on a sideline pass to Gordon Petersen, who made a move to elude safety Tom McGannon and appeared on his way to a thrilling touchdown. But an official ruled that Petersen stepped out of bounds at the 28. The drive then stalled when Berwanger made one of his few mistakes all day and lost a fumble.

Purdue scored again a half-minute before halftime, hurrying through an 81-yard drive. Its last touchdown came with six minutes left in the game, when most Boilermaker starters were watching comfortably from the bench. The final score was 19-0.

On the opposite side, Chicago made few substitutions and Berwanger never left the game. Though they came out on the short end against Purdue for the eighth straight autumn, and were clearly overmatched, the Maroons put up a spirited battle. That was evident when Berwanger was on defense. On a fourth-down play, Purdue sent sophomore Cecil Isbell on a run to the right. He advanced several yards downfield – and then met Number 99. Berwanger lowered his shoulder into Isbell's mid-section and powered the ball carrier to the turf with such force that the Boilermaker's helmet flew off. Berwanger took his lumps, too, courtesy of Skoronski. "After the game, the team doctor asked me how I felt," he said 50 years later. He replied that he was fine but his legs were sore. The way Berwanger told it, the doctor "stuck a pin into my legs, about an inch deep, and I never felt it."[106] Whether the physician actually used a pin as a diagnostic tool cannot be verified, but there was no question that the game took its toll on Berwanger.

As it happened, the game was the last in a Purdue uniform for Berwanger's stalker, Skoronski. A few days after the Chicago game, Purdue's faculty athletic committee declared the team captain ineligible from further competition. A committee investigation confirmed that in 1931, before he had graduated from Chicago's Bowen High School, he played a few minutes for Georgetown University, where he was enrolled as a special student in the foreign service school. Under Big Ten rules, those few plays counted as a full season in calculating eligibility – and therefore Skoronski had already used all of his collegiate eligibility. Skoronski then had a brief stint in the National Football League. Meanwhile, the Boilermakers would win just one of their four remaining Big Ten contests of 1935 to wind up 3-3 in the conference and 4-4 overall.

The Maroons' spirit against the more powerful Purdue squad was noted and appreciated by boosters, including an alumnus who, in a letter to Shaughnessy, complimented the coach for his team's fight and its apparent love of the game, while, the alum observed, Purdue seemed to play like a machine. Observed Edward S. Stern in the campus newspaper, "Such a spirit and love for a sport is the aim of any type of athletics. This is true of the Maroons especially because they can never hope to compare with other conference teams in man-power. Many factors lead to this; chiefly, the small size of the school – Chicago's undergraduate body being from one-half to one-seventh the size of that of the other Big Ten schools. Furthermore, the University draws from metropolitan centers for a large part of its enrollment, and these places do not produce the sturdiest type of athlete."

During the season, University of Chicago officials, accepting their university's fading fortunes in big-time athletics, announced that they would schedule only four conference football games in 1937. (It was too late to change the 1936 schedule, which again featured five conference contests. In 1939, Chicago's last season of major-college football, the Maroons played only three Big Ten games.)

Berwanger and the Maroons prepared for a Big Ten opponent they figured they could beat, Wisconsin, whose coach, Clarence Spears, was in what would be his last season in Madison. His Badgers were 0-4 at that point, having just lost at home to Michigan, 20-12, despite outgaining the Wolverines 342 yards to 173. To the Badgers, Chicago was vulnerable – if they could stop Berwanger. In the week leading up to their "Out-of-the-Cellar" battle in the Windy City, Spears focused on defense, especially defending the pass and containing Berwanger. "The specter of Jay Berwanger and his forward-passing right arm haunts the Camp Randall practice field this week," wrote R.A. Haase, sports editor of the *Daily Cardinal*, Wisconsin's campus newspaper. "'Berwanger, Berwanger, Berwanger,' the scouts have sung who watched the Maroons in action against Nebraska, Carroll, Western State, and Purdue. And 'Berwanger, Berwanger, Berwanger,' has been dinned into the ears of the Wisconsin players throughout the week." The game in Chicago did not hold much attraction for Wisconsin fans; only 600 bought advance tickets. In a scheduling rarity, the teams did not play each other in 1934, but over their previous six meetings, the Badgers were 5-0-1. In the final seconds of their tie in 1933, Berwanger had barely missed what would have been a game-winning 25-yard field goal. The Chicago lineup looked fairly set, though there was some question whether Bob Perretz would start because the eyeglasses ordered for him had yet to arrive. The backfield starters were Ewald Nyquist at quarterback, Skoning at fullback, and Fred Lehnhardt and Berwanger at halfback.

With temperatures in the high 50s and rain in the forecast, the Maroons and Badgers took the Stagg Field gridiron, each squad wearing dark jerseys. Early in the second quarter of a scoreless game, Chicago drove to the Badgers' 15 and faced a fourth-and-two. To no one's surprise, Berwanger got the ball. He started around left end, where Badger defenders threw him for three-yard loss. A few minutes later, the visitors were pinned deep in their own territory after Berwanger's quick-kick punt rolled to the 4-yard line. The Badgers lined up to punt, but the center snap went not to the punter but to blocking back Eddie Jankowski. Near his own goal line, Jankowski attempted a lateral to Johnny Wilson. The ball wound up on the turf, and the best Wilson could do was bat it away from the end zone. Chicago's Nyquist recovered the ball at the 1-foot line. On the next play, Berwanger ran for perhaps the easiest touchdown of his career. The Dutchman's try for the extra-point kick went awry due to a bad center snap, and the Maroons held a 6-0 lead.

Wisconsin scored its first points after Stephen Rondone recovered a Berwanger fumble on Chicago's 20. The Badgers nearly gave the ball back when Jankowski fumbled, but teammate John Fish scooped it up and ran around left end for an 11-yard gain. The Badgers pushed to the 2, where they faced fourth-and-goal. They gave the ball to Wilson, who reached paydirt to tie the game. Lynn Jordan's extra-point kick made it a 7-6 affair.

On the ensuing kickoff, Berwanger unleashed the most exciting play of the afternoon. He caught the kick three yards deep in the end zone and broke into the clear. Racing down the left half of the field, Berwanger covered 78 yards before Fish made the tackle at the 25. Chicago was in business.

Backup quarterback Omar Fareed gained five yards on first down, but then Berwanger lost another fumble at the Badgers' 17. The Chicago defense held, and Berwanger returned the Wisconsin punt to midfield. Fareed

Berwanger's college uniform and College Football Hall of Fame certificate are displayed in the lobby of the University of Chicago's Gerald Ratner Athletics Center. (Author's photo)

connected on a bomb to end Gordon Petersen, who raced along the right sideline to the 10. Fareed then threw to his left, and Berwanger caught the pass at the 3, spun to avoid a tackler, and crossed the goal line for the go-ahead score. Berwanger's kick made it a 13-7 game. Though both teams threatened to score after that, defenses prevailed the rest of the way, and the Maroons had their first conference victory. The winless Badgers were one game from their only victory of 1935 – a stunning 8-0 upset of Purdue at Camp Randall. (After two months of postseason intrigue, Wisconsin fired Coach Spears and Athletic Director Walter E. Meanwell.)

Despite his two fumbles, Berwanger was the game's star. He scored two touchdowns and had a third called back on an offside penalty. His only rest came during the final minutes of the third quarter. His combined yardage – runs from scrimmage and returns of punts and kickoffs – exceeded that of the entire Wisconsin team. He rushed 25 times for 155 yards.

The contest was a breakthrough game for Fareed, the son of a psychiatrist born in Persia (Iran), who had not even joined the team until the fourth week of practice. "Though he is pretty light," Berwanger observed, "he is one of the toughest men on the squad and is hard to hurt." Nearly a year later, Berwanger revealed that Fareed had played 55 minutes in a key game with a punctured trachea but had refused to leave the field.

Fareed, who would go on to a distinguished career in medicine, was driven to succeed. "My father sometimes took advantage of my obsessive-compulsive personality, where there was housework to be done," he told an interviewer 50 years later. "He knew that if he asked me to wash the dishes or vacuum the living room rug, I'd spend an hour or two at it, doing a really thorough job." The speedy sophomore reserve represented an offensive threat who, Maroons fans hoped, might cause opponents to modify their game plan of "stop Berwanger." Instantly, Fareed had a nickname: Omar the Score-maker.

Though Chicago was not winning much, Berwanger's standing on the collegiate scene grew. In late October, the United Press listed early candidates for All-America consideration and offered a few words about each, such as "all-around star, especially good kicker" (William Shakespeare, Notre Dame) or "leading scorer of Big Ten" (Joe Williams, Ohio State). Of Berwanger, United Press simply stated, "The entire Chicago team."

CHAPTER 27

The Chicago Maroons had an open Saturday after their win over Wisconsin, so they had two weeks to prepare for their toughest opponent on the schedule, Ohio State, which had designs on the mythical national championship. The Buckeyes hosted Notre Dame in a marquee matchup in front of a standing-room-only throng of 81,000 fans. The battle lived up to its billing. Ohio State held a 13-0 lead after three periods, but Notre Dame rallied to pull within a point, 13-12, with two minutes to play. Their onside kick attempt failed, but the Irish caught a game-changing break when Ohio State fumbled. Despite losing star running back Andy Pilney to a knee injury, the Irish kept driving. William Shakespeare – yes, that was his name – took the ball on a reverse and then lofted a pass in the end zone where Wayne Millner, a future member of the Pro Football Hall of Fame, caught the game-winning score. The 18-13 loss dropped Ohio State (4-1) out of national championship consideration. Now all the Buckeyes had to play for was the Big Ten title, and Chicago was the next team standing in their way. They didn't expect much of a battle – especially if they could contain Berwanger. During practice sessions, observers heard coach Francis Schmidt frequently invoke one name. The message was clear: "Stop Berwanger."

Back in Chicago, Shaughnessy experimented on defense with his budding star, Fareed, putting him at safety and moving Berwanger closer to the action at defensive halfback. On offense, Shaughnessy listed Fareed as starting right halfback, complementing Berwanger, though he would often take on the duties of quarterback. "Passes are the center of attention now with the new quarterback doing the throwing and Berwanger added to the list of receivers," the student newspaper noted. "At last the Maroons have a method of getting Jay out into the open field without depending on the poor blocking demonstrated so far this season." The Maroons again had the services of end

Bob Perretz, whose shatterproof eyeglasses finally arrived. His return was just in time, because Shaughnessy had to shift Gordon Petersen from end to center to fill a gap created by an injury to Sam Whiteside. Shifts of this sort reflected Chicago's chronic lack of depth. Shaughnessy had to decide what trade-offs would hurt the team the least. Few observers expected anything but an Ohio State victory. The Maroons' primary goal was to avoid another embarrassing rout like the one they suffered in Columbus the previous season, when Berwanger sat out with an injury.

The Scarlet Scourge rode an overnight train from Columbus and arrived at Chicago's Englewood station at 7:30 Friday morning, in plenty of time for an afternoon workout at Stagg Field. Ohio State's 120-piece marching band and entourage of boosters arrived later. The Scarlet Key, the university's senior athletic managers' club, planted a tree at a ceremony to mark the Buckeyes' first visit to the Midway since 1926.

On a rainy, 50-degree afternoon, the Maroons made it clear to the Buckeyes that they would put up a fight. In the first period, Berwanger nearly broke free and was stopped only after gaining 32 yards. Maroon defenders denied Ohio State a touchdown by halting a drive at the 1-yard line. They

The team captain, Berwanger, holds the football in the 1935 University of Chicago football team photo. Front row: Ernest Dix, Stanley Marynowski, Edmund Wolfenson, Robert Perretz, Merritt Bush, Jay Berwanger (captain), Gordon Petersen, Ewald Nyquist, Victor Jones, Paul Whitney, and Daniel Blake. Second row: O.E. Strohmeier (assistant coach), J. Lopez (assistant coach), Murray Chilton, Robert Fitzgerald, Harmon Meigs, Earl Sappington, Sam Whiteside, Clarence Wright, Warren Skoning, Edward Bartlett, Omar Fareed, Prescott Jordan, and Clark Shaughnessy (coach). Third row: Judge R.J. Dunn (assistant coach), William Bosworth Jr., James Chapple, Andrew Hoyt, Nelson Thomas, Woodrow Wilson, Jerome Sivesind, Henry Kellogg, Marvin Channon, Fred Lehnhardt, Robert Shipway, Adolph Shuessler, J.K. Anderson (assistant coach), and Walter Bock (trainer). Back row: Jack Fetman, Robert Wheeler, Paul Antonic, David Gordon, Henry Cutter, William Gillerlain, and Kendall Petersen. (Special Collections Research Center, University of Chicago Library)

did it again in the second quarter, stopping the Buckeyes at the 8. Berwanger's punts denied Ohio State favorable field position, and sportscaster Red Barber later recalled that the Dutchman was involved in three of every four tackles.[107] While making an early defensive stop, Berwanger hurt his shoulder, but he stayed on the field. Meanwhile, Fareed took a severe blow to his windpipe in the first few plays; he stuck it out until the fourth quarter. That same quarter, with the game still scoreless, Chicago's Merritt Bush, standing 6-foot-5 and weighing 245 pounds, crashed through the Buckeye line to block Dick Heekin's punt. The ball bounded out of bounds at the Ohio State 9-yard line. Three plays later, Duke Skoning scored an easy touchdown. The point-after failed, but Chicago gladly took that 6-0 lead into halftime.

In the third quarter, the Maroons' defense stifled another Ohio State drive, stopping the Buckeyes' fourth-down thrust inches short at the Chicago 15. Schmidt sent in Merle Wendt, a future All-America, with the instruction, "Watch Berwanger!" On the next snap, Berwanger unleashed the best individual play of his football career – a feat that some experts described as the best individual performance by any player. Standing in the backfield, he took the center snap and ran through right tackle. With backfield defenders challenging him 15 yards downfield, he took a hard left turn. A defender caused Berwanger to stumble, but he regained his balance and rambled along the left sideline. Two Ohio State defenders angled toward him, apparently intending to shove him out of bounds. With that, Berwanger suddenly stopped and cut a couple of steps to his right. That move caused one of the defenders to fall down, while the other circled back to try again – but Berwanger made another cut that caused him to miss again. Berwanger was in the clear and coasted across the goal line for a thrilling 85-yard touchdown. No fewer than eight Ohio State players had a clear opportunity to make the tackle – one of the defenders tried twice.[108] Wendt was among them. The story was that an angry Schmidt hollered at Wendt, "Didn't I tell you to watch Berwanger?!" to which the player replied, "Yes, Coach. And didn't he look swell?"[109] More than a dozen years later, legendary sportscaster Barber described the play in great detail and called Berwanger "the greatest football player I ever saw."[110]

Still breathing heavily from his thrilling dash, Berwanger kicked the extra point to give Chicago a 13-0 lead and spark the first sense of panic among the mighty Scarlet Scourge. Down 13 points with about 20 minutes to play, Schmidt ripped the trick plays from the playbook and had his Buckeyes execute basic, grind-it-out runs and passes. The coach likewise dropped his plan to rest Heekin, a talented running back. Meanwhile, Chicago's lack of bench strength was taking its toll. The Maroons were becoming drained emotionally and physically. Even Berwanger, who usually played all 60 minutes and would do so this afternoon, was not the same after his thrilling touchdown run. He later admitted he had never felt more tired during a game.

Ohio State mounted an impressive 63-yard drive, mixing passes and runs until Heekin scored from one yard out. Though Sam Busich's extra-point kick missed, the Buckeyes closed to 13-6 and kept the momentum. They tied the game early in the fourth quarter when Stanley Pincura connected with Wendt on a 30-yard pass play. Richard Beltz's kick made it 13-13.

Chicago seemed incapable of accomplishing anything offensively or defensively. Their best hope for preserving a tie came when a beautiful punt by Berwanger rolled to a stop on the Buckeye 10. However, the officials penalized the Maroons five yards for offside, and made Chicago kick again. Ohio State star Joe Williams fielded Berwanger's next punt and returned it nearly to midfield; that transaction cost Chicago 37 yards and probably the game. John Bettridge and Williams took turns chewing up yardage, on the ground and in the air. With the ball on the Chicago 15, Bettridge executed an end-around to his left and was pushed out of bounds at the 1. The Maroons tried to muster one more goal-line stand. Berwanger summoned his remaining energy to burst across the line to throw Williams for a six-yard loss. Chicago fans experienced a moment of excitement on the next play, when Williams fumbled. But as play continued, Williams, still on his feet, picked up the ball, shot through a hole at left guard, and crossed the goal line. Busich made the kick and Ohio State escaped with a 20-13 victory.

Though the Buckeyes collected the "W" to continue their march to a Big Ten co-championship, the headlines featured Chicago's valiant but unsuccessful effort to notch one of the nation's biggest upsets of 1935, including Berwanger's dazzling 85-yard touchdown against one of the country's toughest teams. Statistically, Berwanger amassed 130 yards in just 13 carries. However, Ohio State's defensive strategy of "Stop Berwanger" largely succeeded. Aside from the touchdown dash and his 32-yard burst in the opening quarter, the Dutchman gained only 13 yards on his other 11 carries.

For the rest of his days, Berwanger described his long touchdown against Ohio State as his most memorable play. His effort that afternoon, including defensive stops and playing through a shoulder injury, fortified the case that he was the best player in all of college football.

CHAPTER 28

The University of Chicago won only a moral victory against Ohio State, but even that came at a price. The injury to the windpipe of sophomore Omar Fareed, whom Berwanger described as "hard to hurt," kept him in the hospital all week. A nagging knee injury still had lineman Sam Whiteside hobbling around. Most critical to the team's chances against Indiana, Berwanger's shoulder injury was so severe that he was expected to see only limited action. For the penultimate game of his college career and his final appearance on the Stagg Field gridiron, he was not listed as a starter. Publicly, Shaughnessy expressed no optimism about the Maroons' chances against the Hoosiers, who were improved but still needed victories against Chicago and then Purdue to secure their first winning season since 1920.

With the final home game of 1935 approaching, the Maroon Football Review published tributes to the seniors. Shaughnessy provided this valedictory to the captain:

"I have never met a finer boy or a finer football player than Jay Berwanger. And I don't expect to. You can say anything superlative about him you like and I'll double it. Jay has had a good deal of praise, publicity, and attention. He is completely unaffected by it. But the most significant thing is that there isn't a member of the Chicago squad who is jealous, or who thinks that Jay gets his due, or who doesn't hold him in affection. They are proud to be with him. His abilities as a player speak for themselves. He is not only a wonderful player as an individual but a great team player as well. He's the nicest lad to work with I've ever seen. He has plenty of individuality but he responds beautifully to criticism, and plays his heart out both in practice and in games."

Several events preceded the final home game. Freshmen competed in a pie-eating contest on Thursday. At noon Friday, the student body held a special ceremony to honor the team's 10 seniors. The site was the "C" Bench, the traditional gathering place for varsity lettermen and their invited guests (that is, their girlfriends). Shaughnessy and Berwanger said a few words, and each senior player received a trophy. The same morning, the University of Iowa football team came to campus even though the Hawkeyes were not on the Maroons' schedule. The Iowans disembarked from their train in Chicago and practiced at Stagg Field before continuing to West Lafayette, Indiana, where the next afternoon they would lose to Purdue, 12-6.

The afternoon and evening events on the Midway included the "Victory Vanities" talent show, a pep rally, a parade, a bonfire, and the Victory Dance in Ida Noyes Hall (admission 30 cents.) The cheerleaders and band led the parade, which started outside Bartlett Gymnasium, marched in front of the decorated houses of Fraternity Row, and finished at Campus Circle, where the pep rally and bonfire followed. As the flames danced, students conducted a snake dance to the university's traditional song, "Wave the Flag."[111]

Basketball player Arnold "Bill" Haarlow was Berwanger's Psi Upsilon fraternity brother and lifelong friend. Their junior and senior seasons, both men earned all-America status in their respective sports. Haarlow was one of the first players to shoot the basketball one-handed. Both men moved their families to the Chicago suburb of Hinsdale, where they socialized and golfed regularly. They are charter members of their alma mater's sports hall of fame. (Chicago Tribune photo. Reprinted with permission)

All that enthusiasm did not transfer positively onto the playing field the next afternoon. Despite his injury, Berwanger wound up starting his final home game. However, as the *Chicago Tribune* put it, the captain was "present only in spirit." His shoulder bothered him from the first play, and he was never able to get on track. Meanwhile, Bo McMillen's Hoosiers had their way with the Maroons throughout the chilly, gray afternoon. The only time Chicago had anything going was on their first possession, when the Maroons advanced 60 yards to the Indiana 20. But the drive abruptly ended when William Dileo intercepted a Berwanger pass. The Dutchman was already hobbled when injuries forced Fred Lehnhardt, Ewald Nyquist, and Duke Skoning to leave the game. The Maroons had only 148 yards of offense, compared to 350 for the Hoosiers. The Man in the Iron Mask gained only 24 yards on 10 carries. With the game out of reach at 17-0, Shaughnessy removed the greatest player he ever coached. The Stagg Field crowd gave Berwanger a sustained ovation as he left the gridiron and found a spot on the bench. Irving Vaughan of the *Tribune* said the effort to make Berwanger's final home game memorable wound up being "a swan song out of tune." Wrapped in a blanket against the 41-degree chill, Berwanger sat on the bench and watched the remainder of the game. His brother, 13-year-old Paul, came down from the stands and sat beside him.

What they saw was an Indiana team acting as if it were losing, not winning by a comfortable margin. After making another interception against a bunch of Chicago reserves desperate to pull off a miracle, the Hoosiers were not content to run out the clock. With less than a minute remaining, they connected on consecutive passes. On the second aerial, the receiver stepped out of bounds just two feet from the goal line and with only a few seconds showing on the clock. On the next play, Lewis Walker crashed across for a meaningless touchdown as the official's pistol signaled the end of regulation play. Indiana was still entitled to an extra-point attempt, and the Hoosiers lined up for the place-kick. The holder, George Miller, fumbled the snap, but he picked up the ball and ran. He scrambled around right end and reached the end zone to record the 24th point in an unusual, if not unsporting, conclusion to the contest. All Chicago could do was accept its defeat and hope it would be healthy enough to put up a competitive fight in the season finale.

The Maroons' hosts in their last game of 1935, coach Bob Zuppke's Illini, were having their own troubles. After going 7-1 in 1934, Illinois was only 3-4 overall and 1-3 in the conference entering the Chicago game. Offense was the weakness for the Illini, who had scored only six points in four Big

Ten contests. Their defense kept their games close.

As the banged-up Maroons prepared for the finale, Shaughnessy brought the backfield into the fieldhouse and taught them new plays. Berwanger stood to the side and called the signals while his teammates, including Berwanger surrogate Adolph Schuessler, ran the plays. Outside, the starting linemen scrimmaged against the freshmen. Shaughnessy hoped to try a balanced attack, using still-recovering Fareed and Skoning often enough to cause the Illini to not focus on Berwanger alone.

In advance of his final game, several newspapers published Berwanger tributes. The *Chicago Daily News* presented a multiple-day series, "Berwanger: Genius of the Gridiron." Back home in Dubuque, the *Telegraph-Herald* published its own series on Berwanger's life and achievements, which the University of Chicago newspaper reprinted. (After the season, the *Tribune* carried a long Sunday feature under Berwanger's byline, and ghost-written by Charles Bartlett, "What Has Football Meant to Me?") As he had throughout Berwanger's career, Dubuque sports editor "Scoop" Wilhelm made laudatory remarks:

"The University of Chicago has had better teams than the one that is representing the university now. It had teams that were as much feared of as any in the Western conference. But despite all of this, the faculty, the student body, the ardent Maroon supporters, will rise as one and tell you that as good or as bad as the Maroons have been, they have never had a player like Captain Jay Berwanger, not for a decade or more. Folks who know this Dubuque lad idolize him. He makes them forget defeat, even victory for that matter. ... He's not the kind that 'steals' the

Berwanger as a University of Chicago student-athlete. (Special Collections Research Center, University of Chicago Library)

limelight. He never looks for hurrahs and cheers and even the fuss made over him never bothers him. He treats his football games as he does his daily assignments in his books. He gives his best always. He's the first and last word of the supporters. Not alone is he proficient in football, but on the track as well. He does everything well. He does everything right. That is why they talk about him. Whatever he does, or undertakes, after his school years, he'll never be forgotten. And Dubuque may be proud of him."

Berwanger's final college football game called for special arrangements. A Dubuque contingent, including his family, planned to be in Champaign the Saturday before Thanksgiving. The Illinois Central Railroad scheduled a special train, with service directly to the gates of Memorial Stadium. Passengers could depart the Windy City at 9:15 Saturday morning, disembark at the stadium three hours later, take in the 2 p.m. game, and be back in Chicago by 8 that night. The round-trip fare was a discounted $2.50. Cost-conscious Chicago administrators did not spring for hotel rooms the night before the game. They put the team on the Illinois Central the morning of the battle. The Chicago contingent included boosters, band, Shaughnessy and coaches, and 33 players.

Despite seasonal weather, an in-state rivalry, and Berwanger's swan song, the Illinois-Chicago game attracted only 12,536 spectators, the smallest crowd the Illini would play before all year. In Illinois' two previous home games, a loss to Iowa and win over Michigan, more than twice that number attended. Nonetheless, the turnout for the Chicago contest was half-again more than the 8,135 who showed up for their previous visit in 1933.

The Maroons and their boosters felt they had a score or two to settle with the Illini. Each of their four previous meetings was decided by six or seven points, and Illinois had claimed three straight. The losses during Berwanger's varsity career were particularly difficult to swallow. In 1933, Illinois won 7-0 after recovering a Berwanger fumble on the 3-yard line and, with only seconds to play, stuffing Berwanger on fourth-and-goal from the 1-yard line. In 1934, Chicago lost on a fluke play. Defending their goal line, the Maroons deflected an Illinois pass and the ball fell into the hands of an Illini lineman, Charles Galbreath, who rumbled a few yards for a touchdown and a 6-0 victory. Galbreath, now the team captain, and the rest of the Illini intended to continue their streak of good luck against Chicago.

When Berwanger disembarked from the train, he was already heralded by Big Ten coaches as the conference's best player. The Dutchman was the only unanimous all-conference selection.

Once the battle began, neither team could generate a threat in the early going. Before the end of the first quarter, Berwanger, whose shoulder had improved, exceeded the 33 rushing yards he needed to surpass the one-mile mark (1,760 yards) for his career. By 21st century standards, his rushing totals are not impressive, but amassing that total in 1935, especially on such a middling team, was an achievement.

Among the Illini, Les "Swede" Lindberg, who received All-America mentions the previous year but battled injuries in 1935, returned to the starting backfield and handled punting duties for his final collegiate contest. One of his second-quarter punts helped set the stage for the game's first points. Lindberg, who still holds the Illinois single-game record for punts and yardage (18 for 692 yards), boomed a 72-yarder that came to rest on the Chicago 3. The Maroons couldn't make a first down, and Berwanger punted to midfield with about two minutes left before halftime. Defenders knocked down two consecutive long passes by Lindberg. On third down, Lindberg started to run right, stopped, and tossed the ball 20 yards to Bob Grieve, who caught it while running backward and barely staying inbounds. Grieve, an all-conference sprinter, spun and tightroped the sideline. The last man in pursuit was Berwanger, whose lunge failed to prevent a touchdown. Lindberg's kick for the extra-point missed low and wide, but Illinois held a 6-0 lead.

Chicago responded with some trickery from its own half of the field. Berwanger passed to Bill Gillerlain, who caught the ball and tossed a lateral toward a teammate. However, Illinois' Ken Nelson intercepted the pitch at the 25 and dashed for the nearest corner of the end zone. Had this play occurred in the 21st century, its conclusion would have been the subject of video review from multiple angles. Nelson appeared to simultaneously fumble the ball and go out of bounds at the Chicago 1. The ball rolled into the end zone, where a Chicago player fell on it. What was the call? An Illinois first down at the 1, or Chicago's ball on the 20 due to a touchback? Without benefit of instant replay, the officials convened to discuss what they saw. Finally, referee Fred Gardner announced the ruling: Nelson had fumbled before going out of bounds, and Chicago recovered the ball for a touchback. After the game, Gardner acknowledged that it was his most difficult decision in 23 years of officiating. The Maroons dodged that bullet, but they still trailed 6-0 with two minutes remaining in the third quarter.

The Maroons pinned the Illini deep in their own territory, and Lindberg punted out to Berwanger. The Dutchman caught the ball at midfield and embarked on a return nearly as exciting as his run against Ohio State two weeks earlier. He started left but immediately cut hard to the right and ran directly toward the right sideline. He turned left and headed upfield, shaking off a couple of would-be tacklers. When nearly cornered, he then made a small cut left, slipped through four Illini, turned right, and appeared to be in the clear for the game-tying touchdown. At least seven would-be tacklers got hands on him, three times causing him to stumble. However, an eighth opponent, Nelson, dove and made just enough contact to cause Berwanger to fall as he slid into the end zone. The Chicago contingent thought they had a touchdown, but the officials ruled that Berwanger landed at the 1-yard line. [112]

Though he didn't score on the play, the run was particularly satisfying and memorable for Berwanger because he pulled out an evasive maneuver he had practiced for years but never used in a game. A half-century later, he told an interviewer that during his two summers working at Camp Highlands for Boys, there was an assistant director who also coached football at a prep school. [113] "He taught me – or we worked on – a dodging maneuver. We worked on it for two years," Berwanger said. "It was a maneuver you could only use under certain conditions, and in this game, on that run I used it twice. And that was the first game he had ever seen me play. It was just coincidence. I had known how to do this particular maneuver but the circumstances were not such that I could do it except in that game." [114]

With Chicago in possession, first-and-goal just outside the Illinois 1, few doubted that Berwanger, calling signals in his last game, would get the ball. But Berwanger was a team player, and he figured that the Illinois defense would key on him. So he called

Berwanger posted a career average of 38 yards per punt. (Chicago Tribune photo. Reprinted with permission)

Duke Skoning's number. Fareed, crouching low behind his line, took the snap and handed off quickly to an onrushing Skoning. The Illinois defenders stuffed him. Chicago called the same play. The result was the same – Skoning was stopped. He had advanced the ball one foot on his two carries. Facing third down and about two feet short of a touchdown, Berwanger then took matters into his own hands. Standing five yards behind the center, Number 99 caught the snap, charged forward, and dove over the mass of linemen. No one could stop him. Berwanger rolled into the end zone for the game-tying touchdown. The teams lined up for the extra-point attempt. Center Sam Whiteside snapped the ball to Fareed, the holder, and Berwanger smoothly booted it through the uprights. Chicago moved ahead, 7-6, with the fourth quarter yet to play.

The final 15 minutes featured aerial assaults by Illinois and attempts by Chicago to drain the clock. Ewald Nyquist, like Berwanger playing his final game, was Chicago's defensive star of the quarter, intercepting Illinois passes on three consecutive throws. Chicago worked on a time-consuming ground game, with Berwanger hitting triple digits for the afternoon – 101 yards on 26 carries. Despite being denied twice at the goal line, Skoning had an outstanding afternoon, gaining 78 yards in 28 carries and providing key blocks for Berwanger. Late in the game, laboring to retain the ball, run out the clock, and protect their slim lead, the Maroons twice suffered delay-of-game penalties. But somehow they kept possession. Chicago still was on offense, on the Illini 15, when the official's pistol signaled the end of the game and Berwanger's collegiate football career.

Jubilant Chicago players and fans rushed onto the field. Their celebration was not for a championship. The win only gave the Maroons their third straight .500 season (4-4) and a 2-3 conference record. However, the moment was exciting and historic. In an instant, the celebrants hoisted Berwanger upon their shoulders. After taking in the scene, *Chicago Tribune* sports columnist Harvey Woodruff reported, "Even the majority of Illini rooters among the 12,000 fans present did not seem to begrudge the Chicago leader his hour of triumph in his final appearance, disappointed though they were that Les (Swede) Lindberg could not have had the satisfaction that went to Berwanger."

Disappointed in the loss – the referee's touchback ruling was particularly painful – and with the season failing to fulfill expectations (3-5 overall and 1-4 in the conference), Illinois coach Zuppke showed class. He offered high praise for the Maroons and especially their captain. "I rank Jay Berwanger with Red Grange as two of the greatest backs I have ever seen on a football field," he said. "Their styles were different, but each produced results and always were a constant threat to the competition. Both of them were also great defensive players." Zuppke said that throughout the week of preparation for Chicago, the Illini were in reality preparing only for Berwanger. "When any player asked me what he should do in any given situation, I had only one reply – 'Berwanger, Berwanger, just think of Berwanger.' It was by following that advice that Ken Nelson was able to intercept the lateral pass intended for Berwanger and to score the disallowed touchdown which every member of the Illinois team, myself, and a majority of the spectators think was earned." Nonetheless, as he had in previous years, Zuppke also complimented Chicago's sportsmanship. "It is a pleasure to play teams of their type. They were as gentlemanly a set of players as ever took the field."

Modest by 21st century standards, Berwanger's career statistics were impressive in the 1930s. He rushed for 1,839 yards - more than a mie - on 439 carries for an average of 4.2 yards He scored 22 touchdowns and kicked 20 extra points in his 23 varsity games. Berwanger averaged 38 yards on his punts and booted the ball an average of 46.3 yards on kickoffs.

Berwanger's rushing total would have been greater had he not been so honest. In one game, he tightroped the sideline for a long gain. The opponents complained that he stepped out of bounds early in the rush. The official didn't get a good look at it, so he simply asked him. Berwanger admitted he had, indeed, hit the chalk line, and justice was served.

Repeatedly asked throughout his long life to share his most memorable moment on the gridiron, Berwanger often cited his 85-yard touchdown in Chicago's near-upset of Ohio State. But in his next breath he talked about his final game, the victory over Illinois in 1935.

CHAPTER 29

Postseason honors for Berwanger poured in. If there was an All-America team for 1935, Berwanger was on it. The most prestigious were those picked by committees headed by Christy Walsh and by Grantland Rice, whose All-America program traced its roots to the original Walter Camp squad of 1889. Wrote Rice, "Jay Berwanger of Chicago was the ablest all-around back of the entire crop. He could do more things brilliantly and he had little help. On Minnesota, Princeton or LSU he would still be running." In addition to Berwanger at halfback, the others on Rice's team were ends Gaynell Tinsley of Louisiana State and James "Monk" Moscrip of Stanford, tackles Richard Smith of Minnesota and Truman Spain of Southern Methodist, guards John Weller of Princeton and Inwood Smith of Ohio State, center Darrell Lester of Texas Christian, quarterback Riley Smith of Alabama, halfback Robert Wilson of Southern Methodist, and fullback Robert Grayson of Stanford.

The North American Newspaper Alliance panel – Andy Kerr of Colgate, Dan McGugin of Vanderbilt, James Phelan of Washington, and Gus Dorais of Detroit – said of Berwanger: "Probably the best all-around back in the country. Working with a weak team, and constantly watched by the opposition, he couldn't be checked. He could pass, run, kick, block, and tackle. He gained a mile of ground with the ball and was a menace every minute to Chicago's strongest foes."

Other All-America squads in which Berwanger was a first-team selection were those of the Walter Camp Football Foundation, International News Service, Newspaper Enterprise Association, United Press, Associated Press, Central Press (selected by captains of leading university teams), *Young America* magazine (picked by Princeton coach Herb "Fritz" Crisler), *New York Sun* (which named Berwanger the best all-around player), the international Pathe News (picked by a panel of coaches), and *Kansas City Star*. Even though Berwanger never played farther west than Nebraska, the student newspaper of the University of Southern California, the *Daily Trojan*, made him a unanimous first-team All-America selection. All this came on top of Berwanger's second consecutive first-team all-conference berth, which was announced just before his final game, and coaches' selection as league Most Valuable Player.

Thanksgiving arrived a few days after Berwanger's final collegiate game, and he returned home for the break. Civic leaders hosted a banquet in his honor the Friday night after Thanksgiving at the Dubuque Club, southwest corner of Ninth and Locust streets. Outside the banquet hall, which was decorated in Chicago's colors, Berwanger sat down for an interview with the sports editor of his hometown newspaper, the *Telegraph-Herald*. A few early arrivals for the banquet listened in. "The giant Dubuquer displaying a bronze skin, a pair of massive shoulders and a well-developed neck, appeared in perfect condition and showed not a welt or scar from the three years of Western conference football warring he had concluded against Illinois a week ago Saturday," the scribe noted.

Berwanger denied rumors that he would coach at Princeton or play for one of Chicago's two professional teams, the Bears or Cardinals, mentioning that Big Ten rules prohibit soliciting players in season. He said his attention was turning to graduating and trying out for the 1936 Olympics, noting that he planned to focus on the high jump, where his best mark was 5-foot-10. His small audience was surprised when Berwanger offered a two-pronged answer to the question, "Who hit you the hardest when you were making a tackle?" In a conference game, he answered, it was Ohio State's Dick Heekin. However, he added that the hardest hit he ever suffered occurred in a collision with a 210-pound teammate named Goodsten during a practice session.

When the sportswriter asked about his love life, Berwanger laughed and patiently answered, "No, although my fraternity brothers are willing to bet money I will be married within a year. Of course I date but I have never taken this matter seriously." He finished tongue in cheek: "I used to get fan mail until the metropolitan papers started to run my picture and now never a letter do I get!"

When the banquet began at 7 p.m., every table was filled. Displayed on the wall behind the head table was a Chicago jersey bearing Number 99. The master of ceremonies was Dubuque lawyer Allan Kane, a former state legislator, school board president, and county prosecutor. The program opened with the singing of the national anthem, the college fight songs of Chicago and – after all, this was an Iowa-based group – the University of Iowa. Before the evening ended, alumni of Wisconsin and Michigan had their chances to belt out their fight songs.

The first speakers were C.A. Richards, University of Chicago Class of 1901, who referred to the honor that Dubuque has secured because of Berwanger, and Dubuque dentist Max Kadesky, an all-conference and Walter Camp third-team All-America at Iowa (1922), who shared the "Watch Berwanger" anecdote about the Ohio State game. The Rev. Mathias M. Hoffmann, of Columbia (now Loras) College, stated that Berwanger represented the ideal of modern American youth. A sound mind comes from a sound body, Father Hoffmann noted, and no better example could be found than Berwanger. Lawyer Robert Clewell referred to the rivalry between the University of Chicago and his alma mater, the University of Michigan, and said, "Jay typifies the spirit of Midwestern schools."

With the program in the homestretch, the most moving remarks came from a man who had not planned to give a speech – Berwanger's high school coach, Wilbur Dalzell. However Dalzell stepped up and said that a few years ago he came across a particular poem. He decided to save it until an occasion he was sure would occur – a program to honor Berwanger. The poem was "A Real Man," by Edgar A. Guest. It read in part:

> *Men are of two kinds, and he*
> *Was of the kind I'd like to be*
> *Some preach their virtues, and a few*
> *Express their lives by what they do.*
>
> *That sort was he. No flowery phrase*
> *Or glibly spoken words of praise*
> *Won friends for him. He wasn't cheap*
> *Or shallow, but his course ran deep,*
>
> *And it was pure. You know the kind.*
> *Not many in a life you find*
> *Whose deeds outrun their words so far*
> *That more than what they seem they are.*
>
> *No back door gossip linked his name*
> *With any shady tale of shame.*

He did not have to compromise
With evil-doers, shrewd and wise,

No broken pledge lost him respect,
He met all men with head erect,
And when he passes I think there will be sent
A soul to yonder firmament.

After all the other speeches, master of ceremonies Kane gave a litany of Berwanger's accomplishments on and off the gridiron. Finally, he invited the guest of honor to the microphone.[115] As the waves of applause continued, Berwanger became "visibly affected," the local newspaper noted, "and it was with difficulty he could get through his expression of gratitude so happy was the young man." After all the speeches, Berwanger stuck around "until the late hours" to answer questions from the guests.

After Thanksgiving weekend, Berwanger returned to Chicago and joined

his teammates at a couple of major banquets. The 55th Street Business Men's Association feted them at their 12th annual dinner-dance at the Del Prado Hotel. The next night, a record 1,132 guests jammed the Hotel Sherman ballroom for the Alumni Council's annual football dinner.

The recruiting potential of an event featuring the nation's top football player could not be overlooked; about 60 high school athletes accepted the alumni's invitation to the banquet. Student tickets sold for a dollar. The event was unique in that attendees

After Liberty Magazine named Berwanger to its 1935 All-America team, Thomas J. Courtney, Cook County state's attorney, made the award presentation. Berwanger was the only consensus all-America player that season. (Chicago Tribune photo. Reprinted with permission)

got the silent treatment: No one gave a speech. The entire program consisted of game films from the Maroons' 1935 season. Even the movies were silent. Of course, they featured Berwanger's many outstanding plays, including his 85-yard touchdown against Ohio State and his long punt return and touchdown in the victory over Illinois. Organizers showed every play of the Illinois game.

At the banquet, the Chicago players voted Berwanger their Most Valuable Player – an honor they denied him the previous year, even when he was named captain of Walsh's All-America team. As such, Berwanger became his school's candidate for the *Chicago Tribune's* Silver Football, awarded to the Big Ten player most valuable to his team. He won in a landslide. *Tribune* sports columnist Harvey T. Woodruff presented Berwanger the Silver Football trophy at halftime of the Chicago-Wisconsin basketball game a month later. Before removing the Number 99 jersey draped over the trophy, Woodruff said, "There are many who will think that he is the greatest player who ever won it." That included the inaugural Silver Football winner, Red Grange of Illinois (1924), who himself praised Berwanger, noting that the Dutchman had "that faraway look" that seemed to allow him to assess what was developing for him downfield. "He had a rare gait," Grange said. "A change of pace is not, as some people believe, running slow or medium speed one second and fast the next. It is running hard at top speed and then reaching down within the body and getting an extra burst of momentum to flash past or between defensive men. Berwanger also has an uncanny ability of hitting a hole that was closing on him. His feet would skim the ground lightly, in momentary hesitation when blockers or tacklers were locked in front of him, then he would be away in a flash when a slit of an opening showed."[116] For years afterward, at least until the aura of the Heisman Trophy later elevated his celebrity, Berwanger said that he considered the Silver Football his proudest achievement.

Bob Ray, sports columnist in the *Los Angeles Times*, noted that when Elmer Layden, the Notre Dame coach, included the Dutchman among his All-Midwest picks, he said, "It is said of Berwanger that he never made a mistake in judgment in his football career." Ray responded, "I'll always believe that Berwanger made a mistake when he went to the University of Chicago without taking at least 10 other football players with him." George Kirksey of United Press described Berwanger as the season's "greatest individual player," noting that the Dutchman "made a weak team dangerous." Berwanger was often the top vote-getter in balloting for various all-something teams. When

Hearst newspapers tabulated the more than 200 ballots submitted by grid-iron experts from around the country, Berwanger was a first-team selection on 85 percent of them.

About the only recognition that Berwanger did not receive was an honor he won in 1934: captain of Walsh's All-America team. He made the first team again, but in 1935 its members made Stanford's Robert Grayson the captain. Berwanger received an invitation to play in the Shriners all-star game in San Francisco on New Year's Day, but he had to decline, lest he lose his collegiate eligibility for the 1936 track season.

For the second consecutive year, sportswriters and "other experts" selected Berwanger the Big Ten's top overall athlete. He made most of his headlines in football, certainly, but his efforts on the track complemented his re-sumé. The runner-up for the Big Ten honor was Ohio State track star Jesse Owens. Apparently, the selection panel somehow felt that breaking three world records and tying a fourth in a 45-minute span did not measure up to Berwanger's achievements. Comparing track records to those on the gridiron is an apples-and-oranges exercise, but was racial bias a factor? Owens, the multiple world-record holder, was African-American – as was the runner-up to Berwanger the previous year, Willis Ward of Michigan. There was also the matter of whether Owens' summer job at the Ohio statehouse was on the up-and-up.[117] Seventy-five years later, prejudice has not been proven. How-ever, Owens topped Berwanger in one national vote, The Associated Press poll to select the outstanding athlete of 1935. Boxing champion Joe Louis topped the list with 184 points, followed by amateur golfer Lawson Little (135), Owens (61), and Berwanger (42). Mickey Cochrane, player-manager of the World Series champion Detroit Tigers, rounded out the top five (19).

As football recognition for Berwanger poured in during the first week of December, he was elected president of the University of Chicago Senior Class. No one ran against him. The president's official duties were limited – primarily heading the fund drive for the class gift, overseeing the second annual Midway Fandango fundraiser, and being involved in a high school promotional campaign. Described by the student newspaper as "Chicago's All-American both on and off the gridiron," Berwanger became the third straight football player to serve as the senior class president, following Wayne Rapp and then Ellmore Patterson.

After the release of various All-America teams, another committee went to work on behalf of *Liberty* magazine, polling players who had faced an All-America opponent. After those ballots were tabulated, Berwanger was named the recipient of the Douglas Fairbanks Trophy. He also received a gold medal, two inches tall and seven-eighths of an inch wide. The front depicted the Fairbanks Trophy. The back side of the medal, reflecting some misunderstanding of Berwanger's legal name and nickname, carried this inscription:

JAY J. BERWANGER
HALFBACK
UNIVERSITY OF CHICAGO
1935
ADJUDGED THE MOST VALUABLE
FOOTBALL PLAYER IN THE
UNITED STATES

The Fairbanks Trophy, established four years earlier, was moving toward becoming the nation's foremost award for an individual football player. However, before long, a little-known organization's award eclipsed the Fairbanks.

Inscription on the front and back of the medal that went with Berwanger's selection for the 1935 Douglas Fairbanks Trophy, recognizing his selection as the country's best player. At the time, the Fairbanks Trophy was better known than the Downtown Athletic Club Trophy, which the next year was renamed the Heisman Trophy. (Author's photo)

When Berwanger received the 1935 Silver Football Award, sponsored by the Chicago Tribune, he considered it foremost of all his honors. As time passed, the first Heisman Trophy superseded it. From left: Clark Shaughnessy, Berwanger, Harvey Woodruff of the Chicago Tribune, and athletic director T. Nelson Metcalf. (Chicago Tribune photo. Reprinted with permission)

Of all the awards Berwanger received in 1935, at the time he was most proud of the Silver Football Award, presented by the Chicago Tribune to "The Most Useful Player to His Team in the Big Ten." (Courtesy of the College Football Hall of Fame)

CHAPTER 30

Announcements of Berwanger's selection to several All-America teams, as well as his election by acclamation to the senior class presidency, filled the first week of December 1935. Amid all that, a messenger delivered a telegram for him to the Psi Upsilon house. It was a message of congratulations from an organization that Berwanger likely had never heard of, the Downtown Athletic Club. The New York City-based club, whose athletic director was retired national champion coach John W. Heisman, notified him that he was the winner of the first Downtown Athletic Club Trophy, awarded to the best college football player east of the Mississippi River. Heisman had initiated the process at the direction of club members, who believed such an award would enhance the club's visibility and status. Heisman resisted the idea at first, believing individual recognition ran contrary to the values of team play. He was eventually persuaded.[118] Sixty-five sportswriters participated in the initial selection. Berwanger amassed 84 points, easily beating Monk Meyer, Army's 140-pound junior (29 points), Notre Dame senior halfback William Shakespeare (23), and Pepper Constable, a senior fullback for Princeton (20).[119]

Compared to the All-America teams of Grantland Rice and Christy Walsh and even the award Berwanger so cherished, the *Chicago Tribune's* Silver Football, the Downtown Athletic Club Trophy was second-tier at best. Most sports editors treated the club's announcement of Berwanger's selection as no better than a filler article. The *Washington Post* tucked a one-sentence item about the selection at the bottom of its lead sports page. In the club's host city, *The New York Times* did about the same, squeezing in three paragraphs between a filler concerning Notre Dame's 1936 football schedule and scores of college and prep basketball and field hockey games. *The Chicago Tribune* gave the award two paragraphs at the bottom of its front sports page, under the college basketball scorelines and beside a filler reporting the

When leaders of New York's Downtown Athletic Club decided to establish a college football award, they wanted something special – not just another plaque or loving cup. They commissioned 23-year-old Frank Eliscu, who created what for decades has been the most recognized award in American sports. (Courtesy of Norma Banas, daughter of Frank Eliscu)

New York Celtics' 39-31 basketball victory over Duffy Florals, a Chicago club that had just turned professional, in the 132nd Regiment Armory.[120] Nonetheless, the award generated some buzz. A Heisman history noted that leading comedian Eddie Cantor was excited to use his national radio program to announce Berwanger's selection for the trophy.[121]

The trophy was the creation of Frank Eliscu, a 23-year-old sculptor commissioned by the Downtown Athletic Club. Members believed another plaque or loving cup just would not do. They wanted an iconic award, one depicting a powerful football player. After receiving a club committee's initial approval on his design, Eliscu showed it to Fordham coach Jim Crowley, one of the Four Horseman from Notre Dame, who in turn asked for feedback from his players. Eliscu then made a plaster cast. Less than a month before the award luncheon, the cast passed muster with Notre Dame coach Elmer Layden, another of the Four Horseman, as well as his Irish team, who were in New York to play Army. With the endorsement of leading coaches and players, Eliscu in mid-November 1935 received the club's final go-ahead to make the bronze statue.[122]

Over the years, some contended that it is Berwanger's likeness on the trophy. The chronology is problematic. Eliscu had started work on the statue, using New York University's Ed Smith as his model, months before balloting took place. However, Berwanger claimed in a 1979 interview that the sculptor asked Smith to strike a pose like that he had seen in a publicity photo of Berwanger. However, that pose was one that photographers occasionally set up for publicity shots; it was not unique to Berwanger, though Berwanger's fame caused more people to see him in that pose than other players. For example, *The Herald-Examiner* of October 1, 1934, printed a photo of New York Univerity's Bob Pastor striking a more Heisman-like pose. In any case, years later Eliscu said of the trophy, "It is not my best work but it turned out to be something like the Statue of Liberty. I always thought it was wonderful that I'll be able to leave something like this behind."[123]

At the time, Berwanger considered the real prize of the Downtown

Athletic Club honor not the trophy but the expense-paid trip to New York City for him and his coach, Clark Shaughnessy. Berwanger was thrilled. Like most Americans, he had never been in an airplane. Berwanger and Shaughnessy arrived in New York the day before the award luncheon. Despite being booked for that event plus another luncheon and a banquet, Berwanger found time to see some of the sights of New York City, which was crowded with holiday shoppers. Despite the continuing Depression, retailers were happy: With two weeks remaining, the 1935 Christmas season was shaping up to be their strongest since 1930. Another positive factor was that below-average temperatures in the Northeast contributed to a spike in clothing sales. Macy's Department store featured women's pigskin gloves for $2.98 a pair and hand-knit Shetland cardigans for $9.34. A shopper taking a break could stop in at one of the nine Longchamps restaurants, where the special was a baked spring lamb pot pie "with freshest vegetables" for just 85 cents.

When it was presented to Jay Berwanger in 1935, it was known as the Downtown Athletic Club Trophy. It was renamed the Heisman Memorial Trophy the next year. (Special Collections Research Center, University of Chicago Library)

Berwanger didn't mention partaking in a pot pie, but years later he recalled visits to Times Square; Statue of Liberty; the posh Twenty-One Club, where he toured the former speakeasy's wine cellar; and, of special interest to a 21-year-old American male, a rehearsal of the Rockettes.

Coincidental with Berwanger's visit to New York was news of accusations by the father of former Harvard star George Owen, Jr., that big-time college football was just a racket awash in money. The senior Owen, a professor at the Massachusetts Institute of Technology, excoriated several programs, including Notre Dame, Ohio State, and his son's alma mater, Harvard. Owen, speaking to the Cambridge Industrial Association, alleged that a promising football player was paid $1,000 or handed a job involving little or no work. Owen proposed simply hiring college athletes. "It would be honest, and the public doesn't care who the players are or where they come from. Every college in the country that has a major football team is indulging in commercialism and trying to cover it up." One conference moved toward Owen's solution when the Southeastern decided to out-and-out award athletic scholarships. A few days after Berwanger's trip to New York, the presidents and representatives of Big Ten schools convened and roundly rejected doing likewise; among the minority voters was Glenn Frank of Wisconsin.

The first Downtown Athletic Club Trophy luncheon was held at noon Tuesday, December 10, 1935, in the club's five-year-old structure at 19 West Street in lower Manhattan. Due to high real estate prices, club members could afford only a relatively small lot, so they built their headquarters "up" rather than "out." The 35-story building was narrow, necessitating the placement of various athletic facilities (swimming pool, squash courts, workout rooms) on separate floors.

About 1,000 people attended the luncheon,

Within a year after Berwanger accepted the Downtown Athletic Club Trophy, the award was renamed the Heisman Memorial Trophy. (Corbis Images)

filling two rooms and overflowing into a third. Sportscaster Ted "Mile a Minute" Husing served as master of ceremonies. Radio station WABC opened its live broadcast of the proceedings at 1 p.m. Several active and retired football stars with New York connections attended. Christian "Red" Cagle, who with John Heisman and others had founded the Touchdown Club of New York two years earlier, was on hand. Also present were three members of the New York Giants, Ken Strong, Harry Newman, and Ed Danowski. Paul Moss, the city's powerful License Commissioner, stood in for Mayor Fiorello La Guardia.

Speaker after speaker came forward to sing Berwanger's praises. Alan Gould, general sports editor of The Associated Press, hailed him as the only player unanimously picked for All-America recognition in 1935. In his article, Gould quoted Shaughnessy: "The best thing about Berwanger is that he's unspoiled by all this. He's a great kid as well as a natural athlete and good student." Pat Robinson, covering the luncheon for the International News Service, came away impressed. "Not in many long years has any football star caught the fancy of the American public as has this youngster from the corn belt." After listening to all the adulation heaped on the young man from Iowa, Robinson wrote, "Discounting these rave notices by 99 percent I still believe the young man is quite a footballer. But what impressed me even more – he's quite a man. There is little, if any, of the ego of the run-of-the-mine gridiron star about him. He seems modest, unassuming and as hard-headed as the stock from which he springs." When it was his turn to speak, Shaughnessy talked about the greatest player he had ever coached (and ever would), noting that he was also the finest young man he had ever known.

The guest of honor appeared embarrassed by all the attention. Then again, as a *New York Times* reporter observed, he didn't mind it, either. At last, it was time for presentation of the Downtown Athletic Club Trophy. Club president Walter L. Conwell did the honors. Berwanger's acceptance remarks were delivered in a quiet and modest tone. The afternoon included plenty of picture-taking, with a smiling Berwanger posing with his award, which the *Times* described as "a handsome sculpture." (The *Times* relegated its account to the fourth sports page. The lead story concerned baseball: trades that sent Jimmy Foxx to the Red Sox and Al Simmons to the Detroit Tigers and new leadership for the financially struggling Boston Braves.)

Berwanger's trophy was 14 inches long, 13½ inches high, and, with its onyx base, about 60 pounds. Lugging the trophy around New York was a bit of a problem for the visitors from Chicago, but it was a burden they gladly accepted. (In later years, Downtown Athletic Club officials reduced its weight to 45 pounds by changing the trophy's base from onyx to wood painted black.[124]) Whatever its weight and its base, the trophy has become the most recognizable award in American sports.

Celebration of Berwanger continued that evening. He was the guest of honor at the annual dinner of the Touchdown Club of New York. Heisman presided over the proceedings in the Hotel Martinique, West 32nd Street and Broadway, a block south of the Empire State Building. The banquet attracted about 200 Touchdown Club members and guests. The long roster of speakers included Shaughnessy; coach Arthur "Dutch" Bergman, whose Catholic University team a few weeks later would hold off a Mississippi rally for a 20-19 victory in the second Orange Bowl game; and, of course, Berwanger. On hand were many luminaries from football seasons gone by, including Harry Carr, who in 1906 scored Ohio State's first touchdown on a forward pass, and 72-year-old Hector Cowan, the Princeton tackle who made the first All-America team in 1889.

Shaughnessy and Berwanger were happy to see a familiar face in the banquet hall: Ellmore Patterson, Berwanger's predecessor as Chicago football captain, MVP, and senior class president. Now a New Yorker, Patterson was in the early stages of his rise to the top of the banking profession. The following afternoon, Patterson had the honor of introducing Shaughnessy and Berwanger at a luncheon gathering of the University of Chicago Club of New York. The venue was the 2,000-room Hotel Commodore, 42nd and Lexington, which decades later became real estate developer Donald Trump's Grand Hyatt Hotel.

Reporters in New York, noting that coach Paul Schissler of the National Football League's Brooklyn Dodgers paid Berwanger a call, quizzed the player about his future. He mostly deflected questions about the possibility of playing professionally, allowing only that he might consider it, but that his immediate focus was graduating on time and winning a spot on the U.S. Olympic team. He needed to get busy.

CHAPTER 31

Speculation grew concerning Berwanger's future. Playing pro football? Coaching? Competing in the 1936 Olympics? Working in the business world? Nearly any rumor was worthy of some ink. Edward Stern told his *Daily Maroon* readers that Detroit automaker Walter Chrysler had offered Berwanger a job. There was some basis for that one: Coaches of the National Football League's Detroit Lions hosted Berwanger at a Chicago Bears game and suggested that, if he became a Lion, there could be a job for him with the automaker Chrysler.[125] Other possibilities centered on an individual with a similar last name, Fritz Crisler. The head coach at Princeton and a University of Chicago alumnus, Crisler reportedly was interested in having Berwanger as an assistant coach. Other rumors found their way into the papers. "Professor James Weber Linn and many other followers of Maroon football have stated that they would like to see Berwanger play football for a Chicago professional team at least for a couple of years," Stern noted. "Is this not a selfish attitude to take? For whereas the football fans will lose by not being able to see Berwanger in action on the gridiron, he will gain by the experience he will be getting working in a business which will guarantee him a future." The campus sportswriter noted that the Big Ten rescinded its ban on former professional players from coaching in the conference but added, "In fact, why shouldn't he enter the coaching field immediately? Obviously, this is a possibility, but although the business of coaching offers many unusual opportunities, are not the ones offered by a great corporation more formidable?"

There were many who hoped that Berwanger would not play professionally. They considered pro sports as contrary to the ideals of competing for the love of the game. The rough-hewn status of professional football particularly cast a coarse and a negative reflection on its players. One who held that opinion was Illinois coach Bob Zuppke, who a decade earlier saw his star Red Grange drop out of school after his last collegiate game and join the Chicago Bears. Still, Berwanger did not rule out pro football. He said that after graduating and trying for the Olympics, he would consider the NFL "if there's enough money in it."

Berwanger's celebrity, especially in the Chicago area, was so great that his name was not limited to the sports section. Hugo Westerberg, purportedly an expert in physiognomy, the theory that personality and character could be assessed or predicted by facial characteristics, had a regular column in the *Chicago Tribune*. After expanding upon his previous comments on "light eyebrows" – which he said suggested shyness but also imagination and creativity, Westerberg discussed the best player in college football. "Jay Berwanger … has all the facial marks indicative of business ability and few that may be considered handicaps. The most important part, the mouth, is strongly and harmoniously developed, with a long upper lip (measured from the red part up to the intersection with the lower line of the nose), a solid lower lip, and heavy muscles at the corners of the mouth. His eyes are somewhat covered, indicating an observant but at the same time distrustful attitude."

Chatter about Berwanger entering the professional ranks picked up in early February 1936, when the National Football League made him the first selection in the first-ever player draft. The draft, the brainchild of Bert Bell, owner of the lowly Philadelphia Eagles, allowed the team with the worst record in 1935 to receive first pick among eligible players. Selections continued through several rounds, with teams picking, worst to first, until all the names on the meeting room's blackboard were selected or rejected. Bell had a tough time getting his fellow owners to implement the draft. It took some arm-twisting by George Halas of the Chicago Bears on Tom Mara of the New York Giants for the draft to win approval in May 1935, effective with the 1936 season. Fatigue and alcohol also might have influenced the decision. League meetings were loosely run nocturnal affairs, where drink was plentiful and sleep was scarce, and that played into the hands of Bell, a sober "nighttime" person. Bell's 1935 Philadelphia Eagles finished 2-9, edging the Boston Redskins (2-8-1) for the first pick in the first draft.[126]

League owners conducted the draft the weekend of February 8-9 at the Ritz Carlton in Philadelphia. The hotel was owned by Bell's father, Cromwell, and Bell had served as hotel manager in addition to playing and coaching football.[127] The names of about 90 players went onto the blackboard, and the draft began. To no one's surprise, Bell picked Berwanger.

1936 NFL Draft Round 1

1. Philadelphia Eagles: Jay Berwanger, back, Chicago;
2. Boston Redskins: Riley Smith, back, Alabama;
3. Pittsburgh Pirates: Bill Shakespeare, back, Notre Dame;
4. Brooklyn Dodgers: Dick Crayne, back, Iowa;
5. Chicago Cardinals: Jim Lawrence, back, Texas Christian;
6. Chicago Bears: Joe Stydahar, tackle, West Virginia;
7. Green Bay Packers: Russ Letlow, guard, San Francisco;
8. Detroit Lions: Sid Wagner, guard, Michigan State;
9. New York Giants: Art Lewis, tackle, Ohio University.

There was only one problem with Bell's choice. According to biographer Robert Lyons, the Eagles owner had not bothered to ascertain whether Berwanger was even interested in playing professional football. There are at least two possible reasons for this apparent oversight. One is that Bell hadn't read any of the many sports articles reporting Berwanger's statements indicating limited interest in turning professional – an unlikely prospect for one of the game's management innovators and a future National Football League commissioner. The other, as claimed a dozen years later by Francis J. Powers and Ed Prell in *Sport* magazine, was that Bell never intended to sign Berwanger. Instead, by prior secret agreement with Halas, Bell made the selection so he could trade his rights to Berwanger to the Chicago Bears. There were reports that Berwanger was expecting $1,000 a game – about 10 times the average rate – and that Bell, expecting to be rejected, went through the motions by offering the Dutchman $150 per contest. Whether Halas and Bell had worked it out in advance, or whether Bell listened to overtures from other owners, the Eagles and Bears consummated a deal. Bell received Art Buss, a third-year tackle, plus cash, and Halas got his chance to sign Berwanger.[128] Powers reported that the Bears owner had a conversation with Berwanger several weeks before the draft, "but at that time the Maroon was too busy with his class work and ambitions to win a place on the Olympic track team to bother with football." Powers predicted that Berwanger would join the Bears – not for $1,000 a game but the $500 a contest already paid the league's best players.

Later, Berwanger and Halas engaged in an impromptu conversation in a hotel lobby. Berwanger and a date were heading to a party, and Papa Bear, accompanied by Mrs. Halas, was on his way to another function. After pleasantries and introductions, Halas asked the 21-year-old his contract expectations. Berwanger replied it would take $25,000 over two years – and a no-cut contract. Berwanger recalled Halas' response: "He looked at my date and said, 'Nice to see you. Have a good time at the party.'" That was the extent of their contract negotiations. They never talked about it again. A half-century later, discussing his salary "demands," Berwanger confessed, "I had my tongue in my cheek. I was being facetious when I made that remark. Maybe it was the pixie in me coming out. I wanted it to be known I wasn't interested in playing (pro) ball."[129] In a later interview, he told Beano Cook, "I would have played for that money, but there was no way, because of the Depression, that he (Halas) could have paid it." Asked if he ever wished he had gone ahead and played professionally, Berwanger said he had one regret only: Timing. When his opportunity arrived, there was "no money" for players. "If it had been 30 years later, I would have played pro football."[130] Despite Berwanger's clarifications, contemporary books and blogs still report that Berwanger and Halas engaged in a "contract dispute" and refer to the player's salary "demands."

Berwanger also noted that professional football, which was coming out of its "low-class reputation," was not a full-time occupation. Players couldn't earn enough on their athletic skills alone, so they needed to find supplemental employment. "A good company wouldn't want you if you were a pro football player," he said. It wasn't because the man was a football player as much as it was the employer did not want the distraction and inconvenience of having a worker who needed time away. "They wanted you to work six days a week. They wanted 150 percent out of you, rather than 80 percent. You couldn't hold down a job and play pro football." The marketing opportunities of having a pro football player on the payroll were still limited. For Berwanger, the bottom line was this: "I had other things that I wanted to do, and pro football just didn't fit into the picture."[131]

After trading a player and cash for the rights to Berwanger and coming up empty, Halas handled matters differently when a similar opportunity arose a year later. He traded Bill Hewitt to the Eagles, who again finished last in the NFL, for the rights to the top draft pick of 1937, Nebraska's Sam Francis. This time, Papa Bear made the deal contingent on Francis actually reporting to the Bears. Francis did, and played with three NFL teams over four seasons: Chicago, Pittsburgh and Brooklyn. Hewitt, meanwhile, played his way into the Pro Football Hall of Fame.

CHAPTER 32

At the end of 1935, Berwanger considered temporarily dropping out of the University of Chicago for an academic term or two so he could concentrate on training for the Olympics. Administrators were not enthusiastic about the idea of having their best-known undergraduate – not to mention the president of the senior class – leave the university. Berwanger years later recalled the conversation with a vice president, who, among other points, informed him that he would not be permitted to extend his full academic scholarship. "We had a long discussion around Christmastime," Berwanger said with a wry smile, "and *we* decided I should graduate."[132]

Thus, Berwanger would have to train for the U.S. Olympic decathlon team while representing the Maroons track team, taking classes and serving as class president. In addition to advice from volunteer coach J. Austin Menaul, a former Olympic decathlete, Berwanger received pointers in the pole vault from world record-holder Keith Brown. As a Yale senior the previous season, Brown and his bamboo pole set the world mark of 14-5 ⅛. Brown was part of a long line of outstanding Yale pole vaulters, including 1928 Olympic champion Sabin Carr, who, like Berwanger, was a product of Dubuque High. Having just taken a full-time job in Chicago with Procter & Gamble, Brown received permission to use Chicago's facilities to train for his bid to make the 1936 Olympic team.[133] In late March, a panel of coaches surveyed by The Associated Press predicted that Brown would make the Olympic team; the same coaches picked Berwanger in the decathlon. However, Brown soon concluded, that his job hindered his training, so much he retired.

In his role as president of the Class of 1936, Berwanger had to be out front in one item of unpleasant business – the cancellation of the second annual Midway Fandango, the spring festival and fundraiser. Administrators put its organizers on notice that the university would not tolerate "presence of or association with professional promoters excepting those who may provide the rides concessions" and the presence of any gambling devices "such as slot machines, Chuck-a-luck and others." They also demanded that the festival be cut from three nights to two. Aware that half the $2,400 raised in the inaugural Fandango came from the games of chance, which attracted a substantial number of non-university patrons, student organizers reluctantly threw in the towel.

The senior class was not alone in wrestling with money problems. The track team faced a tight budget. *The Maroon* reported that budget considerations might cause coach Ned Merriam to limit how many athletes he would take on away meets. One story, perhaps embellished but nonetheless reflecting the times, had Merriam handing Athletic Director T. Nelson Metcalf a travel expense report. The administrator scrutinized the document until his eye caught a large number. "What is this for, Ned?" The coach replied that it was the hotel bill. Metcalf set aside the report and said, "In general, it's all very fine, Ned. But in the future don't buy any more hotels." In reality, hotel bills for the track squad were rare. Most of the Maroons' competitions – even

the 1936 national championships – were held on their own campus.

Berwanger no longer raced the high hurdles, and he entered more field events than races, perhaps a concession to the injuries that were pestering him and so he could concentrate on improving in the field events contested in decathlons. He tended to earn his highest places in the shot put; he notched his lifetime best of 48-8½ in February. With 21st

His University of Chicago football career concluded, Berwanger turned his attention to track and field and making the 1936 U.S. Olympic decathlon team. The discus throw is among the decathlon events. (Chicago Tribune photo. Reprinted with permission)

century coaching, conditioning, and athletic training programs, he might have been able to shake his physical problems more quickly. His friend Ernie Dix decades later noted that simply keeping his muscles warm and not sitting around between events would have been a start.[134]

His indoor season opener, a home dual meet loss to Notre Dame, took place the weekend when Berwanger became the first selection of the first National Football League draft. He was shut out in the 60 but collected a first (long jump, 22-7) and a second (shot put, 45-2¼). However, the meet's spotlight landed squarely on Chicago sophomore Ray Ellinwood, a transfer student from Purdue. In his first varsity race ever, Ellinwood ran 440 yards in 49 seconds flat – an indoor world record.

About this time, the anticipated conflict in Berwanger's athletic schedule and other commitments created a minor buzz on campus. He was due to lead the Grand March at the 36th annual Washington Prom at the same time the track team was scheduled to compete at the University of Iowa. Some said that Berwanger would skip the prom in favor of the track meet. Others speculated that the track meet's schedule of events would be changed so that he could speed the highways (or even fly) back to Chicago, where the prom's Grand March was not scheduled to step off until 1:30 a.m. Ultimately, Berwanger did not have to hurry. Chicago and Iowa officials mutually agreed to move up the meet one day. The reason for the change was not disclosed. In his only collegiate competition of any kind in his native Iowa, Berwanger had a busy evening, entering six events and scoring in three of them. He won the shot put (45-10¾), tied for first in the pole vault (11-6), and placed third in the long jump (22-1¾).

The next night, Berwanger donned a tuxedo for the prom at the Lake Shore Athletic Club, a spacious private facility eight miles north of campus along North Lake Shore Drive. The gala, with bids going for $5, started at 10 p.m. on a Friday and ended at 3:30 Saturday morning. Organizers booked two bands. The first was Charles Gaylord's, which played from 10 p.m. until 1:15 a.m. Scheduled to play next, after its final set at the Urban Room in the Congress Hotel, was one of the nation's hottest bands, that of Benny Goodman, the "King of Swing." Goodman's career had taken off the previous summer, and he was wildly popular with the prep and collegiate set. The Benny Goodman Orchestra played for the Grand March, during which Berwanger escorted Barbara Vail.

On the Midway and across the country, Berwanger continued to receive attention. The day of the Washington Prom, a photo of Berwanger, sprinting in his track uniform, appeared on the cover of *Collegiate Digest*, a publication inserted into campus newspapers nationwide. A few days later, at the annual banquet of the University of Chicago Alumni Association, the group presented Berwanger its dreamed-up Master of Football Arts degree. The Dutchman's name continued to appear regularly in the campus newspaper's gossip columns. "The leading rumor in re Jay is that the big boy is turning down the pros to play around in the Loop," wrote "Gulliver" in the *Daily Maroon*. "The other day we saw him fail to bluff the meek little Harper (Library) elevator man into taking up a book for him." "Gulliver" also claimed that when he eats, Berwanger counts his "chews." ("Gulliver" later revealed himself as Cody Pfanstiehl. University officials somehow discovered that Pfanstiehl, who happened to be a relative of Berwanger's future mother-in-law, was not a registered student. However, they liked his work so well that they hired him to do publicity work. For the last 21 years of his professional career, Pfanstiehl was the spokesman for the District of Columbia's Metro transit system.)

After victories over Purdue and Northwestern in home dual meets, Chicago hosted the Big Ten indoor championships. Entered in the 60, shot put and pole vault, Berwanger had a terrible meet, failing to make any finals. His 35-5¾ toss in the shot put, 13 feet short of his lifetime best, brought a dismal end to final season of indoor track.

Whatever troubles the Dutchman had in the Big Ten meet, he left them in the Chicago fieldhouse. Merriam took a small delegation to Texas for a couple of late-March meets – a tune-up dual in Denton and then the Texas Relays. Against North Texas State Teachers College (now the University of North Texas), Berwanger, who had turned 22 years old a few days earlier, was dominant in Chicago's 78½-24½ victory. He won the shot (47-1), long jump (22-6), tied for first in the pole vault (11-0), and anchored the victorious 440-yard relay. His only loss came in the 100, where he placed second. In the Texas Relays at Austin, the Maroons, with Berwanger running the anchor leg, claimed third in the 880-yard relay. In the mile relay, Ellinwood covered the anchor leg in 48.8 and Chicago moved up to fourth place. However, the road trip was already starting to unravel. Merriam spent most of it confined to bed with a lingering case of the flu, and several athletes suffered injuries, including Berwanger. Entered in a half-dozen events, he hurt his back in the shot put and had to withdraw from the javelin and the discus.

Less than two weeks later, Berwanger had recovered sufficiently to enter five events in a dual meet against Northern Illinois Teachers College (now Northern Illinois University). Set for the Saturday before Easter 1936, the meet was to have been an outdoor competition, but the Chicago weather did not cooperate. April 10 was cold and damp, with the mercury never getting above 43 degrees, so the teams agreed to contest all events but the javelin and discus indoors. The meet was close all afternoon. The Maroons needed Berwanger, who was six days away from competing at the Kansas Relays. The Dutchman won the high hurdles and shot put and tied for first in the long jump (21-6½). The visitors amassed points in the middle-distances and held a small lead entering the final race, the mile relay. With indoor world record holder Ellinwood as their anchorman, the Maroons seemed to be a lock for the win; only a pulled hamstring or disqualification would deny them the meet-winning points. Berwanger ran leadoff, John Beal and Quintin Johnstone handled the middle legs, and Ellinwood took care of business on the anchor. Their 3:35.7 win sealed the Maroons' 67-64 victory.[135]

At last, Berwanger could turn his full attention to the Kansas Relays decathlon, a major test of his Olympic potential.

Berwanger (center) was part of the honor court at the University of Chicago's Washington Prom in February 1936. In the same month, he was the first player selected in the first-ever National Football League draft. The women, (from left), are Barbara Vail; Jeanne Stolte; and Cynthia Grabo. The men are Robert Ebert, Rhodes Scholar; Berwanger; and Ralph Nicholson, editor of the Daily Maroon. (Special Collections Research Center, University of Chicago Library).

CHAPTER 33

By the time he packed for Kansas, Berwanger had a couple weeks' growth on his upper lip. He had entered another competition: The Blackfriar Moustache Derby. The men's satirical theatrical group, whose 1936 production was titled "Fascist and Furious," sponsored a contest among seniors. Perhaps knowing his competitive nature, even in moustache-growing, many on campus considered the Dutchman the favorite. Under the rules of the three-week competition, only length mattered: The man with the longest mustache, tip to tip, would be declared the winner. In an upset of sorts, the title went to one Thomas Glassford, whose mustache measured four inches with a length of three-quarters of an inch. As a price of his fame, the 22-year-old suffered a "ducking" in the campus Botany pond. "Seven seniors tried to give Jay Berwanger, husky football star, a ducking, too, merely because he is Jay Berwanger," the *Chicago Tribune* related, "but Berwanger won the tussle." However, "for no apparent reason" – except, apparently, to show he was a good sport – Berwanger then put himself into the pond.

Seventeen decathletes entered the 1936 Kansas Relays, including local favorite Clyde Coffman, a Kansas alumnus and 1932 Olympian. Berwanger, who had finished fourth in the same meet two years earlier, was ready to go head-to-head with some of the nation's best all-around athletes. The competitors enjoyed nearly perfect weather – for April in Lawrence, at least – for both days.

In the first event, the 100 meters, 23-year-old Glenn Morris burst into a 120-point lead with a 10.6-second sprint. Berwanger ran 11 seconds flat to finish second. That race foreshadowed the rest of the two-day competition. Morris, who graduated two years earlier from Colorado State University, where he starred in football and the hurdles, won six of the 10 events, three each day. Coffman won only the long jump. Morris outscored the Dutchman in every event but the long jump – and even then Berwanger's margin was a mere three points, 6.985 meters (22 feet, 11 inches) to Morris' 6.975. Still, Berwanger kept racking up enough points to hold third place after the first day.

Berwanger's best score came in the first event of the first day, the 100 meters, and his worst was in the last of the last day, the 1,500 meters. At the start of the 1,500, he might have known that his hold on third place was secure. But perhaps not. After the ninth event, the javelin, the 14 remaining athletes lined up for the 1,500 without hearing any announcement of the points for the javelin or the overall standings. In any case, Berwanger took his time in the 1,500. He and the man in fourth place, Loyette Burk, formerly of Oklahoma University, crossed the finish line together, dead last, in 5:32.2. Berwanger's time was 21 seconds slower than his effort at Kansas two years earlier. He trailed Morris and Coffman by some 40 seconds. Though Berwanger received only 255 points in the final event, he could have skipped the 1,500 altogether and still retained third place. The athletes had to wait a while for official confirmation of all that. As soon as Berwanger and Burk finished the 1,500, the decathlon judges, professors Guy W. Smith and J.J. Wheeler, decided to go to lunch before figuring and announcing the points for the javelin, the 1,500, and the competition overall. After Smith and Wheeler satisfied their hunger, they disclosed that Morris set an American record (7,576 points) in his first decathlon ever. Coffman (7,136), Berwanger (6,774) and Burk (6,498) rounded out the top four.

A comparison of Berwanger's times and distances at the Kansas Relays of 1934 and 1936 shows that in 1936, he posted better marks in half the events.

Shortly before he graduated from Chicago, Berwanger accepted a University Civic League medal "in recognition of his genuine loyalty to American ideals." (Author's photo)

Comparing his performances on the basis of points awarded in 1934 (7,442) and 1936 (6,774) is misleading, because the scoring tables were toughened between his visits to Kansas. Based on present-day scoring tables, his second appearance in Lawrence was his better meet (6,350 points vs. 6,246 in 1934), despite that indifferent 1,500 meters. He earned a Number 7 ranking among American decathletes.[136] Berwanger's University of Chicago record stood up for more than seven decades, until Zach Rodgers amassed 6,415 points in 2007.

His decathlon performance in Kansas made it clear that Berwanger had to step up his training if he had a prayer to make the Olympic team in two months. That would require more time – a commodity Berwanger lacked. Longtime friend and business associate Ernie Dix recalled that during their final months as undergraduates, Berwanger's mentor from Dubuque stepped in. Ira Davenport had Berwanger move out of the Psi Upsilon house to make it easier for him to focus on academics and earn his degree.[137] His courses the final academic quarter were Survey of Production Management, Survey of Business Finance II, Survey of Personnel Management II, Economic History of Western European Civilization, and, of course, physical education.[138] Dix replaced Berwanger as house president – a position with the perk of free room and board. It was an unbelievable windfall for Dix, whose own modest athletic career was curtailed by finances.[139]

About this time, Berwanger heard tragic news from back home: Oran "Nanny" Pape, who, until Berwanger, was the best running back to come out of Dubuque High, had died in heroic circumstances. Pape, who starred at the University of Iowa and played three seasons in the National Football League, had joined the newly formed Iowa Highway Patrol in August 1935. Responding to the report of a stolen car, Pape stopped a vehicle matching the description. The driver, 23-year-old parolee Roscoe Barton, brandished a gun – it was stolen from a police chief – and took Pape hostage. Soon after Barton started driving, the 29-year-old Pape attempted to overpower him. During their struggle, both men suffered gunshot wounds. The criminal, shot in the head, died soon afterward. Pape lingered with a wound to abdomen, and he succumbed the next day. He was the first member of the Iowa Highway Patrol to die in the line of duty, and more than 75 years later he remains the only member to have been murdered. In mid-2012, the State of Iowa renamed its Department of Public Safety building for Oran Pape.

Perhaps to recover from Kansas, or perhaps to study, Berwanger did not accompany his teammates to the Drake Relays the next weekend. In Des

Moines, Chicago's sophomore sensation, Ray Ellinwood, blazed the 440-yard run in 48.5, chopping 1.2 seconds from the meet record. He also anchored the mile relay, taking the baton in sixth place, churning the cinders with a lap of 47.8, and giving the Maroons a third-place finish. Berwanger was in action the next three Saturdays, when the Maroons recorded dual-meet victories at Purdue, at Western State Teachers College (now Western Michigan), and at Northwestern.

With the Maroons on the road from mid- to late May, work crews had time to dig a new straightaway on the Stagg Field track in preparation for the national collegiate meet. Workers were shocked and excited to unearth a huge jaw with large, square teeth still attached. They came to close to alerting an anthropology professor about their prehistoric find when groundskeeper Jimmy Twohig recalled that, about 50 years earlier, the site was a meadow where about 100 cows grazed. The mystery was solved.

The Dutchman placed in all six of his events at Purdue, winning three (including the mile relay). He won three events in Kalamazoo, Michigan, and placed second in another. Berwanger's final dual meet of his collegiate career was also the closest. Chicago and Northwestern kept the affair tight all afternoon. Berwanger had already won the shot put and taken second in the discus, when, with only two field events to be completed, the host Wildcats held a lead of 5 ⅓ points. (Scoring in dual meets awards five points for first place, three for second and one for third.) However, in the penultimate event, the long jump, the Maroons scored a 1-2-3 sweep, with Berwanger in second, to grab all nine points and pull ahead by 3 ⅔ points. In the final event, the javelin, Northwestern needed to finish 1-2 to win the meet. Anything less would give Chicago the victory. Norm Ogilvie, a Northwestern sophomore, unleashed a toss of 167-7 to win. However, Berwanger beat another Wildcat sophomore, Bob Carter, for second place. His three points gave Chicago the team victory by just two-thirds of a point. As he had in football, Berwanger provided his Maroons their final points for a team victory in his last collegiate competition.

In those dual meets, Berwanger only entered events that would be contested in the decathlon. He improved on his marks from the Kansas Relays in a few events, but not consistently or significantly. To win a berth to Berlin, he would need a breakthrough performance in the U.S. Olympic trials June 26-27 at Marquette University in Milwaukee. Some observers had their doubts. Five weeks before the trials, Berwanger denied rumors that he had given up on the Olympics. Berwanger skipped the Big Ten meet at Ohio

State to start several days of final examinations – after which he planned to train intensively for the trials. However, even he conceded that his chances of making the team were slim. The *Daily Maroon's* Rex Horton came to his defense: "While it is true that Berwanger has not been in particularly good condition lately, due primarily to the pressure of studies, he expects from now on to train seriously for the Olympic decathlon, and may give a surprise to some of the local pessimists."

Meanwhile, Berwanger ended lingering speculation that he might yet play professional football when he disclosed that he had accepted a job. He declined to identify his new employer – the *Tribune* described it as a "Chicago industrial concern" – because he wanted little fanfare about

Berwanger regularly entered multiple events as a member of the Chicago track team. In the field, his best event was the shot put. (Chicago Tribune photo. Reprinted with permission)

it. Berwanger said, should he make the Olympic team, the employer – later identified as Featheredge Rubber Company – would allow him to postpone work until the fall. "You might as well begin forgetting about me," Berwanger told a *Tribune* sportswriter, adding with a chuckle, "The process of forgetting has begun already, I think." Not yet.

Chicago was the site of the Central Amateur Athletic Union meet on the first Sunday of June 1936. In what proved to be his last competition at Stagg Field, Berwanger placed in four events: He won the shot put, took thirds in the javelin and discus, and came in fourth in perhaps his only attempt at the hammer throw. The meet also featured several "special guests" of the host Olde Tymers Track Club – some of the sport's leading African-American athletes, including Jesse Owens and Ralph Metcalfe.

After completing his comprehensive exams, Berwanger received a gold medal from the University Civic League, which each year honored two students, from the University of Chicago and/or Northwestern, who demonstrated a "genuine loyalty to American ideals" and excelled in scholarship, athletics or journalism.[140] The other honoree was Northwestern all-conference tackle Sam Papich, who went on to a 29-year career with the FBI. His assignments included working undercover in South America during World War II, serving as the bureau's long-time liaison to the CIA, and helping investigate President Kennedy's assassination. After retiring from the FBI, he served as a member of the President's Foreign Advisory Board and, later, as a consultant to the Joint Chiefs of Staff regarding Soviet intelligence.[141]

Just before commencement, Berwanger was the honorary host of the university's Senior Day. The Monday affair at a country club in Flossmoor, about 20 miles south of campus, stretched 12 hours – until 2 the morning of commencement. Activities included golf, tennis, horseback riding, a dinner, a dance, and, no doubt, plenty of libations.

Though no doubt sleep-deprived, Berwanger was not about to miss his graduation ceremony, where he received his bachelor of arts degree in busi-

The biggest of the Big Men on Campus in 1935-36, Berwanger and basketball star Bill Haarlow, are joined by young ladies in a photo shoot on the University of Chicago's famed "C" Bench. (Special Collections Research Center, University of Chicago Library)

ness. He was the best known of all the members of the Class of 1936. The *Chicago Tribune* reported his graduation on its lead sports page, and its daily photo page showed the star athlete, in cap and gown, posing with Donald MacMurray, a 21-year-old who managed to earn his undergraduate degree from the University of Chicago in a single academic year. (Apparently a man in a hurry, MacMurray got married two days after that.)

A few days later, Chicago hosted the national collegiate track championships. It was the 15th NCAA meet, and the 13th (and final) time it came to Stagg Field.[142] Berwanger was not entered; the Olympic trials would take place the following weekend. Indoor world record-holder Ray Ellinwood was the only Maroon athlete making the medal podium, placing fifth in the 400 meters.

In the days and weeks before the Olympic trials, an event Berwanger had pointed toward for years, his name appeared in the papers with less frequency and prominence. Ultimately, the rumors were proven true: Berwanger did not compete in Milwaukee. Sportswriters apparently didn't ask him why; they just moved on. In 2013, decathlon expert and historian Frank Zarnowski said Berwanger "appears to be one of the great untapped decathlon talents of the era."[143] Meanwhile Glenn Morris, the decathlon winner at Kansas, broke the existing world record with 7,884 points (a mark never submitted for ratification). In Berlin, Morris won while adding 16 points to his record. His gold-medal decathlon career lasted just three competitions, during which he broke three American records, two world records and the Olympic standard.[144]

While American decathletes Morris, Robert Clark, and Jack Parker turned in outstanding performances to sweep the Olympic medals in Berlin, Berwanger was engaged in performances of a different sort.

CHAPTER 34

With his athletic and academic commitments to the University of Chicago completed, Berwanger went to work. Instead of finding a job, one found him. Sometime before mid-May, Chicago alumnus Benjamin B. Felix called on the star athlete at the Psi Upsilon house. Felix was president of Featheredge Rubber Company, on Chicago's Near North Side, which as recently as the summer of 1933 employed 120. Felix, in his late 60s, told Berwanger he was looking for a third generation of leadership. His vice president was in his 40s, and Felix thought the 22-year-old might fit the bill. "It appealed to me because I was going to learn manufacturing," Berwanger explained decades later. "I would learn the rubber business, then I would go into sales, the idea being that after a while I could get into management." Featheredge's newest employee started at $17 a week.[145] He received some time off during the summer for other endeavors.

Throughout college, Berwanger balanced athletics and academics as well as part-time work to cover his room and board. So it was no surprise that he didn't limit himself to just one job after graduation. In late June, he accepted Clark Shaughnessy's offer to be a part-time assistant coach for the freshman team. Later, he struck a deal with the *Chicago Daily News* to be a part-time football writer. The *Daily News* announced the arrangement the afternoon Berwanger was to play in the all-star game against the NFL champion Detroit Lions – an exhibition sponsored by the rival *Chicago Tribune*. The *Tribune* had featured Berwanger in much of its months-long pre-game promotion, and now he was going to work for the competition.

The Daily News said Berwanger would file daily articles at the start of the Big Ten season and then cover the college game of his choosing each Saturday and "telegraph his reports and comments to *Daily News* in a running fire of frank, accurate language which is so natural to him." The paper's announcement story was accompanied by a photo of Berwanger, wearing a football jersey and helmet (sans faceguard), posing, pen in hand, as if autographing a pigskin. The overline of the photo stated: "Berwanger Writes on Football." For his part, the Dutchman promised that he would do his own work. "It would not interest me merely to sell my name for some ghost writer to use in writing glib, smug generalities about football. But when told that I could write straightforward, frank articles and reports I jumped at the chance, for the next thing to playing football is writing or talking about it." The *Daily News'* John P. Carmichael, on his way to becoming one of the nation's foremost sportswriters, took him under his wing. Berwanger wrote game stories and columns through the 1936 season only. "I could have stayed with the paper," he said, "but that was not what I wanted to do with my life."[146]

He picked up other income by accepting two or three speaking appearances a week. At $50 to $150 per speech, he noted, he was earning more than most pro football players at the time "and I wasn't getting hit."[147]

More money came his way through product endorsements. He pitched Huskies, C.W. Post Company's new wheat-flake cereal introduced to compete with General Mills' Wheaties. Most Huskies campaigns featured sports luminaries in a comic strip format. Endorsers included Berwanger, former Notre Dame standout and Wisconsin coach Harry Stuhldreher, professional star Don Hutson, Notre Dame coach Elmer Layden and Olympic swimming champion Helene Madison. A caricature of a smiling Berwanger enthused, "Huskies taste great fellows ... and you'll sure have fun with us in the Huskies Club."

The advertising campaign coincided with another income-producing endeavor for Berwanger during what was a packed summer of 1936. He and several other college stand-

After declining to play professional football, Berwanger covered college football for the Chicago Daily News. The arrangement lasted only through the 1936 season. (Berwanger family collection)

outs answered Hollywood's call to appear on the silver screen in "The Big Game." (The movie title might have been taken from the name given the annual grudge match between Stanford and the University of California).The RKO-Radio studio shot the movie over a couple of weeks in late July and early August. The screenplay by Irwin Shaw, a future best-selling novelist, was based on a Francis Wallace novel that first appeared in *Collier's* magazine as the serial, "Odds Against Honor."

The story line had crooked gamblers trying to bribe a star quarterback to lose a pivotal game. When their inducements failed, the gamblers kidnapped the quarterback on the eve of The Big Game, intending to hold him until the game was lost and they collected their winnings. The hostage's shorthanded teammates, taking a beating on the gridiron, got wind of the star's whereabouts and raced from the stadium to his rescue. The players' absence was covered, conveniently, by a time-consuming on-field brawl. Once order was restored and the star quarterback was back calling signals, the rest of the game had, as the saying goes, a Hollywood ending.

The cast of college stars included Berwanger, Notre Dame's William Shakespeare, Southern Methodist's Bob Wilson, New York University's Irwin "King Kong" Klein, Ohio State's Gomer Jones, Illinois' Chuck Bennis and a trio from Stanford: Monk Moscrip, Bob "Bones" Hamilton and Frank Alustiza. Klein might have been particularly familiar with the riot scene, which was added into Wallace's story after an actual such altercation occurred a few months earlier between Klein's NYU and Fordham.[148] As it happened, Hollywood made Klein the recipient of numerous punches to the kisser by the character played by squeaky-voiced professional actor Andy Devine. RKO used clips from the 1935 Rose Bowl game for its action-shot segments.

Shortly after arriving on the RKO lot, studio officials introduced the 22-year-old Berwanger to June Travis, a beautiful actress his age from Chicago. Her real name was June Grabiner, and she was the daughter of Chicago White Sox executive Harry Grabiner. Travis got her break after a Hollywood scout spotted her attending a White Sox spring training game. Making her screen debut in 1935, the 5-foot-4 brunette quickly became a queen of B movies. In their introductory conversation, arranged and perhaps coached by an RKO publicist, Travis asked Berwanger if he knew how to apply powder and makeup. A *Chicago Tribune* writer, conveniently on hand for the conversation, reported, "Berwanger's worried grin indicated he didn't." A couple of his compatriots "smiled quite brazenly," because, though they were within the attractive actress' line of sight, "Her eyes were on Jay Berwanger." The article went on to say that Travis, cast as the female lead, agreed to coach Berwanger in matters of acting and makeup. His family also recalls the story that Berwanger, when encountering other Hollywood starlets, took the "twang" out of his last name, put on airs and mischieveously introduced himself with a French-sounding *BEHR-wahn-jhay*.[149] Another actress in the film was pretty 21-year-old Barbara Pepper, who over time lost her looks but gained notoriety as "Doris Ziffel" on the 1960s TV sitcom "Green Acres."

During shooting on the Los Angeles Junior College campus, Shaughnessy paid a visit. The *Chicago Tribune's* George Shaffer, perhaps exercising some artistic license, reported the conversation between the coach and his former star this way:

"Gee, coach," Berwanger exclaimed, "these movies are getting me. When are you going back home? I want to go back to Chicago."

"What's the matter?" Shaughnessy asked. "Haven't you found a lot of pretty girls?"

"I never got along well with girls," the Maroon ace said, "and, besides, there are a lot of pretty girls in Chicago."

Shaffer quoted Shaughnessy further: "These boys certainly look like the

In a publicity shot promoting "The Big Game," a Hollywood film featuring several collegiate stars, Berwanger is greeted by actresses Barbara Pepper (center) and June Travis. Three decades later, Pepper portrayed farm wife Doris Ziffel on the popular television program "Green Acres." (Berwanger family collection)

makings of a great football team. But I don't care who they are, where they come from, or how good they are – they can't play football like Berwanger. My hope is they don't let Jay scrimmage too hard in their movies scenes – or he'll hurt those other boys."

Though Berwanger years later recalled his brief stint in Hollywood as "just a vacation – a great experience" in which he made many friends, at the time he sounded less enamored with the duty, which sometimes lasted 16 hours a day.[150] His few lines came in the scene in which he sat with Pop, played by Devine, as he hatched the plot to start the riot intended to delay the game until their star could be rescued. His longest line: "Pop, I hereby vote you the most valuable man on the squad." No one could have mistaken Berwanger for a professional actor.

"The Big Game" opened in theaters within two months after shooting ended. Reviews for the 74-minute feature were tepid. *The New York Times'* B.R. Crisler was not enthusiastic. "Burdened with a strictly supplementary cast of eight all-American players, Mr. Shaw could hardly have been expected to figure, in his maiden screen effort, as a second George Bernard, and RKO deserves at least half the blame for so flagrant a misuse of talent. An indeterminate film, the beginning of which might easily be mistaken by late-comers for a seasonal newsreel, 'The Big Game' is neither a successful exposé of the college football racket (which it shows timid signs of trying to be) nor a good conventional campus romance, of which it carefully preserves all the ingredients in this case Philip Huston and June Travis." Crisler concluded: " ... 'The Big Game' has about it an air of such grim unreality that even the crescendo voice of MacNamee or a raccoon coat in the neighboring seat would not make it look convincing." The United Press reviewer recognized "The Big Game" for what it was. "One of the best football pictures in many a day, although filled with that same old hokum," the UP said. "Funniest bits are the substitutions, i.e., Jay Berwanger, real-life one-man team, going in for a dud called Jenkins."

Berwanger was not patient with the pace of moviemaking. Asked his impression of the Hollywood scene, he told a reporter, "They are always stalling around." However, he did like the money: He received about $600.[151] The amount seems small by 21st century standards, but his check would have covered full tuition at the University of Chicago for two academic years. Rain had delayed the wrap-up of shooting, so Berwanger took a plane back to Chicago instead of the train. Time was critical. Berwanger had more football to play.

CHAPTER 35

During the summer of 1936, the *Chicago Tribune* sponsored a national poll of sports fans to select a team of college all-stars to play defending National Football League champion Detroit in a late-summer charity game. Some 182 newspapers were part of the *Tribune's* balloting network. During the couple of weeks in which readers could submit ballots, the *Tribune* milked the all-star process for all its publicity-generating worth. The *Tribune* printed daily articles, including summaries of which players various coaches and celebrities picked. Everyday readers received attention, too. The first ballot the *Tribune* opened was submitted by James A. Coughlin, a resident of a Chicago hotel, whose lineup included Berwanger at halfback. Mayor Edward J. Kelly and actor Clark Gable voted the same way. About the only celebrity to leave Berwanger off the ballot was Ginger Rogers. The famous dancer, who had grown up in Fort Worth, picked 10 Texans and Army's William Shuler.

Some fans organized campaigns to get their favorites on the all-star team. University of Iowa boosters staged a drive to promote votes for running back Dick Crayne. It was the sort of ballot box-stuffing that the *Tribune* and its partner papers encouraged. After all, it sold more newspapers. Though the *Tribune* reported that Berwanger appeared to have little or no organized support, after some 3.4 million ballots poured into newspaper offices, he emerged as the top vote-getter among all the all-stars. It was a nice honor, but not wholly unexpected for a leading All-America who starred in the heart of the *Tribune's* circulation area. (From Iowa City, Crayne fell short of starter status but made the all-star squad.) Newspaper readers also had the opportunity to pick the all-stars' coach. Berwanger told a *Tribune* reporter he would have liked to have played one more game under Shaughnessy, but he agreed with his coach that Bernie Bierman of Minnesota would be an excellent choice. The voters concurred.

When Berwanger flew into Chicago after filming of "The Big Game," the *Chicago Tribune* snapped his photo as he emerged from the airplane. The *Tribune* attributed this quote to the Dutchman: "That reminds me of Hollywood. Every time we turned around we bumped into a photographer or a pretty girl." The paper identified Berwanger as the "first all-star ready to drill." Also mentioned for their timely arrival were Darrell Lester of Texas Christian and Don Elser of Notre Dame. The all-stars needed to stay on schedule: Bierman's

Gomer Jones of Ohio State (left), Berwanger, and Notre Dame's Bill Shakespeare join coach Frank Thomas in a publicity photo promoting the 1936 college all-star game in Chicago. (Berwanger family collection)

squad had barely 2½ weeks to get ready for the NFL champs. The coach taught the all-stars his Minnesota system, which featured an unbalanced line and a single-wing backfield. It helped that he had seven of his former players on the squad. Further, Berwanger was familiar with the Minnesota system, which was similar to Shaughnessy's.

In their first team meeting, at Northwestern University, Bierman told the all-stars, "I have found that mental attitude is the most important factor in any game. If you fellows think that you can beat the Lions, you have taken the most important step." He scheduled two workouts a day. Bierman set no curfew, telling his squad, "We will not follow you around to see if you are training. There is no definite hour to retire. That is left to your judgment and discretion, just as the other fundamental training rules are in your hands." Bierman's assistant coaches were Lou Little, Columbia; Elmer Layden, Notre Dame; Bo McMillin, Indiana; and Lynn "Pappy" Waldorf, Northwestern. McMillin worked with the ends and the passers, including Berwanger and fellow Iowa native Mike Layden, Elmer's brother and a Notre Dame standout. (When Layden starred at Davenport High, he graduated a year ahead of Berwanger. However, he attended a prep school for a year between high school and Notre Dame.[152])

A few days into practice, with dog-day heat bearing down on Chicago, the all-stars staged their third scrimmage in four days. The weather eventually got to Berwanger, who, after racking up a couple of first downs, left the field with heat sickness. Nonetheless, the *Tribune's* George Strickler noted, Berwanger was the "chief attraction" among the coaches and pro scouts present. "The public is not permitted to witness the workouts, but locked gates are no barrier to Berwanger's popularity," he reported. "Autograph seekers stop him at every turn. Even a few attempted to follow him into the showers."

Strickler described the former Chicago star as being "reticent, obliging and at times slightly confused" by all the attention, but added, "Berwanger, the nation's most widely publicized player, takes it all good naturedly, although not without some regret." He quoted Berwanger: "All this puts a fellow on a spot. It's worth it though just to be a member of this squad." He raved about the teamwork and camaraderie of the 53 collegians: "The association alone makes the all-star game the outstanding event in a player's career."

Jay Berwanger in December 1935, as his postseason awards, including the Downtown Athletic Club Trophy, were pouring in. (Chicago Tribune photo. Reprinted with permission)

It was hard work. Between the morning and afternoon practices, he usually returned to his room in Northwestern's Hinman House and took a nap. He might have regretted the day he skipped the nap to drive to downtown Chicago, where the Inter-Fraternity Club hosted the all-stars at a luncheon. As he and Vern Oech, a guard from Minnesota, raced back to campus for afternoon practice and his first workout of the day – a night session would follow – a policeman pulled over Berwanger for speeding. Berwanger posted bond on the ticket, news of which made the morning *Tribune*, and the next day paid a fine of $10 (including court costs of $1).

During the run-up to the game against the Lions, former George Washington University back Alphonse "Tuffy" Leemans impressed the coaches. Some sportswriters contended that Leemans was on the all-star roster more because of friends' voting campaign than his abilities. Yet the 18th player selected in the initial National Football League draft earned increased playing time in all-star scrimmages. (Leemans went on to earn induction into the Pro Football Hall of Fame.)

Intermittent showers fell on Chicago throughout the Tuesday morning and afternoon of the third annual all-star game between the collegians and defending NFL champions, saturating the playing surface of Soldier Field. By 5 p.m., a few hours before kickoff, the rain intensified and forecasters said it would continue throughout the evening. Anticipating a gate of 80,000 fans, organizers postponed the game by one day, to 8:30 p.m. Wednesday, September 2. Perhaps demonstrating that there were no hard feelings about his just-announced commitment to write for the *Daily News*, or perhaps reflecting an internal communications breakdown, the *Tribune* published a photo of a pajama-clad Berwanger relaxing in his Hotel Sherman bed as he waited out the postponement.

The *Tribune* used the extra day to promote ticket sales, promising that no fans would be turned away. In addition to reserved seats at $1.10, $2.20 and $3.30, standing room tickets would sell for an even dollar (tax included). Fans driving to the game could find free parking south, east and northeast of Soldier Field. Sportswriters from around the country were on hand, and the game was broadcast live by Chicago radio station WGN for the Mutual network. The National Broadcasting Company and Minneapolis station WTCN also broadcast the game.

The Detroit Lions, coming off their first NFL championship, had as their captain Earl "Dutch" Clark, their only first-team All-Pro selection of 1935. Clark won the pre-game coin toss, chose to defend the north goal and then returned Dick Smith's kickoff 28 yards to the Lions' 43. The all-stars seemed to glow under the Soldier Field floodlights: they wore bright yellow pants and jerseys and light-colored helmets. Their uniform tops displayed red numbers on front and back. Berwanger was easily recognized with his faceguard and familiar Number 99. That enhanced visibility made all-star assistant coach McMillin's work easier. He took a position in the press box, from which he telephoned information and observations to the sideline, where

Waldorf relayed the messages to Layden and Bierman.

As the top vote-getter in the *Tribune's* balloting, Berwanger's place in the starting lineup was guaranteed. Joining him in the first-team backfield were Riley Smith of Alabama, William Shakespeare of Notre Dame, and Sheldon Beise of Minnesota. As was common at the time, in light of substitution rules, Berwanger also prowled the defensive backfield. On the all-stars' first offensive possession, Shakespeare ran for no gain before Berwanger connected on a pass to Smith for 10 yards and a first down. Berwanger on the next play rushed up the middle for three yards. After Beise gained three more yards, Berwanger on third down was stopped for no gain. Just 10 minutes into the game, Bierman sent in Leemans to replace Berwanger. Leemans immediately impressed with his rushes, passes, and punt returns. Berwanger did not return to the field until two minutes remained in the second quarter, when the all-stars faced fourth down on the Lions' 17. Beise tossed a short lateral to fellow Minnesota star Vernal "Babe" LeVoir, who cut through left tackle and eluded Detroit defenders for a touchdown. The kick by Notre Dame's Wally Fromhart gave the collegians a 7-0 lead.

To open the second half, Detroit kicked off to Berwanger, who fumbled but recovered around his own 28-yard line. Neither team could mount a scoring threat in the third quarter, and the massive crowd of more than 76,000 fans buzzed over the prospect of an all-star victory. The Lions stepped up their defensive intensity and put a blemish on Leemans' otherwise outstanding evening. On a running play, Leemans took a hard hit and fumbled. The Lions' recovered at the collegians' 29 and made the most of their opportunity. They drove to the 8, where they pulled off a trick play familiar in the professional ranks. Back Bill Shepherd acted as if he caught the center snap and dove into the defensive line. However, the snap actually went to Clark, who pitched a lateral to Ernie Caddel, who ran around right end for a touchdown. Clark's drop-kick made it 7-7.

Each team had a couple of chances for late-game heroics. Detroit stopped an all-star drive but soon gave up the ball when Crayne intercepted Clark's pass on the all-star 45. The squads exchanged punts, with Berwanger slipping and falling 11 yards into a return, on his own 32. Berwanger was then stopped for no gain. Two plays later, the game ended a 7-7 tie.

The outcome left both teams with degrees of frustration. The all-stars, who beat the Lions in key statistical categories, felt that they were the better team. Leemans was kicking himself for the late-game fumble that paved the way for Detroit's touchdown, but his teammates reminded him that his outstanding play contributed to their own touchdown. The Lions acknowledged that they had their hands full with the collegians. Coach Potsy Clark said, "It was the greatest bunch of all-stars ever assembled. It unquestionably was three touchdowns better than any college team ever assembled." Bierman didn't stick around to deliver a post-game address to his team or give sports-

writers a few quotes. He rushed from the sidelines to the taxi that took him to the railroad depot in time to make his train for Minneapolis. Beise said the Lions did not outplay the collegians. "They weren't as tough as Iowa and Northwestern last year," the Minnesota star said. The evening concluded with a reception for both teams. Gate receipts were more than $130,000.

On that night, the star among the all-stars was Leemans, and much of his acclaim came at the expense of Berwanger, the measuring stick for stardom. Back in the nation's capital, Leemans' stomping grounds, The *Washington Post* stated, "Berwanger, whom many last year acclaimed as the greatest back in America, started the game at left half for the Collegians. But tonight he was only an ordinary back compared with the Capital City's hero …" Other sportswriters offered similar observations. It was not that Berwanger had a bad game; it was a game in which Berwanger did nothing

Direct from Hollywood, Berwanger prepares for his final action in a football uniform – two 1936 exhibitions pitting collegiate all-stars against National Football League teams. (Chicago Tribune photo. Reprinted with permission)

noteworthy while Leemans was outstanding.

Leemans and Berwanger boarded a special train bound for New York, where about half the original all-star squad and others would play the New York Giants in a game sponsored by the *New York Herald-Tribune* for its fresh air fund. Other all-stars reported to their professional teams' training camps or departed for Dallas and a Monday night exhibition game against the Chicago Bears. (The collegians beat the Bears, 7-6, in the Cotton Bowl after blocking Chicago's extra-point kick.)

The northern contingent of all-stars, their ranks diluted, struggled in New York's Polo Grounds. The game had a promising start for the collegians, and for Berwanger, who returned the opening kickoff 35 yards. However, his first-quarter ledger included a couple of rushes for negative yardage and a lost fumble. Leemans, the star of the Chicago exhibition, replaced Berwanger and soon intercepted a pass deep in his own territory. The Giants held a 6-2 lead at halftime; the collegians recorded a safety after Northwestern's Paul Tangora blocked a punt. Berwanger's struggles continued early in the second half, when he threw an interception. The Giants added a touchdown in the fourth quarter to open a 12-2 lead. Berwanger finally got into his offensive rhythm. He powered through several runs, picking up a couple of first downs in the process, and catching a forward pass and immediately pitching the ball to Riley Smith for an eight-yard gain. However, it was too little too late for the collegians. The game ended 12-2. The 30,000 fans in the Polo Grounds had just witnessed Jay Berwanger's final football game. He packed his gear and returned to Chicago for the next chapters in his life.

CHAPTER 36

After Hollywood and all-star football games, Berwanger resumed management training at Featheredge Rubber Company, helped coach the University of Chicago freshmen, and started writing about football for the *Chicago Daily News*. In his debut column, he expounded on the benefits of the game. "College football is the first big test in the average boy's life," he wrote. "He is examined every Saturday for two months before a good many thousand people and they decide whether he has passed. Also he gets his own thrills out of those grueling examinations." He also stated that being a member of a football team helps an athlete focus on academics, immediately develop friendships, and become more independent. He concluded, "I have heard a number of former football players say that they would give 10 years of their lives to be able to relive their college days. They would give anything to hear that opening whistle, to hear the thud as the ball is kicked off and to feel the jarring impact of body contact. These are thrills only a football player experiences and they live within him forever, their memory growing more vivid every year."

As he would often state over decades of interviews, Berwanger wrote that his greatest thrills on the gridiron included the near-upset of Ohio State and the 7-6 victory over Illinois in 1935. Though he returned an Illini punt 50 yards to set up the game-tying touchdown, scored that touchdown, and kicked the game-winning extra point, he gave credit for the win in Champaign to several teammates, including Ewald Nyquist, who intercepted three straight Illinois passes, and fullback Duke Skoning. In subsequent columns, Berwanger discussed injuries and conditioning; how signals are called in the huddle and at the line; and a tribute to Ed Shaughnessy, describing his college coach's brother as "the most remarkable scout I ever saw."

Berwanger's full-time employer, Featheredge Rubber, manufactured the

sponge rubber used to create the moisture-resistant seal around motor-ve-
hicle doors and trunks, as well as gaskets on appliances such as refrigerators
and washing machines. The factory and offices, 340 West Huron Street, were
housed in a multi-story wood-frame building designed by famed architect
Louis Sullivan. The rubber was prepared on the ground floor and sent upstairs for production. Business offices occupied the top floor.

In terms of excitement, the factory was no Stagg Field on an autumn Saturday, but it did have its moments of drama. A few months after Berwanger
started, 18-year-old William Anowski, the night elevator operator, died after
falling four stories in an elevator shaft. A week later, two employees were
shot and a third was stabbed in a late-night street fight outside the factory.
Meanwhile, Featheredge owner Benjamin B. Felix found himself wrapped up
in fights of a civil nature. The 69-year-old businessman's daughter from his
first marriage, Marion Jones, filed a lawsuit seeking to protect what she considered her future share of his estate. A 40-year-old widow, Mrs. Jones sued
her father, his wife of six months (a former employee), and Featheredge for
a half-million dollars.
The plaintiff claimed
that her father was
dominated by his
current wife. Deposi-
tions pointed to Felix'
liaisons years ear-
lier with two younger
women, including an
employee, and pro-
ceedings included the
reading of love poems
Felix sent to the
women. By mid-1938,
the courts had thrown
out the Jones lawsuit.
Father and daughter
remained estranged
for the rest of her
life, which ended in
suicide in 1951.
Felix allowed Ber-

His football days were over, but in the late 1930s Berwanger took up rugby. In 1939, in perhaps the only rugby game featuring two Heisman winners, Chicago defeated Larry Kelley's New York team, 24-9. (Chicago Tribune photo. Reprinted with permission)

wanger to use vacation time to knock off by mid-afternoon so he could travel from the near North Side factory to help coach freshman football at his alma mater on the South Side. Chicago's program was on its decline when Berwanger joined the varsity in 1933. Now, with Berwanger graduated, nothing – not even Clark Shaughnessy's trick plays – could slow the Maroons' free-fall. The varsity went 2-5-1 in the first post-Berwanger season, but their former star did not witness their struggles first-hand. Nearly every football Saturday of 1936, Berwanger covered a key game for the *Daily News*. He also had a one-game stint as a radio commentator. He worked beside freelance play-by-play man Russ Hodges on WJJD's broadcast of host Northwestern's 14-13 victory over Ohio State.[153] Hodges eventually took his talents to New York, where, 15 years later, he delivered perhaps the most famous call in American sports history: "The Giants win the pennant! The Giants win the pennant! The Giants win the pennant! The Giants win the pennant!"

Though he was not getting rich on his $17-a-week salary at Featheredge, Berwanger made enough in his various endeavors to help his sister Eleanor attain her goal of becoming a teacher. After graduating from Dubuque High in 1936, she enrolled at the National College of Education, in north suburban Evanston. He somehow covered all her college expenses and even gave her an allowance. "In 1937, it was very expensive," Eleanor recalled. "The next three years I worked in private homes for my room and board. I was given a scholarship for my senior year, but Jay paid for all my other expenses."[154] During some of her teacher training, Eleanor and Jay shared an apartment.[155] When Eleanor married in 1941, it was Jay, not their father, who gave away the bride.[156]

As he advanced in the sponge rubber business, Berwanger discontinued his *Daily News* relationship but stuck with serving as an assistant coach for the Chicago freshmen. He stayed in relatively good shape and occasionally took an active role in practices. One afternoon in late September 1938, he played for the reserves in a scrimmage against the varsity. Berwanger, showing flashes of his former greatness, had a hand in all seven of the reserves' touchdowns. Joining him in action were former teammates Omar Fareed, Vin Sahlin, and Tommy Flinn. The workout was designed to give the varsity practice in defense – a feature that would be sorely lacking during their 1-6-1 season. After a 0-0 tie in the 1938 opener, the Maroons were outscored 241-75 in their final seven games. By then, whether the University of Chicago should leave the Big Ten or drop intercollegiate football altogether was an open debate. Even the student newspaper called abandoning football as "the wise course."

In 1939, Berwanger found another outlet for his competitive fire – rugby. It was a curious choice for an athlete who twice suffered a broken nose and was the best-known player to wear a facemask. In any case, Berwanger was the headliner on the Chicago team that won 19 straight matches and claimed the national championship of 1939. In mid-November, Chicago posted a 24-9 win over New York before 10,000 shivering fans in Soldier Field. The game featured the first two winners of the Heisman Trophy – Berwanger and Yale's Larry Kelley, representing New York. Another opponent Berwanger faced during his short-lived rugby career – he played again in 1940 – was Joseph Kennedy, older brother of the future U.S. president.

By this time, Berwanger had a serious love interest: Philomela Baker, a vivacious and attractive blonde from Chicago. How the couple met had faded from relatives' memories, but chances are it involved the University of Chicago; Camp Highlands for Boys; or both. The couple had a mutual connection in William "Doc" Monilaw, University of Chicago High School athletic director and owner of Camp Highlands, where Jay worked two summers. Monilaw's daughter Margaret was married to Philomela's uncle Arthur C. Cody, the brother of Philomela's mother, *Chicago Daily News* columnist Helen Cody Baker.

Once financially comfortable, Philomela's parents, Helen and John Cuyler Baker, went bankrupt during the Great Depression. Losing everything forced Philomela to withdraw from prep school in California. She waited tables for college money, and, though originally a member of the Class of 1938, she didn't complete her University of Chicago degree until March 1940. The Bakers made late-summer treks to Northern Wisconsin for "post-camp" events that Monilaw hosted for family and friends at Camp Highlands. Did Philomela and Jay meet there in the summer of 1934 or 1935, when he was a camp counselor? Had they already met on the Midway campus?

Philomela's name, occasionally misstated as Philomena, from time to time appeared in the gossip columns of the *Daily Maroon*. One spring 1935 item suggested that she had three boyfriends simultaneously. None was named Berwanger, but two were his teammates on the football team and the third was a fraternity brother. It is possible, then, that Philomela Baker and Jay Berwanger were already acquainted well before they became "an item" of their own. She probably attended social events at Psi Upsilon, arguably the leading site of fraternity parties. "Hey, call up the Psi U house and find out what happened last Saturday night," gossip columnist Sam Hair once suggested. "They will say nothing." A few weeks later, another entry quipped, "If all the girls at the Psi U Spring Party were put end to end, it might be interesting." A relative remembered "Phil" as a "walking beauty queen," tall and slender, who had a "great laugh, a sophisticated giggle." She had a tendency to find many events and situations to be hilarious.

A college classmate and life-long friend, Mary Jane Dix, remembered Philomela's "wonderful sense of humor." While Jay and Philomela were dating, Mary Jane was going out with Jay's friend Ernie Dix. Mary Jane recalled her confidential conversations with Phil: "We decided it would be wonderful if she married Jay and I married Ern."[157] That came to pass. Philomela and Jay's engagement was announced in May 1940, and it made all the Chicago papers. Jay Berwanger was still news in the Windy City. She was working as

a secretary for her alma mater and he was assistant sales manager at the rubber company.[158]

"Dutch" Berwanger and "Phil" Baker exchanged vows on the University of Chicago campus at 8 p.m. Saturday, October 12, 1940. Doctor Herbert Prince, rector of the Church of the Holy Spirit in north suburban Lake Forest, performed the ceremony. The setting was Bond Chapel, a small place of worship just a few steps east of the "C" Bench. Matron of honor was Patricia Davis Bethke, for

Philomela and Jay were married on the University of Chicago campus on Saturday evening, October 12, 1940. (Chicago Tribune photo. Reprinted with permission)

whom Phil was maid of honor a year earlier. The groom had as his best man his 18-year-old brother Paul, a star fullback at Western Reserve Academy near Cleveland.[159] Groomsmen were Jay's former college classmates Bill Haarlow, Richard Cochran, Robert Upton and John Baker (no relation to the bride). John Berwanger attended his son's ceremony, as did the groom's sisters Eleanor, Dorothy, and Betty. However, poor health forced Jay's 59-year-old mother, Pauline, to stay home in Dubuque.

After the wedding, the Bakers hosted a small and informal reception in their apartment at 5648 Dorchester Avenue, just east of the Chicago campus. The newlyweds took a short wedding trip and then moved into an apartment on 75th Street near Jeffrey Street. Six months after the wedding, they enjoyed a delayed honeymoon in Havana. In a postcard to her parents, whom she greeted as "Darlings," Phil wrote of Cuba, "This is a lovely, fantastic country." In another dispatch a couple of days later, she apologized to her parents for not phoning once they returned stateside, but they determined that it was too expensive to make the call from Florida to Chicago.

A few months after their wedding, Jay and Philomela enjoyed a delayed honeymoon in Cuba, from which she told the folks back home, "This is a lovely, fantastic country." The couple at right are not identified. (Berwanger family collection)

Their wedding took place during the first autumn without University of Chicago football. The 1939 season had been another disaster. The Maroons managed to defeat two small colleges, Wabash and Oberlin, but were 2-6 overall and lost all three of their Big Ten games by a combined score of 192-0. In its four post-Berwanger seasons (1936-39), Chicago won exactly one Big Ten game, a 7-6 decision at Wisconsin in 1936, and, despite intentionally softening its schedule, was just 6-23-2 overall. University officials, starting with President Robert Maynard Hutchins, no fan of big-time athletics, had seen enough. In December 1939, to the shock and outrage of many alumni, university trustees voted to drop intercollegiate football immediately. Though the possibility of dropping the sport entirely had been discussed, many observers anticipated that the university would continue football but schedule lesser foes. (Chicago departed the Big Ten Conference entirely in 1946.) Though not necessarily opposed to the decision, athletic director Nelson Metcalf and coach Clark Shaughnessy expressed surprise at the suddenness of the trustees' decision. Shaughnessy landed on his feet, moving on to Stanford, where his 1940 team capped an undefeated season with a Rose Bowl victory. Called the Father of the T Formation, Shaughnessy, who also coached and advised in the National Football League, entered the College Football Hall of Fame in 1968.

Meanwhile, Amos Alonzo Stagg took his College of the Pacific team to the Midwest to open Notre Dame's 1940 schedule. The University of Chicago lettermen's club, the Order of the "C," planned a halftime ceremony to honor the 78-year-old Stagg. Berwanger was co-chair of the planning committee. The Grand Old Man and his squad received permission to conduct pre-game practice at Stagg Field. On the gridiron in South Bend, the Irish cruised past Stagg's squad, 25-7.

In July 1941, Berwanger traveled to Dubuque for the funeral of his mentor, Ira N. Davenport. A loyal alumnus of the University of Chicago and a 1912 Olympic track medalist, he not only greatly influenced Berwanger's decision to become a Maroon but continued to counsel the young man during college. The owner and general manager of Dubuque Boat and Boiler Works, Davenport was 53 years old.

He was not a member of the military, but with Europe already at war and pressure mounting for the United States to enter the fray, Berwanger in the fall of 1941 visited the University of Chicago campus as a "liaison officer" to talk up the university's newly created Institute for Military Studies. The institute was a night school of sorts, offering 10 weekly sessions in basic military instruction and occasionally culminating in a "war game" in a nearby forest preserve.

By that time, as Jay and Philomela Berwanger marked their first anniversary, they were expectant parents, with their first child due in the spring of 1942. Autumn 1941 was also when Berwanger became a football official. He received assignments for Big Ten games right away, despite having little or no experience in a striped shirt. Apparently, being the college game's best player at one time was sufficient qualification for the conference. After just one season at the major-college level, his officiating career was put on hold. Everything changed on December 7, 1941.

One month after the Japanese attack on Pearl Harbor, Berwanger was back on the Midway, discussing hand grenades with University of Chicago students. A couple of months earlier, Berwanger was on campus to promote enrollment in a basic military course. "I'm not an interventionist by any stretch of the imagination," he said in mid-November 1941, "but most military experts agree that we'll be in this war from six months to two years." (Special Collections Research Center, University of Chicago Library)

CHAPTER 37

Soon after the Japanese attack on Pearl Harbor, Berwanger enlisted in the U.S. Navy Reserve. His official appointment as a lieutenant (junior grade) was dated March 9, 1942. Ten days later, he participated in a swearing-in ceremony at Northwestern University and entered active duty. Former Chicago teammate Bill Gillerlain, an ensign with the Navy's Aviation Cadet Selection Board, administered the oath. Berwanger's swearing-in made national news. A photo of Berwanger and civilian Red Grange shaking hands went out over The Associated Press national wire.[160] Having in its ranks one of college football's all-time greats helped the Navy's publicity machine. Berwanger was assigned to procurement – recruitment and selection of Navy pilots. Men were jamming into Chicago and suburban recruiting offices for the various military branches and Berwanger's job was to make sure the Navy got more than its share in quality and quantity.

The Navy sent Berwanger to speaking appearances in and around Chicago, and he posed for lots of photos. In August, as it launched a drive to recruit 1,000 air cadets a month, the Navy assembled current and former football players for a publicity shot. To depict the "kickoff" of the recruiting campaign, the photographer had civilian recruiter Don Hutson, the Green Bay Packers end and place-kicker, kick a ball from the hold of former Wisconsin letterman Claude York. Flanking them were Berwanger and Clifford Phillip, another ex-Wisconsin player. (Hutson's 11-year career with the Packers went on without war-related interruption.) A few days later, Berwanger stood at home plate of Comiskey Park to participate in a ceremony between games of a doubleheader inducting Bob Kennedy, 21-year-old third baseman of the Chicago White Sox, into the naval air corps, effective at season's end.[161] A few months later, Berwanger returned to Comiskey Park for a halftime ceremony at a Chicago Cardinals-Chicago Bears football game. He administered the oath of induction to 70 naval aviation cadets recruited by the Cardinals and Bears. The Cardinals won the recruiting competition, 37-33, but the Bears won the game, 21-7.

For more than a year after joining the Navy, Lieutenant Berwanger lived at home with Philomela and followed an unusually domestic schedule for a new serviceman during wartime. About this time, the Berwangers lived at 1372 E. 57th, in the Hyde Park neighborhood, near the University of Chicago and her parents' apartment. Except for wartime relocations, it would remain their address until 1950.[162] In mid-April 1942, he spent two full days in Dubuque, visiting the campuses of Loras College and University of Dubuque and meeting with prospective Navy flyers at the recruiting office in the Dubuque post office. One evening, he addressed the Dubuque YMCA's annual athletic banquet, where he showed a Navy promotional movie, "Navy Wings of Gold." About six weeks later, he addressed the Dubuque Noon Lions Club and that evening spoke to about 300 Elks Club members and potential recruits.[163] He no doubt visited his ailing mother. Pauline Berwanger's poor health had prevented her from attending his wedding in Chicago a year and a half earlier. That visit probably included Jay showing his mother a photo or two of her first grandchild. On May 8, 1942, Jay and Philomela had become first-time parents. They named him John Jay Berwanger.[164] Pauline Berwanger died at home, of colorectal cancer, on November 6, 1943. She was 62.[165]

Recruiting and photo opportunities were Berwanger's assignment in 1942, but his desire was to fly. There was an obstacle: The military initially said that married men were ineligible for flight training.

Berwanger enlisted in the U.S. Navy in 1942 and served through the end of World War II. After initially working in recruitment, he became a flight instructor. (Berwanger family collection)

Berwanger is in control while training at Instrument Flying Instructors School at the Atlanta Naval Air Station in February 1944. (U.S. Navy photo)

However, the brass amended that order and allowed ensigns and lieutenants (junior grade) with 50 hours of flying time to receive training. When he wasn't handling his military assignments, Berwanger took private pilot lessons and practiced. Most of the lessons took place on Sunday mornings. "I went out and bought it," he said of his pilot's license. "It cost me money."[166] His wife, not content to be, as her mother phrased it, an "earth-bound wife," also took flying lessons. Grandmother Baker baby-sat with infant John.[167] In August 1942, while he was assigned to a recruiting campaign in and around Gary, Indiana, Berwanger completed his initial solo flight. Once he was safely back on the ground, his fellow Navy cadets soaked him with water – an aviation tradition after a pilot's first solo. Predictably, a Gary newspaper was tipped off and had a photographer on hand to capture a damp Berwanger shaking hands with Nick Jankovich, the airfield's operator and senior instructor.[168] Having his pilot's certification took Berwanger out of the publicity and recruitment role and into that of flight instructor. In late October 1943, after attending classes in New Orleans, he earned his wings as a Naval flight instructor – reportedly, he graduated at the top of his class – and started his assignment at Lambert Field in St. Louis. Philomela and the baby lived with him in St. Louis much of his time there.

Though he was serving stateside and not facing enemy fire, Berwanger nonetheless faced constant danger. Crashes and other accidents involving

Berwanger trained Navy pilots during World War II, during which he rose to the rank of lieutenant commander. (Berwanger family collection)

military student pilots were common, especially with the skies around training bases crowded with inexperienced aviators. In February 1944, Berwanger spent a month at the U.S. Naval Air Station in Atlanta, where he completed an instructors course in instrument flying. He then returned to St. Louis and served as a primary flight instructor with a promotion to lieutenant commander.

During the build-up of naval aviation forces, many instructors worked a schedule of 10 days on and two days off. However, by 1944, as the Allies continued to score victories against Japan and Germany, the military anticipated needing fewer pilots to complete the war. Whereas the Navy set estimated pilot output for 1944 at 20,000, they planned to need just half that number in 1946. That translated to higher performance standards for pilots, fewer students, and a reduced need for flight instructors.[169] In early 1945, the Navy switched Berwanger's assignment to the newly created Bombing Fighting Squadron 3 in the Atlantic Fleet. He was in line to see combat in Japan. Meanwhile, Philomela was pregnant with their second child. The war in the European theater ended on May 8. Three months later, on August 10, 1945, Japan agreed to surrender and the Berwangers' son Cuyler arrived.

With the war over, the military could not move quickly enough to discharge its active personnel. One month and one day after Japan surrendered, Berwanger reported to Separation Center at Glenview Naval Air Station north of Chicago to receive his release from active duty.[170] His 3½ years of active military service concluded, Berwanger anticipated the resumption of business career. However, it would not be easy.

CHAPTER 38

In September 1945, when the U.S. Navy discharged him from active duty with the rank of lieutenant commander, 31-year-old Jay Berwanger had a wife and two sons but no job. He could not return to Featheredge Rubber Company because owner Benjamin B. Felix had closed it during the war. Some people said that Felix lacked the energy or enthusiasm to retool for post-war production, but others said that Felix closed the business due to his concern that the war would ruin the sponge rubber industry, a field in which he was once an innovator.

However, Berwanger believed that rubber would bounce back. He scraped together and borrowed about $10,000 and established his own sales agency, brokering sponge rubber and other components to manufacturers of various consumer products. One of his early backers was Louis C. Upton, whose son Robert was Berwanger's Chicago classmate, post-college roommate, and groomsman. The senior Upton in 1947 co-signed a $3,000 loan for Berwanger at Boulevard Bank in Chicago.[171] The loan was not too great a gamble. Not only was Louis Upton betting on a young man who had always been a winner, he also could afford the risk. He was a co-founder of Upton Machine Company, forerunner of Whirlpool Corporation.

To help pay his debts, Berwanger also coached intramural football at his alma mater, gave after-dinner speeches, and resumed officiating college football. In his primary occupation, he sold sponge rubber and other rubber parts, plastic parts, and raw materials. The rubber products were molded rubber, extruded rubber, and sponge rubber. For many years, Upton's Whirlpool was Berwanger's biggest customer. Whirlpool contracted with Sears Roebuck to manufacture Kenmore appliances. Other early customers included Roth Rubber in suburban Chicago; Geauga Industries, of Middlefield, Ohio; and automakers. Most of the items and materials Berwanger sold wound up as gaskets on Whirlpool refrigerator doors and washing machine lids. As automakers geared up to meet post-war demand, Berwanger sold the sponge rubber for the seals that kept rain and snow from seeping in as well as the padding for armrests and dashboards.

By 1948, Berwanger had taken in his father-in-law, John Cuyler Baker, as an investor and partner. They named their enterprise Jay Berwanger, Incorporated. Jay was president and his wife's father was vice president. About the same time, Berwanger and three former Featheredge employees bought the Featheredge factory, 340 West Huron Street, and restarted production. The majority owner, former plant manager Harry M. Hood, served as president of Hood Sponge Rubber Company and supervised operations. Berwanger was sales manager and corporate secretary, and he simultaneously operated his sales agency. He added Hood Sponge Rubber to his list of clients and moved Jay Berwanger, Incorporated, into the Hood building, 340 W. Huron

When Berwanger borrowed $3,000 to establish his own business, Louis C. Upton, the father of a Chicago classmate, co-signed the loan. Upton co-founded a company later known as Whirlpool Corporation. (Berwanger family collection)

Street.

During this period, Berwanger hired his old pal Ernie Dix, who was unemployed and nearly broke, with a wife and three children, after the failure of a soft-drink venture he started with a brother-in-law. Dix had sales experience; for a decade after graduating from the University of Chicago, he worked for a corn products company. The friends discussed the advantages and disadvantages of one going to work for the other. "Jay asked him what he needed to live on and gave him that as a draw against his sales commissions," said Bill Dix, Ernie's son. "Fortunately, one of his early customers was Whirlpool ... Given the post-war boom in housing, the need for appliances grew rapidly. Dad had early success, and together he and Jay built a prosperous manufacturers' representative business."

As he had at Featheredge, Berwanger stayed familiar with the operation and capabilities of all the equipment on the Hood factory floor. That experience served him well in operating both companies – to ensure that Hood products met his customers' specifications and to know the factory's capabilities and limitations. In its early days, Hood Sponge Rubber rode the crest of pent-up demand for cars and other consumer products in post-war America, and as early as 1951, the company had 200 employees, production of three million pounds of rubber products and gross revenues above the million-dollar mark. A visitor noted Berwanger's personable management style, where factory workers interacted with him on a first-name basis. "We're small enough so that while our prices are just competitive, we can beat the big firms any day on service," he explained. "We can give a customer his finished product while the order is still being processed in the office of a big company."[172] Among Berwanger's business accomplishments is inventing two products receiving U.S. and international patents – one for a sponge rubber weatherseal (1965) and the other for a sponge rubber insulated pipe wrap (1972).[173]

Still, business success came at a price. Family life suffered. Berwanger for many years maintained a rigorous travel schedule. Sales calls frequently involved Whirlpool in St. Joseph, Michigan, and Evansville, Indiana. (Evansville, home to other appliance manufacturers, was once known as the Refrigerator Capital of the World.) It was common for him to leave the house on Monday, make sales calls all week, and not return home until Friday. During the football season, his schedule was even more jammed. Friday nights found him in a hotel of a Big Ten city, where he officiated the following afternoon. Otherwise, weekends centered on playing a round or two at Hinsdale Golf

Club. In the early years of running his own businesses, the former Naval flight instructor piloted himself to his appointments. By 1951, he had decided that keeping up his pilot's license was not worth the time and expense. "Flying," he later told an interviewer, "is for the birds."[174]

The dynamics of Berwanger's enterprises changed in the last half of the 1950s. The 70-year-old vice president of his manufacturers' rep agency, father-in-law John Baker, died in mid-1955. Four years later, when business partner Harry M. Hood died at age 65, Berwanger purchased a majority stake in Hood Sponge Rubber Company. In the 1960s, Berwanger expanded his business holdings when he bought a firm renting space in the Hood building, Winner Cutting and Stamping. The firm, which performed die cuts and produced ink stampers and stamp pads, remains a wholly owned subsidiary of Jay Berwanger, Incorporated.

As Berwanger's enterprises became more prosperous, he entertained thoughts of at least one of his sons following him into the business. A teenager and young man during the Great Depression, Jay remained locked into making money and building wealth. John was going to be a lawyer, so income was not likely to be an issue. However, Jay was concerned about Cuyler's interest in a teaching career. Jay didn't apply excessive pressure on his younger son to join him in the business. That was left to Ernie Dix, who had a talk with his godson. "Ernie pulled out a wad of cash and said, 'See this? You'll never make money as a teacher,'" Butch said years later. "'You only get – what? – $6,000 a year? You've got to make more money!' I said, 'You've also got to be happy. You've got to do what you like to do.' And Dad was fine. He said, 'Do what you want to do.'"

The Simpson family has played a role in Jay Berwanger, Incorporated, for more than 60 years. Duncan Simpson joined the rep agency in the early 1950s. In 1973, Simpson's son Bob came on and learned the business top to bottom. After a dozen years, as Berwanger transitioned toward retirement, Bob Simpson succeeded him as company president. He credits the former Heisman Trophy winner with teaching him many things, including keeping a calm demeanor and coolly working through difficult issues while remaining competitive.[175]

Berwanger believed that success had to be earned. For example, in 1980, his second wife's son-in-law, Greg Gerwig, had been unemployed for some time. Berwanger offered him a job with the caution, "You'll have to start at the very bottom." Gerwig's first position was machine operator, and from there he worked his way up the ladder of responsibility. Some 33 years after

Berwanger gave him a chance, Gerwig still works for the company, where he is production manager.

In 1975, Berwanger sold Hood Sponge Rubber to Schlegel Corporation and moved his rep agency and subsidiary Winner Cutting and Stamping to 1245 Warren Avenue in Downers Grove, a western suburb of Chicago. The location was a few minutes' drive from his home in Hinsdale (and a subsequent residence in Oak Brook). The single-story building with a dark brick exterior has never displayed the name of the 17-employee businesses operating inside.

Berwanger was a modest man. He did not throw his name around to gain attention or exact favors at ticket windows or restaurants. But if his name got his foot in the door on a sales call, well, that was another matter. Many

After military service during World War II, Berwanger (shown about 1951) returned to the sponge-rubber manufacturing business and also established Jay Berwanger, Incorporated, a manufacturers representative firm specializing in molded rubber and plastic parts. (Berwanger family collection)

a factory manager feeling too harried to see a salesman making a cold call suddenly found the time when he learned that the man waiting in the outer office was the winner of the first Heisman Trophy. Regular customers looked forward to his visits, when they could talk about sports, get an autograph, and perhaps discuss sponge-rubber products. Though his employees and partners, starting with father-in-law John Baker and Dix, did not enjoy the same high level of customer access, the Jay Berwanger name on their business cards was a great ice-breaker. In later years, Berwanger handed out golf balls imprinted with his company name and a drawing of his famous trophy.

Name recognition provided other benefits. After Berwanger moved his company to the Chicago suburbs and started producing parts, a large corporation sent out a man to conduct a surprise inspection of the manufacturing facility. The auditor never made it to the factory floor; he spent all his time in Berwanger's office, shooting the breeze with the sports legend before filing a favorable report with his superiors.[176] It's likely the company would have passed its audit anyway. Jay Berwanger, Incorporated, has maintained its reputation for quality products and service at competitive prices.

After Bob Simpson assumed presidency of the company, and even after Berwanger sold Simpson the business in 1990-91, Berwanger kept coming to the office. He was always welcome. He would hold court in his old office, chatting up customers and talking business with employees. Berwanger usually had lunch at his desk, and the menu always included a milkshake. "He was our entertainment committee," Simpson reflected. In 2013, more than a decade after Berwanger's death, his desk and memorabilia remain on display at Jay Berwanger, Incorporated, arranged in a way that an observer might think that the Heisman legend had just stepped out to play another round at the country club.

CHAPTER 39

Berwanger's 1941 debut as a football official coincided with a youth movement. "The Big Ten gradually is reconstructing its staff of officials to bring in younger and faster men and reward some its greatest stars, and Berwanger is one of the new crop," noted the *Chicago Daily News*, which featured him as a photographic model to illustrate officials' signals. (In later years, he demonstrated various signals for features in the *Chicago Tribune* and, curiously, *Popular Mechanics*, which examined gestures as a means of communication.) His qualifications as an official were limited to being a star player and college assistant coach. By the 1942 football season, however, Berwanger was not in a sports official's uniform but that of the U.S. Navy.

After his wartime service, Berwanger returned from a four-season officiating hiatus and tuned-up with the Northwestern spring game in May 1946. That fall, he served as line judge when Pitt visited Illinois. He fulfilled the same role in Evanston a few weeks later, when Northwestern handled College of the Pacific, 26-13. The visitors' coach was still the Grand Old Man himself. Former Chicago icon Amos Alonzo Stagg was roaming the sidelines at age 84. Berwanger was making the grade as an assistant official, and in 1947 the Big Ten moved him up to referee for many games. The next season, he received his biggest assignment yet: Line judge for the 1949 Rose Bowl. As events played out, however, he might have regretted going to Pasadena. The game pitted undefeated California of the Pacific Coast Conference against 7-2 Northwestern, the runner-up in the Big Ten.[177] The game was played before 92,000 fans in the stadium and as many viewers as KTTV could attract in the television station's very first day of on the air.[178] Cal coach Pappy Waldorf previously coached Northwestern (1935-46). The Wildcats were coached by one of Waldorf's former All-America players, 32-year-old W. Robert Voigts, whose players included many war veterans who called

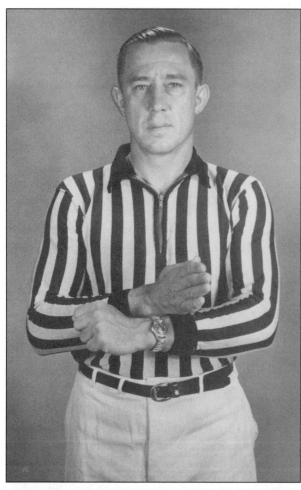

From the mid-1940s to mid-1950s, Berwanger officiated Big Ten games. Chicago news-papers and even Popular Mechanics asked him to demonstrate officials' various signals. (Top photo, Special Collections Research Center, University of Chicago Library, and, bottom row, Chicago Tribune. Reprinted with permission)

their coach "Bob." Northwestern, which had rebounded from a 3-7 season in Voigts' first year, finished 7-2 and one game behind Michigan in the Big Ten. However, the conference allowed only one member to play in a postseason bowl game – the Rose Bowl and only the Rose Bowl. Further, the conference restricted a school that had made the appearance in Pasadena to wait at least two years before going again. Thus, Michigan, which had completed its second consecutive undefeated season, had to stay home, satisfied with memories of its 49-0 thrashing of Southern California in the Rose Bowl of New Year's Day 1948. Illinois, which whipped UCLA 45-14 in the 1947 game, likewise knew throughout the 1948 regular season that it was not bowl-eligible.

Early in the 1948 campaign, *Chicago Tribune* sports editor Arch Ward quoted Berwanger on what he considered the toughest judgment on the gridiron. He cited the occasion when the passer loses the ball upon being hit by a defender. It is a fumble or an incomplete pass? It depends on the passer's motion immediately before the ball leaves his hand. Berwanger might have amended that answer in light of his controversial decision in Pasadena.

With the game tied 7-7 in the second quarter, Northwestern drove to first-and goal at the Cal 1. The Wildcats' Art Murakowski powered toward the goal line, where he lost his grip on the ball while being tackled by Norm Pressley. The Golden Bears' Will Lotter fell on the loose pigskin in the end zone. Was it a Northwestern touchdown? Or was it a touchback, denying the Wildcats a score and giving Cal the ball on its 20-yard line? As line judge, Berwanger gave the referee the signal for a touchdown. He believed that Murakowski lost possession of the ball *after* it hit the plane of the goal line. A sportswriter who afterward studied the Pathe Newsreel film of the play said referee Jimmy Cain moved up from his position behind the offensive team, turned to his right and conferred with Berwanger, who nodded his head. Cain then signaled a touchdown. The Golden Bears argued, to no avail. Their only consolation was that Northwestern missed the point-after kick, making their deficit only 13-7 at halftime.

It was a big decision, but it loomed even larger after Northwestern and California traded second-half touchdowns and the Wildcats claimed a 20-14 victory. The Murakowski fumble/touchdown became the epicenter for rumblings by unhappy California backers and West Coast sportswriters. The *Los Angeles Times* published a photo of the play taken from behind the end zone. It shows a forward-leaning Murakowski being tackled with his feet outside the end zone and the ball free. The photo showed how close a play it was, but Cal supporters saw it as conclusively showing a fumble before the goal line. The Californians piled on Berwanger, the official from the Midwest. Paul Zimmerman, sports editor of the *Los Angeles Times*, led the charge. In a column discussing the Murakowski play in particular and photography's impact on sports officiating in general, Zimmerman said that Berwanger, straddling the goal line during the play, had his head turned toward the end zone. "Berwanger, today, stands over in the corner with the dunce cap on," he wrote. California writers also complained of an apparently illegal block on the play by Northwestern's Tom Worthington.

Zimmerman's counterpart in Chicago, the *Tribune*'s Arch Ward, saw it differently. He expressed no doubt that it was a touchdown, reporting that Murakowski was a yard into the end zone when the ball came loose. Ward attributed the furor to West Coast sportswriters who were "becoming increasingly disturbed" about the Pacific Coast's lack of success in postseason competition with the Big Ten. Northwestern's win was the conference's third straight in the Rose Bowl. Immediately after the game, Cain, who was assigned to the game by the Pacific Coast Conference, told reporters, "Jay

Berwanger's career as a college football official was interrupted by World War II. Posing during their certification exam in 1947 are three former star players. From left: Mike Layden, Notre Dame; Berwanger; and Herb Steger, Michigan. In high school, Iowa natives Berwanger and Layden competed against each other in football and track. (Chicago Tribune photo. Reprinted with permission)

Berwanger was in a position to see the play and he called Murakowski over the goal line for the touchdown." That brought a response from the Big Ten, whose supervisor of officials, Jim Masker, charged Cain with attempting to deflect criticism for a final decision that is the referee's alone. "The camera is tricky on goal line plays," Masker observed. "Movies usually are taken at a bad angle on touchdowns and still shots may be snapped a second before or after the farthest advance of a ball carrier." If any sportswriters reached Berwanger immediately afterward, he didn't talk to them. Berwanger headed to San Francisco to visit friends for a few days. Nearly a week after the Rose Bowl, Berwanger surfaced and told sportswriters, "All we can do is call them as we see them. On whether it is right or wrong depends on what part of the country you belong, I guess. The game has been played, and I think myself and every other official in the game did his job as well as he could." He also spoke at length with Masker, who subsequently told reporters that the former Heisman winner had no doubt about the Murakowski play, including the Worthington block. Several weeks later, after that controversy largely faded and fans turned to other issues, the men of Cal's Sigma Nu fraternity made good on their friendly wager with their counterparts at Northwestern. The prize, a fraternity blanket from the losing chapter, arrived from Berkeley. It was embroidered: "Northwestern 14, California 14, Berwanger 6."

Berwanger officiated several more seasons of college football, then hung up his whistle around 1954. He nearly didn't make it that long. After the 1952 season, he suffered a heart attack, though at the time it was not disclosed as such. The *Chicago Tribune* said it was a virus infection and added that the former football star would spend up to six weeks in Naples, Florida, to regain his health and to decide whether to continue officiating. "He was just worn out," recalled his son Butch, who added that after the health scare his father started watching his diet and made butter and fried foods a thing of his past.[179] However, Jay still regularly enjoyed a milkshake with his lunch, and he never shook his life-long relationship with cigarettes.

Berwanger's officiating resumé included many Big Ten games, a few minor bowls (such as the Refrigerator Bowl in a city he frequently visited on business, Evansville, Indiana) and serving as line judge for the NFL-College All-Stars game in 1951, when the Cleveland Browns spanked the collegians, 33-0. But he handled no games bigger or more controversial than the 1949 Rose Bowl. In 1984, when Northwestern players held a reunion commemorating their championship in Pasadena 35 seasons earlier, they made a plaque to honor Berwanger. It was inscribed, "Courageous Call 1-1-49."

CHAPTER 40

In 1950, the Jay and Philomela Berwanger family moved from the Hyde Park neighborhood in Chicago to 404 East First Street in Hinsdale, a well-to-do western suburb featuring big houses on large, shaded lots. The family now included a daughter, Helen, born in 1949 and named after her maternal grandmother, and her brothers John (1942) and Cuyler (1945). The Berwangers also bought the lot behind their home and installed a tennis court. Some winters, the family flooded the court to provide the children with an area for ice skating. Jay joined Hinsdale Golf Club, a private club established in 1898, where he fed his lifelong passion for the links. In later years, he became a member of one of the nation's premier country clubs, Pine Valley, in southern New Jersey.

For several years, the family home displayed no evidence of Dutch Berwanger's storied past. No framed photos of Berwanger scoring a touchdown, the *Chicago Tribune* Silver Football Award, or the plaque recognizing his selection as captain of the All-America Team. That was not his style. The Heisman Trophy wasn't even in the home. For years, what today is America's most-recognized award was a doorstop in the Chicago home of Aunt Gussie, his mother's sister. He was modest as an athlete, and he remained so throughout his life. His friend of 70 years, Ernie Dix, said, "In all those years – though he had a right to do so – not once did I ever hear him brag."[180] However, fortunately for his family, he was a bit of a pack rat. He left behind boxes of newspaper clippings, telegrams, correspondence, trophies, game films, and even track and wrestling ribbons and medals dating back his days at Dubuque High.

When John was in preschool or kindergarten, he came home one day with a question that gave his parents pause. He asked, "What is a Heisman?" Recalling the exchange decades later, Berwanger said, "My wife and I looked at each other. It was time to tell him who I was." They got out the scrap-book documenting his Heisman-worthy athletic career. Jay also went to the telephone. "I called Aunt Gussie and got the Heisman Trophy back."[181] Even then, his children recalled, the trophy for years gathered dust in their basement.

Not long after their move to the suburbs, the family acquired an unusual pet – a baby squirrel that apparently had fallen out of a nearby tree. They managed to domesticate it. Johnny liked to walk around the house with the squirrel tucked in the pocket of his bathrobe. One day, the squirrel suffered a serious injury after some rough treatment by a neighbor boy. A distraught Phil contacted another neighbor's acquaintance for some expert advice: Marlin Perkins, a zoologist who would become famous through the "Wild Kingdom" television program (1963-72). Perkins was aghast to learn that the Berwangers kept a squirrel in their house. The pet did not survive, and Perkins gave clear instruction: "You are lucky. Don't try that again!"[182]

When John and Cuyler (Butch) were old enough for the experience, Phil and Jay sent them to Camp Highlands for Boys. The summer camp on Plum Lake in Northern Wisconsin was owned and managed by a distant relative of Phil's, Doc Monilaw. It was also where Jay worked as a counselor in 1934 and 1935. Loyal supporters of Camp Highlands, the Berwangers for many

Jay and Philomela pose outside their home in the Chicago suburb of Hinsdale in the 1950s. (Special Collections Research Center, University of Chicago Library)

summers used the camp's lodge for their family vacation after the boys' regular stint at camp. Butch liked Camp Highlands so much that he was a staff member for 23 summers, 1963-85.[183]

John was at camp in 1953 when a ferocious afternoon storm hit with straight-line winds. The storm downed thousands of trees, including one that crashed onto a cabin occupied by five campers. Four of the boys escaped, but the fifth, Bruce Allen, was killed. His bunk was the farthest from the door. John was in the cabin next door. "There was so much noise from the wind and the branches hitting our cabin that we didn't know it had happened," he said. "We didn't hear about it until the kids from the cabin came into our cabin." Back in Illinois, Jay and Phil heard that a severe storm ravaged Northern Wisconsin with tragic consequences, but they had no details. Was Johnny all right? They loaded Butch and Helen into the car and drove all night to Sayner, more than 350 miles away. A dozen miles from Camp Highlands, Jay dropped off his passengers at Coon's Franklin Lodge and drove on. A few miles later, uprooted trees blocked the road, so Jay parked and walked about five miles – over and around downed trees – to reach Camp Highlands. John was shaken but unhurt, and Jay stayed on to help the staff deal with the aftermath.

While Phil, Butch and Helen waited for Jay to return, they acquainted themselves with Coon's Franklin Lodge. Owned by the Coon family since 1892, it sits on the shore of Trout Lake about 10 miles north of Minocqua. The Berwangers decided that they preferred Coon's over the Camp Highlands facility for their family vacation. For many summers afterward, they hauled their motorboat to Coon's, where they enjoyed fishing and skiing. Most of the family spent all August there, but Jay felt he could not spare a full month away from work. His departures for Chicago or customers' locations caused some family stress. He simply was not around his family all that much – at any time of year – leaving it to Phil to manage the household.

Over several summers in Northern Wisconsin, Phil, despite her expressed determination to catch a muskie, came up empty day after day. She worked hard at it, going out early in the morning and following all sorts of fishing advice. But she still couldn't land her prize. Meanwhile, success had a way of finding her husband. His routine was to sleep in, play nine holes of golf and, finally, in the late morning, wet a line. On one such morning, he landed a muskie. He teased Phil about his success. It was bad enough (for Phil) that it happened once, but he pulled out a muskie on at least two other occasions. Phil couldn't conceal her frustration. "They nearly got divorced over those muskies," chuckled John years later. However, that was not Jay's biggest "catch" ever. His children remember the time they watched from land as Jay, normally a conservative boat operator, sped the craft into shore. They figured he had a trophy to show them. They rushed to the dock and excitedly asked him what he caught. He tersely replied, "Your mother." While casting, Jay had snagged Phil in the back of her head. The episode concluded with a hospital visit.[184]

The three Berwanger children attended Hinsdale Township High School. "Butch and Helen were much more athletic than I was," John said. "I played a little football, but I gave it up in high school. But Dad didn't really pressure us. He would love to see us play football. He'd gotten a lot out of it, he knew what you could get out of it, but we did what we wanted to do. I ended up playing a lot of tournament bridge, and that was fine."[185] Interscholastic sports for girls were still years away, but Helen was a member of the country club's swim team. Butch played varsity tennis and football. Being a Berwanger on Chicago-area gridirons brought Butch some notoriety, but the Red Devil teams were outstanding, and he was not a star, so sportswriters rarely made the literary link to his famous father. It did happen once, during Butch's junior year, when Hinsdale's senior-dominated football team won every game and was Illinois' top-ranked team. After Butch scored a touchdown in a close game, a newspaper played up the son-of-a-Heisman-winner-leads-Hinsdale-to-victory angle. After the paper came out, Butch recalled, "I came back to my locker and there were 10 of these articles posted on my locker. I did not need that, not at all. I knew my place as a junior on this very senior team. So it wasn't always easy being a football player following Dad in Chicago."

In addition to being the manager of the household. She also served as travel agent, Phil arranged family vacations and outings, including train trips to New York City, where the family attended Broadway shows (including "Camelot" and "West Side Story") and the 1964 World's Fair. A winter vacation in the Miami area was memorable. Though Phil faced health issues with some regularity, she enjoyed tennis and horseback riding and raised Drahthaar dogs; Suzy was a favorite. The family pointer Duke often accompanied Jay and the boys on excursions to the suburban hunting club where they were members.

With her husband away so much due to business, officiating, and golf, it fell to Phil to handle most matters of discipline. However, as teenagers the Berwanger boys had to face their father after some memorable incidents involving automobiles. In one case, when John was just learning to drive, he accepted the invitation of his mother, who was seated beside him, to drive the car into the garage. That's what he did – literally. John hit the accelerator instead of the brake and propelled the car into the garage's back wall. Failing to survive the crash were Jay's prized ladders – the ones he needed for installing and removing storm windows. "There was this horrendous crash as I hit the back of the garage, and it opened up like a door," John remembered. "I was screaming and mother was screaming. Dad came out, and his famous line was, 'How are my ladders?' Jay deflected criticism that he was more concerned about his ladders than his family. "He said later that he knew we were all right because he could hear us," John said. "But the ladders were kindling wood."[186]

In another incident, a teen-age Butch and a buddy watched a neighbor friend park his family's new car in his driveway and enter the house. The pair thought it would be a great joke to sneak behind the wheel and move the car. The neighbor saw what was going on and, as Butch backed out of the driveway, he started a chase. Butch backed the car down the street. But the chase was short-lived: Butch crunched the neighbor's car into a telephone pole. The crash was so loud that a policeman in the vicinity heard it – as did

For a time in the early 1950s, the Berwangers kept a squirrel as a household pet. They considered it domesticated, but the noted zoologist Marlin Perkins told them otherwise. Shown with their parents and sister Helen are Cuyler (left) and John. (Special Collections Research Center, University of Chicago Library)

Jay from inside his house. Butch recalled what happened next. "So my Dad runs out, looks around and says, 'You all OK?' I said, 'Yeah, we're fine.' He says, 'All right. You'll have to pay for it,' and goes back to the house." He left it to Butch to explain things to the policeman and, later, to the family whose car he damaged. Jay paid for what insurance didn't cover, but he made Butch reimburse him. "With my summer paychecks, I paid for the car, over like three years," he said. However, that negative turned into a positive of sorts. "Dad took the money and put it in the stock market, or put it someplace. Then, after I paid for the car, he said, 'OK, here's the money. I invested it for you.'"

On those and other occasions when he advanced his children money – to cover damage, help them purchase a home, or some other purpose – the story was the same. He insisted that the debt be repaid, but when it was settled, he returned the money, often in the form of a college fund for his children or grandchildren.

The Berwanger children's involuntary investments and their father's business success allowed them to attend prestigious private colleges and universities. John received his undergraduate degree from Princeton University (1964) and then earned a law degree from his father's alma mater, the University of Chicago. Butch attended Stanford University one year before transferring to Denison University, of Granville, Ohio, where he received his bachelor's degree in 1968. When Butch was a senior, his sister joined him at Denison; she earned her degree in 1971. It was at Denison where, with Butch playing the matchmaker, Helen met her future husband, John Tierney. (John's wife, Patricia, also graduated

John (left) and Cuyler pose with their parents after an outing on the water. Philomela's frustrations over her failing to land muskies in northern Wisconsin, while her husband seemed to catch them at will, became part of family lore. (Berwanger family collection)

from the Ohio institu-
tion, though the couple
met while working sum-
mer jobs in Chicago.)

Jay kept his cool on
most occasions, but there
were exceptions. "He
had a temper once in a
while," Butch said. "We
had an expression when
he got mad: 'Walking
the dog.'" When she
saw her husband getting
riled up about something
or another, Phil would
tell him, "Go walk the
dogs." Butch said, "He
would take our two large
hunting dogs for a long
walk and often come

Philomela, shown in a 1962 publicity shot promoting a society fundraiser, donated her time and her name to several charitable causes. (Chicago Tribune photo. Reprinted with permission)

back much calmer." His daughter observed, "He could be quite demanding, both of himself and others. This sometimes made dinners out or checking into hotels an adventure." In his later years, restaurant servers who brought him a wine glass that wasn't filled sufficiently or a plate where the food items touched each other were likely to hear about it. "But he was willing to give 100 percent of himself and asked the same of others."[187] Occasional flare-ups notwithstanding, he was so well thought of at Hinsdale Golf Club that, even a decade after his death, the menu still lists "The Berwanger." It was his standard order at lunch: half a cold deli sandwich and a cup of soup.[188]

By the time Helen was in middle school, her father was spending more time at home. He was retired from officiating and had less business travel. "Dad was the one who got me up in the morning and made me breakfast," Helen said. "He believed in a hearty breakfast long before it was fashionable. Why I didn't weigh 400 pounds, I don't know." By the time she was a sopho-more at Hinsdale High, her brothers were away at college. "So it was just Dad and me in the mornings. I liked that." He was a dedicated father. On the day of Helen's "coming out" party, a dinner-dance a couple of days before Christmas 1967, Jay battled a 104-degree fever. Despite feeling dead to the world, he got into his tux and attended the Hinsdale hospital benefit at the Drake Hotel in Oak Brook. He was determined to not spoil his 18-year-old daughter's special evening.[189]

Jay and Phil came to love winter vacations in Mexico. They visited Acapulco, Puerto Vallarta, and Cozumel, and eventually bought a condominium near Monzanillo, on the Pacific coast. As the only child still living at home during her school years, Helen accompanied them. "Dad tried valiantly to learn Spanish, but evidently foreign languages were not his forté. He and Mom had tapes and books, but ended up mostly only saying, "¡hola!" and "gracias." All their lives, the Berwangers were a personable couple who made friends easily, Helen said, "especially Dad. He would talk to anyone, find out where they were from, what they did, and all about their families." On one occasion, while Phil and Helen were sunbathing on the beach, Phil saw her husband and another man approaching. "Quick! Turn over," Phil instructed her daughter. "Here comes Insurance from Peoria!"[190]

Tragedy struck the family in early February 1969. Jay's brother, Paul, a television salesman for Goldblatt's Department Store, was found dead in his Chicago apartment with a self-inflicted gunshot wound.[191] Jay told a Chicago newspaper that his brother never regained his health after service in World War II.

The Berwanger family in December 1967. From left: John; John's wife, Patricia; Helen; Jay; Philomela; and Cuyler (Butch). (Berwanger family collection)

Jay and Philomela in 1966, 30 years after his graduation from the University of Chicago. (Berwanger family collection)

Though the newspaper article was not specific, Jay most likely was referring to his only brother's mental health. Today it might be diagnosed as post-traumatic stress disorder. Wounded in the Battle of Guadalcanal, Paul witnessed nearly all the other members of his unit perish. He returned to action – only to again witness carnage among his new unit.[192] Paul Berwanger, who never married, was 46 years old.

Phil's health issues were a continual concern. A cold that might sidetrack most people for a day or so would hit her so hard that she'd spend a week in bed. Her doctors were so concerned that they told her to quit her Salem cigarettes and alcohol. She didn't. In the early months of 1975, she experienced a serious kidney infection. Surgeons removed the kidney, and Jay and Phil soon headed to Florida for recovery and relaxation. Things did not go as expected. Jay's concern heightened when Phil didn't rebound. Back in the Chicago area, she reentered the hospital, where she received a diagnosis that was tantamount to a death sentence: pancreatic cancer. She died within a week, on August 26, 1975. Philomela Baker Berwanger was 59.[193]

CHAPTER 41

In 1977, Jay Berwanger did perhaps the most impulsive thing of his life: He secretly remarried. The bride was Jane Fulton Temple, whom he had known for some 45 years, going back to their time at the University of Chicago. Jane's late husband, Joe Temple, had "rushed" Jay into Psi Upsilon fraternity. After college, Joe Temple struggled personally and professionally. He held several jobs over the years. When he died at age 58 in late 1968, he

Jane Berwanger in 1988.

was a security guard at a suburban Chicago hospital. The Temples and Berwangers had remained marginally connected through a large circle of friends with ties to the University of Chicago. Described by a daughter as a "people person," Jane was a successful real estate agent in Chicago's southside Beverly neighborhood.[194] When Philomela died in 1975, Jane was among those paying her respects at the funeral home.[195] Around 1977, when a widowed friend the Berwangers also knew well became seriously ill, Jane moved in to help

provide care. "Dad would stop over and see if they needed any help and that's kind of how they reconnected," Butch said. Jane and Jay hit it off from the start, and, though their families were aware that they were spending time together, they had no idea how serious the relationship had become. Jay's three children heard about the marriage after the fact. They were stunned. Jane had informed her son and two daughters just before the wedding, and, though it struck them as "kind of sudden," daughter Marianne Gerwig said, "I was just really happy for her."[196] The bride was 65 and the groom was 63.

After they had been married two or three years, Jay and Jane moved from

Hinsdale to a gated community in the suburb immediately north, Oak Brook. As the new Mrs. Berwanger, Jane accompanied her husband to Heisman ceremonies, University of Chicago events and countless other social occasions. As had Philomela, Jane enjoyed winter vacations with Jay in Mexico. They took excursions sponsored by the University of Chicago, including a trip to Russia and an African safari. Jane came to feel comfortable in her new role as the wife of a Heisman Trophy winner. Apparently, she adapted to it more readily than did the second wives of other recipients. Rudy Riska, the retired executive of the Downtown Athletic Club, tells the story of Les Horvath, the 1944 winner, who explained to his new wife that the Heisman Trophy was a very exclusive award. Not long after that, the Horvaths visited the homes of Tommy Harmon (1940) and Glenn Davis (1946), each of whom had his Heisman on display. Driving home after the second visit, the new Mrs. Horvath turned to her husband and said, "What's this about your trophy being so exclusive? I'm seeing them all over!"[197]

Several years before their mother died, the Berwanger children completed their education and embarked on their chosen paths in life. For John, it was a stint in the Air Force and then a career as an attorney in Chicago. For Butch, it was working with young people as a teacher, coach, and school counselor

Most of the time he attended University of Chicago football games, Jay was sitting in a place of honor. However, on this occasion in 1978, he and Jane enjoyed relaxing in general seating. (Chicago Tribune photo. Reprinted with permission)

in the Chicago suburb of Riverside. Though Jay initially had misgivings about his younger son's career direction – would it be enough to pay the bills? – he supported Butch's decision. One of the hallmarks of Butch's career was founding the Hauser Junior High food drive, a program he directed for more than four decades. He retired in 2011.

Helen took a less predictable path. After marrying John Tierney, whom she met at Denison University, she left the bustling Chicago suburbs for the

After they married in 1977, Jay and Jane frequently traveled, including this excursion to Africa. (Berwanger family collection)

Northern Michigan town of Onaway, population 920, where they owned and operated a resort. Soon afterward, they acquired a bar and expanded it into a restaurant. At first, her parents had their doubts, but they kept their own counsel, even as their daughter and son-in-law struggled to make their business successful. "To their credit, my parents never expressed any misgivings about the move, until much later, and supported our decision," Helen said. "One time when Dad came to visit he took me aside and told me he was very proud of me because I had learned to accept people for what they were, and not where they came from. He was like that – always looking for common ground with someone new. He could talk to anyone about anything."

The Tierneys' community lacked a natural gas utility. In the early 1980s, John Tierney and friend Delmer Porter lobbied Michigan Consolidated Gas to extend service to their region. The big utility scoffed at the idea. "They said natural gas will never come to the little town of Onaway, Michigan, because Onaway is on the end of the road from nowhere," Helen said. "It kind of made my husband and his friend Del mad. So they decided they were going to bring natural gas to Onaway." However, money was an obstacle. That was when Jay offered to become a partner, and, with his financial investment,

Aurora Gas Company became a reality in 1984. Jay came to enjoy visiting Onaway, where he became a local celebrity. He loved staying at Helen and John's resort, holding court in their 211 Bar & Grill, and speaking to high school athletes from Onaway or neighboring Cheboygan. Most likely, he is the only football player in the Cheboygan Sports Hall of Fame (1987) to have never played a down within 450 miles of town.[198] Nearly 30 years later, John and Helen still own and operate the natural gas distributorship. They sold the resort in 2000 and the restaurant in 2004.

"I'm sure that there were many times in our early struggles that he worried about our success, but he never second-guessed our decisions," Helen said of her father. "He would offer advice only when asked, and gave financial help under the guise of 'birthday presents' or 'anniversary presents' or 'sweetest day gifts.' We knew he was there if we needed help, but he never made us feel he was giving us a hand out. Having worked hard to get where he did in life, he appreciated anyone who did the same, even if they lived in the 'sticks.'"[199]

With the passage of time and his second marriage, Jay Berwanger's family and extended family grew. He became stepfather to Jane's son and two daughters. At the time of his death, his combined family included 20 grandchildren and 13 great-grandchildren. When he attended weddings and other special occasions, attendees from outside the Berwanger circle were often excited to have a celebrity in their midst. At several wedding receptions, it became necessary to set up two receiving lines – one to congratulate the new bride and groom and another for guests to shake hands and to have their picture taken with the first Heisman Trophy winner. At one such reception, the wedding photographer on duty was so caught up in the moment that he asked a wedding guest to take his camera and snap his picture with the sports legend.

In the early 1990s, Jane began showing indications of Alzheimer's Disease. She and Jay continued to travel until her health prevented it. He maintained the role of caregiver as long as he could. He took her shopping and took her to an adult daycare program a few days a week. Finally, it became necessary for her to receive professional care, and she moved into Manor Care Nursing Home in Hinsdale. Jay was there every day, and he saw to it that a stylist did Jane's hair every week. Jane Berwanger died on the last day of 1997 at age 85 years old. Jane's family has only positive memories of her 20 years as the wife of Jay Berwanger. "He was so good to my mom," Marianne Gerwig said. "He was the nicest man I've ever known."[200]

CHAPTER 42

Berwanger's name was well-known to football fans when he played in the mid-1930s and won acclaim as the nation's best player, but it understandably faded as later stars took over the headlines. However, Berwanger's fame experienced a rebound of sorts as the status of the Heisman Trophy grew. Generations later, people who did not know or recall the name Jay Berwanger certainly knew of the Heisman Trophy, and they were honored to shake the hand or secure the autograph of the man whose name appeared at the top of the Heisman honor roll.

Starting around each Thanksgiving, Berwanger anticipated phone calls from sportswriters requesting interviews. "Every year about this time, I become famous," he told *The Washington Post* in 1976, a few days before he was a guest on NBC television's "Today" show. "They dig me out of the record books and a lot of kids – even the winners – ask, 'Who's Berwanger?'" Journalists considered Berwanger a good interview. His voice was gruff and his manner direct, but they appreciated his modesty, his intelligence and his accessibility. Whether the reporter represented a big-city daily or his paper back home in Dubuque, he was always accommodating.

Even after being asked the same questions over and over, year after year, Berwanger was a patient interview subject. His answers became rote: At the time, the best part of his Heisman experience was not his selection but the airplane trip to New York. Greatest thrills: the 85-yard touchdown against Ohio State and the victory over Illinois in his final game. The brief "negotiation" with George Halas. Why he didn't play professionally. His observations about the contemporary game. His only "regret" was being "born 30 years too soon" and missing out on the high salaries paid to the professional stars of subsequent generations. Still, he offered that comment more as a quip than a genuine regret. In 1969, he told a reporter, "For years, nobody mentioned the

Heisman Trophy very much, and then the (world) war started and we all had other things to think about. But then football started to blossom. The older I get, the more effect the Heisman has on my life."

Still, long before the Heisman solidified its place at the pinnacle of college football honors, Berwanger continued to receive acclaim and attention for his gridiron achievements of years past. As the 1940s came to a close, sportswriter and All-America coordinator Christy Walsh named him one the greatest players of the quarter-century (1925-49). Twenty years later, the Football Writers of America named him to its All-Time All-America team.[201] Ever modest, Berwanger often credited his coaches for the honors. Berwanger and his favorite coach, Clark Shaughnessy, were reunited in January 1970, when Berwanger was honored as a member of the NCAA's "all-time" team. Four months later, Shaughnessy died at age 78.

In 1954, Berwanger was among the second class inducted into the College Football Hall of Fame. That December, he was among the speakers at the 20th Heisman Trophy presentation ceremony, honoring Wisconsin's Alan Ameche. Berwanger attended nearly every Heisman Trophy ceremony, his

In the 1970s, retired Dubuque High coach Wilbur Dalzell poses with his most famous athlete and the replica of the most famous award in American sports. (Telegraph Herald photo)

presence added an important historical touch to the proceedings. Downtown Athletic Club officials reserved a front-row seat for him.

Before the early 1980s, Heisman officials usually announced their winner at a midday news conference, with the black-tie presentation ceremony occurring a week or 10 days later. Exceptions occurred in 1971, when they announced Auburn's Pat Sullivan on national television during halftime of a Thanksgiving night college game. In 1977, Heisman officials sold TV rights to CBS, which planned to make it an entire program during prime time on a Thursday night in December. Before the program, O.J. Simpson, the program's master of ceremonies, was scheduled to present the trophy. Simpson demurred, saying in so many words, "Why me, when you have the first Heisman winner here?" Berwanger wound up presenting the trophy to Earl Campbell of Texas. It was the only classy aspect of CBS' telecast, which was muddled with comedy sketches, sexy actresses, chorus girls and very little football. The hour-long TV program carried only 3½ minutes of game action, broken up into disjointed half-minute segments. *New York Times* columnist Dave Anderson panned the program, complaining that the award should be

renamed the "Schlockman Trophy." Johnny Majors moved to organize his fellow members of the American Football Coaches Association into a protest of the show-biz takeover of what were previously dignified proceedings. Noted Anderson, "Perhaps the nicest touch was having Jay Berwanger, the first winner in 1935, present the trophy."

On a trip to New York in December 1961, Berwanger was on hand when President John F. Kennedy addressed the National Football Foundation and Hall of Fame banquet. In his opening remarks, the president re-

At a January 1970 ceremony marking college football's centennial, the NCAA honored Berwanger as a member of its "all-time team." Joining him in Washington was his college coach, Clark Shaughnessy, who died four months later. (Capitol & Glogau photo, courtesy of Cindy Bertaut)

ferred to several former
and current players in
the audience. "Then,
Jay Berwanger, who is
here tonight, who, when
Chicago was tenth in
the Big Ten, was every-
one's All American."
(For the record, the
Maroons were never
tenth in the Big Ten
during Berwanger's
career, but they were
close – either seventh or
eighth his three varsity
seasons.) Later in his

In 1984, President Ronald Reagan said, "Jay Berwanger of the University of Chicago, was a powerful halfback and a hero to millions of football loving Americans, including a certain sportscaster named Dutch Reagan." (White House photo)

speech, Kennedy expressed concern about the growth of professionalism and specialization in sports, as well as the Americans' lack of physical fitness. He said he would not weigh in on the debate whether baseball or football was the national sport, but stated, "The sad fact is that it looks more and more as if our national sport is not playing at all, but watching. We have become more and more not a nation of athletes but a nation of spectators." Kennedy pitched his platform of improved physical fitness among all Americans.[202]

That night, Berwanger attended a reception and found himself standing a few feet from the president. The man talking to JFK stepped away and Berwanger stepped up. "President Kennedy, I'm Jay Berwanger from Chicago." The president took his arm and shook his hand. "Oh yes, Jay, I remember you," Kennedy said. "You played rugby with my brother Joe in Chicago." Recalled Berwanger decades later, "That took me back a bit…"[203] It was a memorable experience, but not enough to convert the dedicated conservative Berwanger into a Democrat. The next afternoon, Syracuse's Ernie Davis became the first non-white player to accept the Heisman Trophy.

In December 1975, three months after Philomela died, he traveled to New York for the 18th annual National Football Foundation awards dinner and the 41st annual Heisman Trophy presentation. The honoree was the first and (through 2012) only two-time recipient, Ohio State's Archie Griffin. He and Berwanger initially met the previous year, when Griffin received his first Heisman. Griffin's 1975 installation came 40 years after Berwanger accepted the Downtown Athletic Club Trophy. Over the years, Griffin and Berwanger become friends through joint appearances at Heisman ceremonies, golf outings and other events. They rarely discussed their respective gridiron days. "Jay was not one to talk about his athletic career," said Griffin, noting that Berwanger preferred to listen to stories rather than tell them. "He loved to laugh."[204] Berwanger went into the National Football Foundation Hall of Fame in 1958.

He was not exceptionally skilled at golf, but Berwanger loved the game, and he played as often as his schedule allowed – at Hinsdale Golf Club, Pine Valley, and at various charitable outings. In July 1995, he attended the outing to celebrate the 100th anniversary of the Big Ten Conference, but hot weather in suburban Chicago caused the 81-year-old to stay in the clubhouse and visit with friends and well-wishers. He played in two outings in June 1999. He was one of four celebrity guests at the Clarke College Classic in his hometown of Dubuque. Also featured were Tom Davis, University of Iowa basketball coach; Lou King, Iowa quarterback in the 1940s; and fellow Dubuque native Dick Hoerner, a retired National Football League fullback

In 1988, when Oklahoma State's Barry Sanders won the Heisman, Jay and Jane Berwanger were in New York to congratulate him. (Photo courtesy Charles Benson)

(1947-52). Later, he traveled to Omaha for the Husker-Heisman golf event, where his Heisman brethren, including host Johnny Rodgers (1972) and Billy Simms (1978), congratulated Berwanger on reaching his 85th birthday. [205]

Berwanger proudly supported his alma mater throughout his life. John Davey, who secured his bachelor's degree (1959) and law degree (1962) from the University of Chicago, noted that loyalty was not as prevalent among some of Berwanger's contemporaries. Many remained estranged and bitter about the university's decisions regarding intercollegiate athletics, particularly killing the football program in 1939. "Jay didn't show antagonism," said Davey, an attorney in Chicago, who described him as "an extremely humble man."

Davey likes to tell the story about an incident at the University Club of Chicago, where he and Berwanger were members. Davey's guest was a die-hard Notre Dame fan who boasted at length about the Irish. In so many words, he told Davey, "There is nothing to talk about regarding University of Chicago football except Jay Berwanger." Little did the Notre Dame alum know that Berwanger was seated within arm's reach. Davey turned to Berwanger, at the next table, and said, "Jay, we were just talking about Notre Dame football. Did Chicago ever play them?" In his gravelly voice, Berwanger gruffly responded, "Beat them four times. They never rescheduled." Davey said of the surprised Notre Dame booster, "The guy's jaw just dropped."[206] Berwanger knew his Maroons history: Chicago did beat Notre Dame in their only four meetings (1893-1899).

In addition to his familiarity with Maroons football history and his financial donations to the University of Chicago, Berwanger served as member and chair of various fund drives and special events, including his 60th class reunion. The university reciprocated with several honors and recognitions, including its Alumni Service Medal in 1984. However, Tom Weingartner said that when he became athletic director in 1990, university officials were not making the most of their association with their noted alumnus. Their reluctance might have been a reflection of a campus culture that long (especially after the Berwanger era) downplayed athletics.

Weingartner recalled the time, early in his tenure at Chicago, when he was among university representatives asked to provide assistance at Berwanger's appearance at a downtown Chicago department store. He arrived well before the appointed hour to find the venue empty. "I thought, 'Will there be anyone at Carson Pirie Scott who has heard of Jay Berwanger? No one is going to show up for this thing,'" Weingartner said.[207] "I didn't want him to be embarrassed." The administrator left the area for a half-hour and returned to witness a remarkable transformation. "There was this line all the way through the men's section, into another section of Carson's. People are waiting hours for his autograph. … I said, 'When am I going to learn my lesson? I'm always worrying about Jay, and here are all these people who get who he is,'" Weingartner said. On another occasion, in October 1995, the university athletic department plastered the campus with posters announcing a halftime ceremony honoring Berwanger on the 60th anniversary of his Heisman. It also scheduled a post-game reception in the Trophy Room of Bartlett Gymnasium. After the Maroons' 35-21 loss to Carnegie Mellon, Weingartner walked to the gym and became concerned when he observed the scene. People were lined up out the gym door and down the sidewalk. The athletic director assumed something had gone wrong – a problem with the caterer or some such – and he would have to go in and straighten out the mess. He worked

his way through the crowd to the Trophy Room. "And here are all these people with the poster of Jay, standing in line, waiting for him to sign autographs." Berwanger stayed until he signed every poster of every guest in line. "I said to myself, 'We're going to use Jay more often.'"

Dubuque honored Berwanger on several occasions, and he returned the favor. The City Council named him an Honorary Citizen in 1972. Seven years later, Berwanger came to town and donated an official replica of his Heisman Trophy to Dubuque Senior High in tribute to his prep coach, Wilbur Dalzell.[208] At the presentation ceremony, during halftime of a Rams football game, Berwanger stood at the microphone with his arm around

In 1999, an 85-year-old Berwanger poses with the honor that he most coveted at the time, the 1935 Silver Football awarded to the most valuable player in the Big Ten. In time, the Heisman would be the award that brought him perpetual fame. (Chicago Tribune photo. Reprinted with permission)

During a halftime ceremony in September 1979, Berwanger donated his replica of the Heisman Trophy to his prep alma mater, Dubuque Senior High. At right is Wilbur Dalzell, his prep coach in football, wrestling, and track. At left, holding the trophy, is Don Kolsrud, principal. (Courtesy of the Telegraph Herald, Dubuque)

a frail Dalzell. The trophy is prominently featured in a secured display in the gymnasium lobby. In 1992, Dubuque Senior High established an Athletic Hall of Fame, and Berwanger was an easy choice to be a charter inductee. At the induction banquet, Berwanger was gracious, humble, and humorous in his remarks. Other charter inductees included Dalzell; Johnny Orr, major college and former Dubuque High basketball coach; and three cousins: for-mer NFL players Dick Hoerner and Mike Reilly, and former major league baseball reliever Joe Hoerner.

Elsewhere in his native state, Berwanger is a charter member of The Des Moines Register Sports Hall of Fame (1951) and enshrined in the Iowa High School Football Players Hall of Fame. Illinois and Chicago organiza-tions also honored Berwanger: Illinois Sports Hall of Fame, Sports Lodge B'nai B'rith's first "Inspiration to Youth Award" (1985), Chicago Sports Hall of Fame (1983), and Chicago Park District Senior Citizen of the Year (1989). The University of Chicago posthumously made him a charter member of its athletics Hall of Fame in 2003. Certainly, these recognitions considered Berwanger's athletic achievements, but they also reflected what he accomplished with the rest of his life – his many civic contributions and

Private donations in 2013 paid for a larger-than-life bronze statue of Berwanger in the recon-structed public-school stadium in Dubuque, Dalzell Field. Standing beside a one-third-size clay model of her creation is Vala Ola. "To capture Mr. Berwanger in bronze is compelling for me as a sculptor," she said. "What a superb specimen of our human kind." (Vala Ola Studios)

business success. Sports Illustrated ranked him fifth among the greatest Iowa-born sports figures of the 20th century. (The top four: wrestler Dan Gable, pitcher Bob Feller, 1939 Heisman winner Nile Kinnick, and football legend Elmer Layden.)

Back in Dubuque, the public school district in the fall of 2013 dedicated a multi-million-dollar reconstruction Dalzell Field. Included were a memorial wall dedicated to Berwanger and his beloved coach, Wilbur Dalzell, plus a 7-foot-tall statue of Berwanger. The wall and statue came through private donations.

The statue was created by award-winning artist Vala Ola, a native of Iceland who has lived in the American Southwest for two decades. "To capture Mr. Berwanger in bronze is compelling for me as a sculptor," she said. "Speed, power, muscles, movement - he had it all. What a superb specimen of our humankind. Outstanding athletes have been a favorite subject matter for sculptors going all the way back to the classical Greek monuments of ancient times." Ola added, "Mr. Berwanger will inspire young athletes for generations to come. He has been an invigorating inspiration for me as a sculptor."

CHAPTER 43

For most of the 4½ years after his second wife died, Berwanger maintained an active schedule for a man in his mid-80s. Much of it involved golf. After playing a round one day in 1999, he returned home to keep an appointment with a photographer representing *ESPN: The Magazine*. Working in Berwanger's backyard, Chicago-based freelancer Jeff Sciortino captured the incongruous image of a somber and shriveled 85-year-old man wearing the uniform of a young man's game. Berwanger donned his uniform from the All-Star games of 1936 — a yellow jersey and pants – and leather helmet (without faceguard). The red number stitched onto his jersey was, of course, 99. Nestled in his left arm was an old and cracked football. "Jay was an amazing character. He was more than pleased to put on his uniform," Sciortino said. "He was, however, a little skeptical that he would actually fit into it." The photographer recalled that his subject was a great sport. "He was very comedic, cracking little jokes." More than a dozen years after the shoot, Sciortino still considers it one of his favorite images. "It's a timeless portrait."[209]

In mid-October 1999, Berwanger was the guest of his alma mater as it celebrated the 30th anniversary of the resumption of University of Chicago football (after a 30-season absence). When the women's basketball coach had asked one of her players, Liz Corken, to serve as Berwanger's student guide for the day, she was unaware that both Berwanger and Corken hailed from Dubuque. "Mr. Berwanger didn't know, either, so he was pretty surprised when I gave him a Senior High T-shirt and hat when I met him," Corken said at the time. "We tried to make sure everything was about the University of Chicago. But, like he told me, 'Dubuque's not a bad place to be from.'" Corken enjoyed her day with Berwanger, though it required pulling him away from autograph-seekers and keeping him on a tight schedule, which included the football game against Carnegie Mellon. She escorted the

Heisman legend to midfield for the pre-game coin toss and sat with him during the game. "When I played at Wahlert (Catholic High School in Dubuque), and long before Chicago recruited me, we'd go play at Senior, and we'd see his Heisman Trophy in the trophy case. We always thought it was pretty cool," Corken said. "It was amazing to be walking around with the guy who won that trophy. "He's such a nice man, and he's so down to Earth. It's pretty amazing how much the people at Chicago respect him." Today,

In October 1999, when the University of Chicago celebrated the 30th anniversary of the resumption of interscholastic football (after a 30-season absence), Berwanger was on hand. His student host, Elizabeth Corken, presented him with a shirt from his prep alma mater. She also hailed from Dubuque but attended another high school, Wahlert Catholic. (Photo courtesy of Elizabeth Corken Deegan)

Elizabeth Corken Deegan is an attorney based in Cedar Rapids, Iowa.

Age and a lifetime of cigarettes were catching up to Berwanger as the 21st century arrived. He had a heart pacemaker and his emphysema was evident in his smoker's cough. Yet he still made a few public appearances. When he attended a Heisman-related golf outing in Connecticut in 2000, he only felt up to chipping and putting at each green. His partner on the golf cart that day, then-Heisman director Rudy Riska, recalled the excitement when Berwanger holed a putt from 80 feet.[210] Berwanger served as grand marshal of the 2001 Independence Day parade in suburban Downers Grove, where the business bearing his name has operated since the early 1950s. A few months later, he returned to the University of Chicago campus where he was honored during the Homecoming football game. Wearing a brown sport coat over a sweater and sporting a brown cap, he appeared frail that afternoon as he acknowledged the crowd's applause. Accompanied by the university president, Don Randel, he then rode a lap around the field in the dark blue 1922 Milburn Light Electric car once owned by Amos Alonzo Stagg. It was his last documented visit to the Midway.

Berwanger's health in early 2002 was more fragile than his family realized. He didn't reveal to them that he had been coughing up blood. The first indication of the seriousness of his condition occurred in the spring, when he cancelled his golf trip to Pine Valley at the last minute. He phoned Butch and asked to see the doctor. Tests revealed the worst. The diagnosis: lung cancer. The prognosis: grave. The cancer was too far along to consider treatment for an 88-year-old man. All he and his family could do was prepare. Seven weeks later, it was over.

Jay Berwanger died at home Wednesday night, June 26, 2002.

Virtually every daily newspaper in the United States reported on the passing of the first Heisman Trophy recipient. Chicago newspapers gave news of Berwanger's death prominent display on their lead sports pages. It was the top story on the front page of the University of Chicago's *Daily Maroon*, which seven decades earlier enthusiastically regaled readers with accounts of Berwanger's gridiron heroics. "Jay Berwanger's extraordinary athletic prowess was left on the playing fields of the University of Chicago more than a half-century ago," said Randel. "But in the 60-plus years since then, he has meant much more than athletic achievement to thousands of students and fellow alumni. He was an old-fashioned gentleman whose modesty was never

Berwanger in October 1985 congratulates University of Chicago back Bruce Montella, who earlier that season rushed for a school-record 305 yards. Montella was the top rusher in NCAA Division III that season, averaging 152.4 yards per game. For the Maroons, playing at the alma mater of the first Heisman Trophy winner was "a real source of pride," Montella said. "Everybody felt good being part of a Division III program with that history." (Jim Wright photo)

corrupted by his fame." University of Chicago officials lowered the flag in the center of the Quad to half-staff in honor of their lifelong friend.[211]

The memorial service in Hinsdale's Grace Episcopal Church attracted friends and neighbors and a range of people representing the worlds of sports, business and higher education. Among the mourners were three former Heisman winners: Johnny Lattner (1953), Gary Beban (1967), and Johnny Rodgers (1972). His remains were interred in a plot beside both his wives, Philomela and Jane, in Bronswood Cemetery. Beside the simple grave marker for all three is a statue of a favorite chocolate lab, CoCo, sitting at attention and seemingly standing watch over its late owners.

The family asked that well-wishers not send flowers but instead make memorial donations toward the University of Chicago Athletic Hall of Fame, now located in the lobby of the Gerald Ratner Athletics Center (2003), where the first Heisman Trophy is the focal point.

Other tributes came in from the prominent and common person alike. An anonymous contributor on a website chronicling celebrity gravesites left a message on Berwanger's page recalling his performance in a 1934 game. "I saw you run against U. Of Minn. Your reputation preceeded you and you were all that had been said. You didn't win the game but you won a lot of respect from all of the Gopher fans. May you now rest and peace." The Illinois Senate passed a resolution mourning his passing.[212] The family received a touching letter from a Florida man whose wife had died of cancer a few years earlier. Their son, not yet 10 years old, in 2000 had written to the Heisman legend to ask for a donated item for an American Cancer Society fundraiser. "Mr. Berwanger, to our amazement, sent the football he had received at the Heisman ceremony that year. I was not fortunate enough to meet Mr. Berwanger, but he was a wonderful man to help my son in the way he did."[213] In Briarwood Lakes, the gated community where Berwanger lived, the association flag was lowered to half-staff and its president sent a letter to all members. "To the rest of America, Mr. Berwanger was a sports legend. He meant more than that to us in Briarwood. To us, he was the friendly neighbor on Briarwood Loop who waved as we passed, had a ready smile and a strong handshake. To us, he was a wonderful family man, a successful businessman and a mentor to those who sought his advice. The occasional newspaper stories heralding his sports success were interesting facts about someone we respected for what he did with the rest of his life. Mr. Berwanger was able to keep it all in perspective."[214]

Back in his native Dubuque, the local newspaper reflected on his life and death in an editorial:

As October's vivid foliage gives way to November's blustery winds, thoughts of football turn serious.

That is when the season has taken shape, and there are no more throw-away games for late-bloomer teams. That is when speculation begins in earnest about who might win the Heisman.

In some circles, talk of Heisman history goes back no further than Ron Dayne, the Wisconsin running back who won it in 1999. Those with longer memories might talk about Barry Sanders (1988) or Earl Campbell (1977).

But in Dubuque, football fans speak with pride of a piece of homegrown Heisman history – the man who was the first. Each December, when the Downtown Athletic Club of New York City announces its pick for the nation's outstanding football player, Dubuque fondly recalls Jay Berwanger. Its native son won the first award in 1935. (The name Heisman was not associated with the award until a couple of years later.)

Reminiscence came early this year. Berwanger succumbed to cancer Wednesday at the age of 88.

Seven decades ago, Berwanger took Senior High School's Rams, under Coach

Berwanger poses in 1996 with his historic trophy and the game ball from Chicago's 39-0 win over Dartmouth. In that 1933 game, Berwanger, a sophomore, scored two touchdowns. (Chicago Tribune photo. Reprinted with permission)

Wilbur Dalzell, to the 1931 Mississippi Valley League championship. Though college football powerhouses pursued him, Berwanger chose the University of Chicago because of its business education. He liked the idea of not getting special attention as a football star.

That is the kind of man Jay Berwanger was – a guy who had his priorities straight and was never arrogant. For years, his Heisman trophy served as a doorstop at his aunt's house. (Now its home is the University of Chicago. A replica is on display in the Senior High trophy case.)

Berwanger passed on competing in the 1936 Olympics to graduate with his college class. He eschewed the National Football League for a career in business. In a 1999 interview with the Telegraph Herald, Berwanger said that he had enjoyed a full life and had absolutely no regrets. 'I got recognition in football and track and got a college education," he said. "I played for the love of the game and because it was a means to an end.

He never won an Olympic medal or played in the NFL. So his will never be a name recognized like some of the others on the list of Heisman winners. But there will likely never be a winner as humble as the Dubuque native. And few will be the role model for young athletes that he has been.

Come the crisp days of late autumn and talk of the Heisman resumes, Dubuquers will once again feel a sense of pride – tinged with a sense of loss – over its hometown Heisman winner, Jay Berwanger.[215]

In 1999, Berwanger agreed to suit up in Number 99 for a photo shoot for ESPN: The Magazine. The uniform was from the all-star games of 1936. Photographer Jeff Sciortino considers his picture of Berwanger, then 85, "a timeless portrait." (Jeff Sciortino photo)

BIBLIOGRAPHY

NEWSPAPERS

Four publications were the primary sources of newspaper articles for this biography: *Chicago Tribune*; *Daily Maroon*, the University of Chicago campus newspaper; *Telegraph Herald*, Dubuque, Iowa; and *Chicago Daily News*.

The complete list: *Chicago Daily Defender*; *Chicago Tribune*; *Chicago Daily News*; *Chicago Sun-Times*; Clinton (Iowa) *Herald*; *Daily Maroon*, University of Chicago; Davenport (Iowa) *Democrat and Leader*; Daytona Beach (Florida) *Morning Journal*; Des Moines (Iowa) *Register*; Des Moines (Iowa) *Tribune*; *Hyde Park Herald*, Chicago; Iowa City (Iowa) *Press-Citizen*; LaCrosse (Wisconsin) *Tribune* and *Leader-Press*; *Los Angeles Times*; Miami (Florida) *Daily News*; *Milwaukee Journal*; The *New York Times*; Oelwein (Iowa) *Daily Register*; Orlando (Florida) *Sentinel*; *Philadelphia Inquirer*; *Reserve Record*, Western Reserve Academy, Hudson, Ohio; and *Telegraph Herald*, Dubuque, Iowa.

Articles by *The Associated Press*, *United Press* and other wire or syndicated services also were accessed. Newspapers publishing those dispatches are not included in the list above.

BOOKS

Brady, John T. 1984. *The Heisman: A Symbol of Excellence*. New York: Atheneum.

Brichford, Maynard. 2009. *Bob Zuppke: The Life and Football Legacy of the Illinois Coach*. Jefferson, North Carolina: McFarland & Co.

Didinger, Ray and Lyons, Robert S. 2005. *The Eagles Encyclopedia*. Philadelphia: Temple University Press.

Dzuback, Mary Ann. 1991. *Robert M. Hutchins: Portrait of an Educator*. Chicago: University of Chicago Press.

Gems, Gerald R. 2000. *For pride, profit, and patriarchy: football and the incorporation of American cultural values*. American sports history series, Number 16. Lanham, Maryland: Scarecrow Press.

Lester, Robin. 1999. *Stagg's University: The Rise, Decline and Fall of Big-Time Football at Chicago*. Champaign, Illinois: University of Illinois Press.

Lyons, Robert S. 2010. *On Any Given Sunday: A Life of Bert Bell*. Philadelphia: Temple University Press.

McNeill, William H. 1991. *Hutchins' University: A Memoir of the University of Chicago, 1929-50*. Chicago: University of Chicago Press.

Newhouse, Dave. 1985. *Heismen: After the Glory.* St. Louis, Missouri: The Sporting News Publishing Company.

O'Connor, Candace. 2005. *Meet Me in the Lobby: The Story of Harold Koplar and the Chase Park Plaza.* St. Louis, Missouri: Virginia Publishing Company.

Papas, Al Junior. 2009. *Gophers Illustrated: The Incredible Complete History of Minnesota Football.* Minneapolis: University of Minnesota Press.

Park, Jack. 2003. *The Official Ohio State Football Encyclopedia.* Champaign, Illinois: Sports Publishing LLC.

Schaap, Jeremy. 2007. *Triumph: The Untold Story of Jesse Owens And Hitler's Olympics.* New York. Houghton Mifflin.

Stagg, Amos Alonzo and Stout, Wesley Winnans. 1927. *Touchdown!* New York and London: Longmans, Green and Co.

Theoharis, Athan G., editor. 1999. *The FBI: A Comprehensive Reference Guide.* Phoenix, Arizona: Oryx Press.

Umphlett, Wiley Lee. 1992. *Creating the Big Game: John W. Heisman and the Invention of American Football.* Westport, Conn. : Greenwood Press.

Walsh, Christy. 1949. *College Football and All America Review.* Culver City, California: Murray & Gee, Inc.

Watterson, John Sayle. 2000. *College Football: History, Spectacle, Controversy.* Baltimore, Maryland: The Johns Hopkins University Press.

Wilkie, William E. 1987. *Dubuque on the Mississippi.* Dubuque, Iowa: The Loras College Press.

Wilson, Kenneth L. "Tug," and Brondfield, Jerry. 1967. *The Big Ten.* Englewood Cliffs, New Jersey: Prentice-Hall.

Wolfe, Rich. 2004. *For Hawkeye fans only: Rousing toasts from loyal sons.* St. Louis, Missouri: Lone Wolfe Press.

MAGAZINES AND JOURNALS

Bamberger, Michael. "The Invisible Man." *Sports Illustrated*, December 11, 2000.

Barber, Red. "The Greatest Football Player I Ever Saw: Jay Berwanger." *Sport Magazine.* December 1948.

Berwanger, Jay and Graf, Bob Junior. "I Was So Scared." *The Saturday Evening Post.* December 5, 1936.

Brady, Tim. "Historical Highlights" *Minnesota Magazine,* University of Minnesota Alumni Association. Accessed online November 13, 2010.

Citizens Historical Association, Indianapolis. Biographical profile of Ira

Davenport, January 27, 1940.

Cohen, Sheldon S. "The Genius of the Gridiron." *Chicago History.* Winter 1986-87.

Jordan, Edward S. *"Buying Football Victories." Collier's.* November 11, 1905, and November 18, 1905.

King, Peter. *"Inside the NFL." Sports Illustrated,* Fall 1995. Vol. 83, Issue 15. 63.

Lester, Robin. *"Legends of the Fall." The University of Chicago Magazine,* October 1995.

Mandenach, Mark. *"Jay Berwanger: First Heisman Trophy winner took a pass on professional football." Sports Collectors Digest,* April 4, 1997.

Masin, Herman L. *"Miami and Chicago, a Couple of Hit Shows." Coach & Athletic Director,* September 2003.

Newhouse, Dave. "Breakaway Jay and the First Heisman." *University of Chicago Magazine,* Winter 1986.

Portz, Matt. *"Aviation Training and Expansion." Naval Aviation News,* September-October 1990.

Rappoport, Ken. *"The Heisman Trophy – Up for Grabs." The Saturday Evening Post.* December 1984.

Schmidt, Raymond. *"The 1929 Iowa Football Scandal: Paying Tribute to the Carnegie Report?" College Football Historical Society Newsletter.* Volume 34, Number 3 (Fall 2007).

Zarnowski, Frank. *"History of the Decathlon at U.S. Olympic Trials."*

OTHER

Cohen, Sheldon, interviewer. Loyola Oral History Project. Interview of John J. "Jay" Berwanger, August 1985.

College Football Historical Society. Various newsletters.

Donnelley, Reuben H., compiler. The Lakeside Annual Directory of the City of Chicago, 1910.

Dubuque Senior High pamphlet, "Housewarming for Senior High School," March 9, 1923.

Encyclopedia Dubuque, Carnegie-Stout Public Library, Dubuque, Iowa. www.encyclopediadubuque.org

History of Santa Clara County, California. Published by Historic Record Co., 1922, Page 511. (Accessed through www.mariposaresearch.net/santaclararesearch/index.html.)

IAAF Scoring Tables for Combined Events 2001 Edition. www.iaaf.org.

Illinois High School Association website.

Illinois Senate Resolution 473. Approved November 7, 2002.

JCM Productions, "Heisman Heroes: Berwanger." November 22, 1994. Beano Cook interview, broadcast on ABC Television.

Lyons Township High School, La Grange, Illinois. Hall of Fame web site.

National Collegiate Athletic Association. 2002. "Football's Finest." Indianapolis, Indiana: NCAA.

Nauright, John. Theatrice Gibbs: "An Africa-American Football Pioneer in Iowa." Academia.edu accessed December 29, 2012.

The NCAA News, January 4, 1984.

Reagan, Ronald. "Remarks on Congratulating Doug Flutie, the 1984 Heisman Trophy Winner." Public Papers of Ronald Reagan. December 6, 1984.

Reagan, Ronald. "Remarks at a Senate Campaign Fundraising Reception for Pete Dawkins of New Jersey." Public Papers of Ronald Reagan. April 19, 1988.

Stolteben, Hildegarde M. "Dubuque Senior High School History," 1958.

University of Chicago web site.

ENDNOTES

1 Louis Siems was born in Hamburg in 1854. His wife, the former Maide (also listed as Metha and Meta) Schulte, was born in 1855 in Mecklenburg.

2 Wilkie, William E. Dubuque on the Mississippi.

3 Berwanger interview with Sheldon Cohen, August 1985. Loyola University of Chicago archives.

4 Indiana University yearbook, 1918.

5 A reference to Dalzell as a 1917 "star halfback" trying out at fullback appeared in *The Christian Science Monitor*, October 19, 1918. Dalzell's name does not appear on Indiana University's all-time list of football letter-winners.

6 Interview with Beano Cook, ABC-TV's "Heisman Heroes," 1994. JCM Productions.

7 The incident received wide coverage, including in *The New York Times* (December 9, 1923), *Chicago Tribune* and *Washington Post* (both December 11, 1923).

8 The *Dubuque Telegraph-Herald* of November 8, 1929, reported that Berwanger "needs another week before he gets into action."

9 *Davenport* (Iowa) *Democrat* and *Dubuque Telegraph-Herald*, November 17, 1929. The *Telegraph-Herald* of November 3, 1929, similarly referred to a pair of Cedar Rapids Grant running backs as "dusky mates." The article also appeared the same day in the *Cedar Rapids Gazette*.

10 Permanent record, Dubuque Community School District.

11 College Football Historical Society newsletter, February 1990.

12 Eleanor Berwanger VonPein, unpublished remembrances, September 2000.

13 Dubuque Senior High yearbook, 1930-31.

14 Iowa High School Athletic Association archives, Dubuque Senior High yearbook 1930-31. Dubuque Telegraph-Herald, May 10, 1931. Page 16. January 26, 1932.

15 Berwanger wrote that it was 92 degrees, bylined article, Chicago Daily News, November 19, 1935. Official readings in Davenport, Iowa (90 degrees) and Peoria, Illinois (92) support that recollection.

16 The Dubuque High School News, May 19, 1932.

17 John Nauright's paper on Theatrice Gibbs, "An Africa-American Football Pioneer in Iowa." Accessed on academia.edu December 29, 2012.

18 Lester, Robin. *Stagg's University: The Rise, Decline & Fall of Big-Time Football at Chicago.* Pages 55-56 and 60-61.

19 Stagg, Amos Alonzo and Stout, Wesley Winnans. *Touchdown!* Pages 180-181.

20 Watterson, John Sayle. *College Football: History, Spectacle, Controversy,* citing

Savage, Howard J. et al, American College Athletics, Bulletin 23, New York: Carnegie Foundation for the Advancement of Teaching, 1929.

21 A feature in the article in the *Chicago Tribune*, January 5, 1997, listed as the leading suitors Northwestern, Iowa, Michigan and Purdue.

22 Lester. Page 159.

23 Berwanger's interview with Beano Cook, ABC-TV's "Heisman Heroes," 1994.

24 Biographical profile of Ira Davenport, Citizens Historical Association, Indianapolis, January 27, 1940.

25 Davenport profile, Citizens Historical Association; and Encyclopedia of Dubuque web site.

26 Berwanger, in interview with Beano Cook, 1994.

27 Berwanger, in interview with Sheldon Cohen, August 1985. Loyola University of Chicago Archives.

28 Berwanger to Cook, 1994. He had told Cohen essentially the same thing in 1985.

29 Berwanger to Cohen, 1985.

30 Berwanger's permanent student record, Dubuque Community School District.

31 *New York Times*, January 20, 1890.

32 Stagg, A.A. and Stout, W.W. *Touchdown!*, Pages 143-144.

33 Lester, Robin. *Stagg's University*, Page 17.

34 Miller, Donald L. City of the Century, Page 394, citing the unpublished memoir of Robert Herrick.

35 Miller, Donald L. Page 399.

36 Lester, Robin. *Stagg's University: The Rise, Decline and Fall of Big-Time Football at Chicago*. Page 22.

37 Stagg, A.A. and Stout, W.W. *Touchdown!*, Pages 154-155.

38 Stagg and Stout. Page 157.

39 Lester. Page 34.

40 University of Chicago athletics web site, early era year-by-year scores.

41 Lester. Page 33.

42 Stagg and Stout. Page 237.

43 *Los Angeles Times*, June 2, 1932. Page 11. Lester. Page 72.

44 Gems, Gerald R. *For Pride, Profit and Patriarchy: Football and the Incorporation of American Cultural Values*. Page 92.

45 Jordan, Edward S. "Buying Football Victories," *Collier's*.11 November 1905. Page 19. Lester, Robin. Page 88.

46 Lester. Page 90.

47 Watterson, John Sayle. *College Football: History, Spectacle, Controversy*. Pages

69-73.

48 Watterson. Pages 37 and 40.

49 Summary based on information from Victor C. Winnek, NCAA football official and rules historian.

50 *Chicago Tribune*, January 15, 1908. Page 10.

51 *Chicago Tribune*, October 6, 1906. Page 8.

52 Lester. Page 116.

53 Lester. Page 90.

54 Lester. Page 120.

55 Berwanger's official transcript, University of Chicago.

56 Berwanger to Sheldon Cohen, 1985.

57 Author's interview with Ernest Dix, October 25, 2009.

58 Lester, Robin. Stagg's University: The Rise, Decline and Fall of Big-Time Football at Chicago. Page 144.

59 Lester. Pages 147-149. *Chicago Tribune*, December 13, 1932.

60 *Chicago Tribune*, December 13, 1932.

61 A.A. Stagg letter to Clark Shaughnessy, dated February 17, 1933. University of Chicago Library.

62 Frank Zarnowski, decathlon expert and historian, email to the author, January 21, 2013. Zarnowski interviewed Menaul's son Richard in 1987.

63 Theoharis, Athan G., editor. *The FBI: A Comprehensive Reference Guide*. Phoenix, Arizona: Oryx Press. Page 339. This reference list Lopez's first name as Julius, though sportswriters and the University of Chicago 1934 team photo stated it as Julian.

64 Berwanger to Sheldon Cohen, 1985.

65 Undated article, circa June 1933, Berwanger family scrapbook.

66 Berwanger, interview with Beano Cook, 1994.

67 Berwanger to Cook. The Chicago trainer's name was reported as Bill Bock in the *Chicago Tribune* of November 9, 1934. Captions on various University of Chicago team photos show various first names, including Wallace, Walter, and W. After more than two decades as their trainer, the Cleveland Indians released Bock. *Chicago Daily Defender*, August 14, 1971. In 1971, Cleveland baseball writers honored Bock. The Washington Post, February 2, 1971.

68 Shaughnessy's letter to Stagg, dated October 8, 1933, is held in the Special Collection archives of the University of Chicago Library.

69 Morgenstern, William V. *University of Chicago Magazine*, November 1933.

70 *St. Louis Post-Dispatch*, October 15, 1933. Game accounts also taken from the *Chicago Tribune, Chicago Herald-Examiner, Daily Maroon*, United Press wire service,

and several undated articles found in a Berwanger family scrapbook.

71 Helen Berwanger Tierney, Jay's daughter, interview with author, July 14, 2009, citing her father.

72 Michigan also defeated Chicago 28-0 in 1903.

73 *Dubuque* (Iowa) *Telegraph-Herald*, December 1, 1935.

74 Article in *Detroit News* and box score in *Chicago Tribune*, October 29, 1933.

75 Dix, Ernie. Interview with author. October 25, 2009.

76 University of Chicago and University of Illinois online archives.

77 Brichford, Maynard. 2009. *Bob Zuppke: The Life and Football Legacy of the Illinois Coach.* Jefferson, North Carolina: McFarland & Co. Page 27.

78 IlliniHQ.com, maintained by the *Champaign* (Illinois) *News-Gazette.* Accessed September 25, 2010.

79 *Chicago Tribune*, May 4, 1932. Page 21.

80 *Chicago Tribune.* February 25, 1934. Page A1. A photo shows Berwanger slightly ahead of three competitors in the high hurdles. University of Chicago archives. Department of Physical Education papers.

81 University of Chicago archives. Department of Physical Education papers.

82 Decathlon expert and historian Frank Zarnowski, email to author, January 21, 2013.

83 University of Chicago official transcript.

84 Camp Highlands for Boys website. Accessed October 9, 2010.

85 Berwanger to Sheldon Cohen, 1985.

86 The medal is still part of the Berwanger family collection.

87 "Michigan 1934," College Football Historical Society newsletter, November 1994.

88 Watterson, John Sayle. *College Football: History, Spectacle, Controversy.* Pages 316-318.

89 Berwanger, John. Interview with author. July 14, 2009.

90 University of Missouri football "Records and History," accessed online November 2, 2010.

91 Chicago History Museum website displays a season-ticket book, which was good for 50 admissions.

92 Chicago History Museum website, accessed November 6, 2010, and *Chicago Tribune,* November 2, 1934. Page 3.

93 Lester, Robin. Stagg's University. Pages 103-105.

94 Opening years of other new stadiums in the Big Ten: Ohio State, 1922; Illinois, 1923; Minnesota, 1924; Purdue, 1924; Indiana, 1925; Northwestern, 1926; Michigan, 1927; and Iowa, 1929. Sources: University websites.

95 Lester. Pages 128-131. *Year of fieldhouse completion: University of Chicago archival photographic files.*

96 Brady, Tim. *Minnesota Magazine.* University of Minnesota Alumni Association. Fall 2009.

97 Advertisement in the *Walnut Grove* (Minnesota) *Tribune*, March 27, 1930, and several other newpapers.

98 Berwanger to Sheldon Cohen, 1985.

99 Collier's, December 22, 1934.

100 Walsh, Christy. College Football and All America Review. 1949.

101 Associated Press report. *Christian Science Monitor*, January 3, 1935. Page 12. Albert W. Keane, sports editor of the Hartford Courant, said he had an "unimpeachable source" that Shaughnessy topped Bingham's list. January 5, 1935. Page 13.

102 Official transcript, University of Chicago.

103 McNeill, William H. Hutchins' *University: A Memoir of the University of Chicago 1929-50.* Pages 63-65.

104 Ernie Dix, letter to Helen Berwanger Tierney, July 24, 2002.

105 Berwanger to Sheldon Cohen, 1985.

106 *University of Chicago Magazine,* Winter 1986. Dave Newhouse article adapted from his book, "Heismen: After the Glory."

107 Red Barber, CBS sports director. *Sport magazine.* December 1948.

108 Author's review of game film.

109 *Dubuque* (Iowa) *Telegraph-Herald*, December 1, 1935.

110 Barber.

111 *Maroon Football Review*, by Edward Stern, November 16, 1935, and *Daily Maroon*, University of Chicago, November 15, 1935.

112 Game films, reviewed by the author 75 years later, showed that the officials were correct.

113 Timothy Bachmann, of Camp Highlands for Boys, identified the camp official as Angus M. Frew, of Western Reserve Academy in Hudson, Ohio. Like many at Camp Highlands, Frew had a University of Chicago connection, having previously taught and coached at University of Chicago High School, where camp director Doc Monilaw was athletic director. A half-dozen years later, Berwanger's brother, Paul, transferred from Dubuque High to play for Frew at Western Reserve Academy.

114 Berwanger to Sheldon Cohen, 1985.

115 Less than a month after serving as master of ceremonies, Kane died of a heart attack at age 49. *Dubuque* (Iowa) *Telegraph-Herald*, December 27, 1935.

116 Wilson, Kenneth and Brondfield, Jerry. The Big Ten. Page 193.

117 Schaap, Jeremy. Triumph: The Untold Story of Jesse Owens and Hitler's

Olympics. Page 102.

118 Brady, John T. The Heisman: A Symbol of Excellence. Page 13.

119 Heisman Memorial Foundation, heismantrophy.com. Accessed January 16, 2011.

120 All appeared in the morning editions of December 5, 1935.

121 Brady, John T. *The Heisman: A Symbol of Excellence.* Page 13.

122 The final inspection of the cast was made after a dinner at the McAlpin Hotel on November 16, 1935, according to the Heisman Trophy Trust website, Heisman. com, accessed December 1, 2012.

123 Official Frank Eliscu website, accessed January 19, 2011. www.frankeliscu. com

124 Tim Henning, Heisman Memorial Foundation, email to author, February 1, 2011.

125 Berwanger to Sheldon Cohen, 1985.

126 Lyons, Robert. On Any Given Sunday: A Life of Bert Bell.

127 Didinger, Ray and Lyons, Robert S. 2005. *The Eagles Encyclopedia.*

128 Lyons.

129 Berwanger to Cohen, 1985.

130 Berwanger to Beano Cook, 1994.

131 Berwanger to Cohen, 1985.

132 Berwanger to Sheldon Cohen. 1985.

133 Decathlon expert and historian Frank Zarnowski interviewed Menaul's son Richard in 1987. *Chicago Tribune,* January 21, 1936.

134 Dix, Ernest. Interview with author, October 25, 2009.

135 At some point, a scoring discrepancy was discovered. It appeared to have involved three points initially awarded to Chicago. The *Chicago Tribune* of April 11, 1936, reported the final score as 70-61, but the results form in Department of Physical Education papers, held in the University of Chicago archives, list the score as 67-64.

136 Frank Zarnowski, decathlon expert and historian. Email to author, January 21, 2013.

137 Dix to author, October 25, 2009.

138 Official transcript, University of Chicago.

139 Dix.

140 The Berwanger family still has the medal. The inscription reads, "Awarded to Jay Berwanger in recognition of his genuine loyalty to American ideals."

141 *Northwestern magazine,* Summer 2005. *Washington Post,* December 28, 2004.

142 Trackandfieldnews.com

143 Zarnowski.

144 Morris parlayed his Olympic glory into a stint as an NBC radio announcer. He also appeared in three Hollywood movies, including one in the leading role as Tarzan, and played in four games with the Detroit Lions. He was wounded during his World War II military service, after which he struggled with employment and finances. Morris, who died of congestive heart failure in 1974 at age 61, was inducted into the USA Track & Field Hall of Fame in 2007.

145 From two interviews of Berwanger: By Sheldon Cohen in 1985 and Beano Cook in 1994. Berwanger did not mention Felix by name, but several *Chicago Tribune* articles in 1937-38 identified Felix as the Featheredge president.

146 Berwanger to Cohen.

147 Cohen.

148 IMDb.com entry on "The Big Game."

149 John Berwanger, Cuyler Berwanger, and Helen Berwanger Tierney, interview with author, July 8, 2012.

150 Cohen. Arch Ward quoted Berwanger regarding the long days, adding that the athlete was "through with the movies." *Chicago Tribune*, August 15, 1936.

151 Cohen.

152 *College Football Historical Society Newsletter*, February 1990. "An Interview: Mike Layden."

153 During the 1936 season, others who provided color commentary with Hodges included Red Grange, former Northwestern star Wally Cruice, and Chicago Bears standout Bronco Nagurski.

154 Eleanor Berwanger VonPein, unpublished recollections, September 2000.

155 Ernie Dix, letter to Helen Tierney Berwanger, July 24, 2002.

156 VonPein.

157 Mary Jane Dix, to the author, October 25, 2009.

158 Two undated newspaper articles, Berwanger family scrapbook.

159 Paul Berwanger might have arrived in Chicago with a headache. In the final quarter of his football team's previous game, a 19-0 win over Orange High, he was knocked unconscious.

160 In addition to the Chicago papers, others publishing a photo included the *Milwaukee Journal* (March 20, 1942) and *New York Times*, (March 22, 1942).

161 Kennedy missed three seasons of baseball (1942-45) due to military service.

162 If not for the war, their location would have allowed Phil and Jay to be close to his brother, Paul, who enrolled at the University of Chicago and was a member of the freshman track team. However, Paul withdrew to enter the military, where he experienced close combat.

163 His visit took place on May 27, 1942.

164 John Jay Berwanger interview July 14, 2009. St. Luke's Hospital palmprint document.

165 Death register, Dubuque County, Iowa. A Congregational minister officiated at the service at Egelhof Funeral Home, and she was laid to rest in Linwood Cemetery.

166 Berwanger to Sheldon Cohen, 1985.

167 Undated article by Helen Cuyler Baker. Berwanger family scrapbook.

168 Undated newspaper datelined Gary, Indiana. August 11, 1942.

169 Portz, Matt. "Aviation Training and Expansion." Naval Aviation News, September-October 1990.

170 Official orders dated September 5, 1945.

171 The Berwanger family has retained the loan document.

172 *University of Chicago Magazine*, November 1951.

173 U.S. Patent 3167824 (weatherseal) and U.S. Patent 3654061 (pipe wrap). www. prior-ip.com.

174 *University of Chicago Magazine*, November 1951.

175 Robert Simpson interview with author, August 16, 2011.

176 Robert Simpson interview with author, November 28, 2011.

177 The Big Ten was also referred to as the Big Nine in the years between Chicago's withdrawal in 1946 and the addition of Michigan State in 1950 (1953 for varsity sports).

178 Northwestern University archives online and *Los Angeles Times*, Jan. 2, 1949.

179 Cuyler Berwanger interview with author, November 7, 2009.

180 Ernie Dix. Letter to Helen Berwanger Tierney, July 24, 2002.

181 *University of Chicago Magazine*, Winter 1986.

182 John and Cuyler (Butch) Berwanger, interview with author, November 7, 2009.

183 Cuyler and Jay Berwanger are enshrined in the Camp Highlands for Boys Hall of Fame.

184 Jay's children – John Berwanger, Cuyler Berwanger, and Helen (Berwanger) Tierney – interview with author, July 14, 2009.

185 John Berwanger, interview with author, July 14, 2009.

186 Berwanger children. July 14, 2009.

187 Helen Berwanger Tierney, written comments to author, November 11, 2010.

188 Hinsdale Golf Club, email to author, November 11, 2009.

189 Helen Berwanger Tierney, telephone interview with author, July 8, 2012.

190 Helen Berwanger Tierney, November 11, 2010.

191 *Chicago Tribune*, February 6, 1969.

192 Berwanger children, July 14, 2009.

193 After private funeral services, Philomela was laid to rest in Bronswood Cemetery in Hinsdale.

194 Marianne Temple Gerwig, interview with author, November 2009.

195 Helen Berwanger Tierney, interview with author, July 14, 2009.

196 Gerwig.

197 Rudy Riska, interview with author, October 11, 2009.

198 In competition, the closest Berwanger ever came to Cheboygan was Columbus, Ohio, some 450 miles away, in 1934.

199 Helen Berwanger Tierney, letter to author, November 11, 2010.

200 Gerwig.

201 Framed certificate, dated September 24, 1969.

202 John F. Kennedy Presidential Library and Museum archives. Address at the National Football Foundation and Hall of Fame banquet, December 1961.

203 Berwanger to Sheldon Cohen, 1985.

204 Archie Griffin, telephone interview with author, February 16, 2010.

205 His birthday was in March, three months earlier.

206 John Davey to author, November 1, 2011.

207 Tom Weingartner to author, September 22, 2009. A Chicago area native who played football at Stanford, Weingartner in mid-2012 accepted a newly created position with the University of Chicago to work full-time on fundraising and alumni engagement for athletics.

208 Dalzell died less than a year afterward, in July 1980, at age 82.

209 Jeff Sciortino, email to author, April 20, 2012.

210 Rudy Riska, telephone interview with author, October 11, 2009.

211 University President Don M. Randel, letter to Cuyler Berwanger, July 1, 2002.

212 Illinois Senate resolution, November 7, 2002.

213 Mack Sturdivant, letter to Berwanger family, 2002, regarding his son Matthew.

214 Constantine P. Xinos, Briarwood Lakes Community Association president, letter, June 29, 2002.

215 *Telegraph Herald*, Dubuque, Iowa. June 30, 2002.

About the Author

For nearly 28 years, **BRIAN E. COOPER** has been executive editor of Dubuque, Iowa-based TH Media, whose products include the *Telegraph Herald* daily newspaper, magazines, specialty publications and THonline.com.

As a free-lance writer of non-fiction, Cooper is the author of two other sports books – *Ray Schalk: A Baseball Biography* (McFarland & Company, 2009) and *Red Faber: A Biography of the Hall of Fame Spitball Pitcher* (McFarland, 2007) — and a commissioned work, *McCoy Group: A History of Commitment to the Customer* (2012).

Of Cooper's four decades in journalism, most have taken place in Iowa, where he was editor of *The Ottumwa Courier* four years before joining the *Telegraph Herald*. He also held newsroom management positions in Quincy, Illinois, and Winona, Minnesota. He is a journalism graduate of the University of Missouri.

In addition to state and regional writing awards for editorials and columns, Cooper is the recipient of the Iowa Newspaper Association's two most prestigious honors, the Master Editor-Publisher and Distinguished Service awards. He is a past president of the Iowa Newspaper Foundation and the Iowa Freedom of Information Council.

Cooper and his wife, Ann, reside in Dubuque.